Panda
THE l

About the Authors

Yue Nan was born in 1962 in Zhucheng, Shandong Province, where he completed his middle school education. Then he served in the armed police for a dozen years and studied for two years in the literary department of the People's Liberation Army Arts College. He is now a member of the Chinese Writers Association and works as a magazine editor in Beijing.

Dr Yang Shi was born in Linqing, Shandong Province. She graduated from the stomatological department of Beijing Medical College in 1957 and has worked as head of a dental clinic. A history buff, she has cherished a great interest in the Ming Dynasty.

About the Translator

Zhang Tingquan began his career as a journalist after graduating from Beijing Foreign Studies University in 1954. Working for the overseas news service and English sports service of Xinhua News Agency, he has been writing in English for 40 years. His earlier translations include H. G. Wells' *Love and Mr. Lewisham*, *China's Socialist Economy* and the classic *Book of Filial Piety*.

Yue Nan & Yang Shi

THE DEAD SUFFERED TOO

The Excavation of a Ming Tomb

Translated by Zhang Tingquan
English text edited by Bertha Sneck

Panda Books

Panda Books
First Edition 1996
Copyright © CHINESE LITERATURE PRESS, 1996
ISBN 7−5071−0298−X
ISBN 0−8351−3179−3

Published by CHINESE LITERATURE PRESS
Beijing 100037, China
Distributed by China International Book Trading Corporation
35 Chegongzhuang Xilu, Beijing 100044, China
P.O. Box 399, Beijing, China
Printed in the People's Republic of China

Landscape view of Ding Ling. From fore- to background: the stone bridge, the stone tablet without inscription, the tomb precinct and the stele pavilion.

The inverted-V opening of the diamond wall of the underground palace.

The third prospecting ditch, which led to the gate of the underground palace.

One of the three blue and white porcelain dragon vats discovered in the underground palace.

Coffins of Emperor Wanli (centre) and his two empresses (left and right) at the moment the underground palace was first opened.

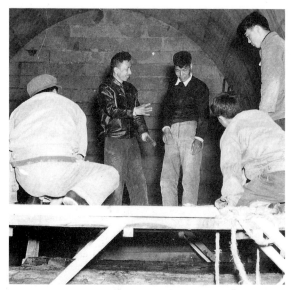

Xia Nai (second left) and Zhao Qichang (centre) on the wooden stands from which they reached down to remove objects from the emperor's coffin.

Yang Shi (left) interviewing Zhao Qichang (right) and Wang Yan.

Photos courtesy of Zhao Qichang

Contents

Preface		1
Chapter 1	Zhou Enlai's Choice	5
Chapter 2	Piercing the Miasma of History	22
Chapter 3	Ding Ling, Choice of the Emperor	43
Chapter 4	Excavation of Ding Ling	64
Chapter 5	Love in the Imperial Tomb Precinct	86
Chapter 6	The Diamond Wall	103
Chapter 7	The Underground Palace Opens with a Bang	125
Chapter 8	The Perplexing Dais	155
Chapter 9	Two Female Corpses	190
Chapter 10	Audience with the Emperor	214
Chapter 11	A Tragic Legacy	235
Chapter 12	Skeletons in Flames	253
Concluding Remarks		259
Postscript		273
Appendix 1	Location of the 13 Ming Tombs	278
Appendix 2	Plan of the Ding Ling precinct	279
Appendix 3	Plan of the underground palace	280
Appendix 4	Illustration and drawing	281

PREFACE

THIS book about Ding Ling, a Ming Dynasty tomb, came to be written at the prompting of history: it was exactly 400 years since its completion in 1590.

The vicissitudes of the past 400 years have hidden this magnificent imperial tomb under layers of neglect, just like verdigris on the bronzeware buried in its mysterious underground vaults. The legendary lives of the tomb's occupants remain enveloped in a mist so obscuring that today scholars still argue endlessly about them.

As we walk into the underground halls of the ancient tomb and gaze at the three coffins painted bright red, we seem to hear a voice from the nether world uttering sounds of sorrow and regret. Where are the three original *nanmu* (Phoebe) coffins of exquisite workmanship unearthed from the tomb? Where are the three corpses which had already decomposed but had miraculously emerged into the light again? Where are the glossy, priceless brocades which embodied the silk-weaving techniques of the Chinese nation in the Ming Dynasty and which exemplified a peak in the development of textile art worldwide?

Mist again confuses people's minds.

Scientists outside China kept a close watch for the issue of a report on the excavation of Ding Ling in the hope of solving the many puzzles.

Thirty years elapsed, but strangely enough not a single academic report was published on this subject. Gradually the hopes of people in the East and the West lapsed into disappointment.

Finally, those who could no longer endure the silence began to explore the cause of this "enigma". Letters poured in from all over the world, some expressing perplexity, some anger, some even resorting to caustic remarks... A female scientist in Hong Kong wrote: "No academic report has been published in nearly 30 years since Ding Ling was excavated. This is unprecedented in the world history of archaeology. I fear that the splendid 5,000-year-old civilisation of the Chinese nation and the achievements of our ancestors will crumble at the hands of their unworthy descendants..."

Such reaction was a shattering blow, but the Chinese archaeologists remained strangely silent. They could not but keep silent. How could they do otherwise? In the eyes of those living outside China, full of sincerity and expectations, even the great archaeologist Xia Nai was either unable, or ashamed, to explain. The excavation of Ding Ling was interwoven with a number of historical incidents. In the minds of Xia Nai and his students, this great excavation and their outstanding finds seemed like a dream, far off and long ago. In silence, they were thinking of the destroyed coffins and the burnt skeletons. Some of the excavators have passed away, while some saw their families broken up during the "cultural revolution".

Thirty years passed in a flash.

What history has given us is not the long awaited scientific report of the excavation, but the sad news of the death, illness or aging of the witnesses to it. Wu

Han, Guo Moruo, Shen Yanbing, Deng Tuo and Fan Wenlan, who originally proposed the excavation and wrote a joint letter to the Administrative Council (predecessor of the State Council prior to 1954), and the two great scholars Zheng Zhenduo and Xia Nai, who took part in guiding the excavation, are all gone; those ardent young people then in their twenties who took an active part in all aspects of the work have already turned grey. In this way, as if by an irresistible law of nature, History creates, then willfully destroys its creations.

This dreadful "death cycle" has left a void; it is now up to us. We can no longer remain silent. Since history has bequeathed us this rare opportunity, we ought to take it as a lofty mission, using our pens as plough-shares to turn up the layers of mystery deposited by time, picking up the pieces shattered by history to repair and restore its original brilliance. In this way, the dead will be exonerated and those still alive will have no more regrets.

Chapter One
ZHOU ENLAI'S CHOICE

A Letter to the State Council

It was in the early summer of 1935. Xia Nai, a student in the department of history at Qinghua University in Beiping (today's Beijing), had been assigned to archaeological field work in Anyang, Henan Province, and was leaving shortly. On the green lawn of Gu Yue (Ancient Moon) Hall, he was chatting with his close friend and classmate Wu Han about their future work. Xia Nai asked Wu Han, who was then preparing to teach at Qinghua: "If you could choose, at which site would you want to dig?"

Wu Han, who had already distinguished himself in historical research into the Ming Dynasty, replied lightheartedly: "The Ming Tombs". Exchanging knowing looks and meaningful smiles, they shook hands and said goodbye. They never dreamed that this remark, seemingly off-hand and far-fetched, would 20 years later turn out to have been prognostic and, moreover, lead to a dispute.

In October 1955 a report requesting instructions on the excavation of Chang Ling of the Ming Dynasty was put before Premier Zhou Enlai of the State Council. It had been signed by Guo Moruo, Shen Yanbing, Wu Han, Deng Tuo, Fan Wenlan and Zhang Su on

October 3, 1955.

When the news spread, it astonished Zheng Zhenduo, director of the Bureau of Cultural Relics under the Ministry of Culture, and Xia Nai, deputy director of the Institute of Archaeology under the Chinese Academy of Sciences. On learning that the report had been initiated by Wu Han, vice-mayor of Beijing, they tried to persuade him to withdraw it. This led to a dispute.

"After we excavate Chang Ling, we can use the burial objects of Ming Emperor Chengzu (better known by his reign title Yongle) to study the politics, economy, military affairs and culture of the dynasty, and at the same time establish a museum at the tomb site in which to place a selection of the objects unearthed that will be useful for educating the people about history and enriching their cultural life."

Zheng Zhenduo became impatient with Wu Han's explanations. He rose from his chair: "With the present technical level of our archaeological work, it is still difficult for our country to carry out large-scale excavations of tombs," he said. "The problems of preserving and restoring unearthed antiques have not yet been solved. Even technologically advanced countries would find it a headache to excavate and preserve a tomb as large as this."

Before Zheng Zhenduo finished, Wu Han broke in: "It has been five or six years since the country was liberated. We have the older generation of archaeologists and also a good number of university graduates trained in recent years. We have both the human and material resources to cope with such a gigantic project."

They seemed to have reached a stalemate, but then

Xia Nai came out to give Zheng Zhenduo a helping hand. With a calm look at Wu Han, his fellow villager and schoolmate, he said: "Large-scale construction is now being carried out throughout the country. A request for urgent help comes from the northwest today, another request from the southeast tomorrow. Even if we send all our people out, we can not begin to cope. All unearthed burial objects have to be preserved and restored. We do not have enough trained people. The question should be considered according to the importance and urgency of archaeological work countrywide, not just from the viewpoint of an expert in Ming Dynasty history. Think it over; you're no longer the Wu Han of your student days at Qinghua."

The argument lasted an entire afternoon without any agreement being reached. On the question of excavations at the Ming Tombs, Wu Han, vice-mayor of Beijing, who was in charge of the city's cultural and educational work, had made up his mind; there was little possibility of any outside influence changing it.

After Zheng Zhenduo and Xia Nai left, Wu Han went to see his close friends Guo Moruo and Deng Tuo, and made every effort to explain the importance of excavating the tomb to the leaders of the central government. At the same time, Zheng Zhenduo and Xia Nai likewise presented their opposing views indirectly. Both sides placed their hopes on a favourable decision from Premier Zhou Enlai. In five days, word came of the Premier's choice. The report was signed:

I APPROVE THE EXCAVATION.

The choice of this great man opened an exciting, new

page in the history of China's archaeological work. At the same time, on the same page there would be recorded many unforeseen events.

In early December 1955 Chang Ling Excavation Committee was set up under the chairmanship of Wu Han. The members of the committee were:

> Guo Moruo, President, Chinese Academy of Sciences,
> Shen Yanbing, Minister of Culture,
> Wu Han, Vice-Mayor of Beijing,
> Deng Tuo, President of the *People's Daily*,
> Fan Wenlan, Director, Third Division of the Institute of History at the Chinese Academy of Sciences,
> Zhang Su, Deputy Secretary General of the Standing Committee of the National People's Congress,
> Xia Nai, Deputy Director, Institute of Archaeology under the Chinese Academy of Sciences,
> Zheng Zhenduo, Director, Bureau of Cultural Relics under the Ministry of Culture,
> Wang Kunlun, Vice-Mayor of Beijing.

A work team directed by Chang Ling Excavation Committee was made up of personnel from the Bureau of Cultural Relics, the Institute of Archaeology, and the Beijing Cultural Relics Investigation and Research Group.

Its members included:

> Zhao Qichang, leader, 28-year-old graduate of department of history, Beijing University,

specialising in archaeology;
Bai Wanyu, deputy leader, 58-year-old, with primary school education;
Yu Shugong, 52-year-old, graduate of the Sun Yat-sen University in the Soviet Union;
Liu Jingyi, 23-year-old, undergraduate in the department of history, Nankai University;
Xian Ziqiang, 17-year-old,
Cao Guojian, 18-year-old,
Pang Zhongwei, 19-year-old,
Li Shuxing, 19-year-old, and Wang Jie, 19-year-old, all with junior middle school education.

Providing precise details concerning members of Chang Ling Excavation Committee and the work team serves to record as fully as possible the history of the planned excavation of the first imperial tomb following the founding of New China. Politicians, historians, archaeologists and other research workers need much food for thought, an abundance of facts, to make a trustworthy and scientific assessment of its gains and losses.

Snowy Days at Heavenly Longevity Hills

Since approval for the excavation was given, Xia Nai, deputy director of the Archaeological Institute who was in charge of excavations, was duty-bound to give personal guidance to the work. He urged Zhao Qichang to conduct an on-the-spot investigation of the Ming Tombs as soon as possible.

On the last day of 1955, in the midst of a snowstorm Zhao Qichang and a prospector named Zhao

Tonghai went to the imperial area of the Ming Tombs, carrying their special tools and implements.

Snowflakes danced in the howling wind. The undulating hills and the desolate tombs were blanketed in white. The imperial tombs, undisturbed for hundreds of years, had become ever more silent and forbidding. Zhao Qichang tramped through the thick snow, crossed the Hall of Heavenly Favour and climbed the Chang Ling tumulus sheltering the majestic Tomb of Emperor Yongle (Zhu Di).

From the top, looking south, he saw a seven-kilometre-long central axis running to the foot of the hills like a broad silver chain falling from the sky. Flanked by two rows of ministers and generals carved in stone, it formed the ceremonious Divine Road. Snow clouds shaded the sun. It looked as if across the chilly northern wilderness, Zhu Di, prince of the Yan State, was setting out on a military expedition to conquer the country under the banner of "ridding the emperor of his evil ministers"...

In the 5th month of 1398 Zhu Yuanzhang, the founding emperor of the Ming Dynasty, was confined to his bed in the Western Palace in Nanjing. Straining to keep his eyes open, he gazed at his grandson Zhu Yunwen, with sadness and apprehension. He twitched his lips as if to speak to him, but could not utter a word. This was how the founder of the Ming Dynasty departed, leaving behind the feats of his lifetime. Eventually he was buried in a huge, magnificent tomb set at the foot of Zhong (Bell) Mountain on the outskirts of Nanjing.

After news of the death of the emperor reached

Beiping (today's Beijing), a contingent of horses and soldiers left the ancient city for Nanjing. Travelling ahead of them was Zhu Di, prince of the vassal state of Yan. He had first become prince in the 13th year of the Hongwu Reign (1380) of Zhu Yuanzhang and, during the following 18 years, the dream of rising from prince of a vassal state to emperor had become rooted in his heart. At this moment, he was desperate to reach the capital city to learn more of the situation in the palace and estimate his chances of turning his dream into reality.

Zhu Di pressed southward in high spirits. Outside of Huai'an, an imperial edict reached him: Acting upon the order of the deceased, Royal Grandson Zhu Yunwen has ascended the throne and the title of the new reign is to be Jianwen; all princes stationed outside are asked not to return to the capital city for the funeral. Zhu Di was alarmed. The intention of the imperial edict was unmistakable: princes of vassal states were forbidden entrance to the centre of power at the capital city to contest the official transfer of power.

Suppressing his anger, Zhu Di returned to Beiping with his entourage.

The Zhu Di of that portentous day was no longer the Zhu Di of his early years. It was now difficult to find in this middle-aged awe-inspiring personage astride his war-horse any shadow of the stripling who was first appointed prince of the Yan State at the age of 21. He was now 39, the golden age at which to strike out on a grand venture.

Long years of fighting in the northern wilderness had imbued him with all the qualities displayed by the great soldiers of ancient times: as a strategist, he was masterful and farsighted; as a military planner, he was as sly as a fox; as a combat man, he was fearless and highly skilled. Best of all, as a military leader he could inspire his soldiers to perform great feats. What was of the utmost importance to him now was that the situation at the Imperial Court was highly advantageous to him. Zhu Biao, the crown prince who had won favourable comment from both the court and the commonality, had died long before. Zhu Shuang, prince of the Qin State, and Zhu Gang, prince of the Jin State, whose forces were by no means inferior to his own, had both died of illness. The founding generals of great renown in strategy had all been put to death one after another by Zhu Yuanzhang on various pretexts. Now the almighty emperor had passed away, and the new successor, Zhu Di's nephew, was only 16 years old. Surrounding him were only a few pedantic scholars who appeared wise and capable but who were in fact useless, paralysed followers of traditional rites. All this created a good opportunity for Zhu Di to usurp the throne. After waiting in abatement for a long time, the dream buried in his heart was rekindled again, spurring him to strike out for the realisation of his great ambition, even at the risk of his life.

Now that the royal grandson, Zhu Yunwen, had already ascended the throne, it would have been most unseemly to say the least, and against all accepted codes of conduct, for an uncle to usurp the throne from his nephew. Accordingly, 14 months after Zhu Yuanzhang's death, Zhu Di proclaimed firmly his righteous expedition to "rid the new emperor of evil ministers" and to rescue the country from "disaster" on the pretext that treacherous court officials were stirring up trouble.

Once the wind began blowing, the brave soldiers spread out like clouds. Zhu Di personally commanded his troops and left Beiping in full regalia. After four years of battles, he finally captured Nanjing.

As soon as his troops entered the city, he sent an armed contingent to the palace to arrest Emperor Jianwen. Amidst the fracas, a huge fire broke out in the palace, flames rising sky-high. No trace of the emperor was to be found in the mêlée. A bold eunuch, pointing to a burnt body, vowed that it was the emperor. Other court attendants assuringly echoed their agreement. Zhu Di ordered his men to place this corpse in a luxurious coffin. But no one could authoritatively confirm that it was indeed the emperor. Some eunuchs claimed that the emperor had died in the fire, while others reported that he had fled, spinning out the details with great precision.

According to one story, when informed that Dongchuan Gate had fallen, Emperor Jianwen paced his antechamber sighing helplessly and contemplating suicide. At this moment, a eunuch came forth with a sizeable iron box. Handing it to the emperor, he said it had been given to him by the founding emperor before he died. The grandfather had left his successor some special advice: "Open only when in great danger." Emperor Jianwen opened the box and found three official personal identification documents issued to monks with three names: "Ying Wen", "Ying Xian" and "Ying Neng". There were also three Buddhist robes, three Buddhist caps, three pairs of Buddhist shoes, one razor and ten silver ingots. A personal letter was found, written in red by the former emperor:

"Ying Wen should leave through Devil's Gate, and the others through the trench." It so happened that there were two eunuchs in attendance on Emperor Jianwen, one called Yang Yingneng and the other Ye Xixian. On reading the letter, both volunteered to be tonsured and become monks together with Zhu Yunwen. They fled from Nanjing according to instructions in Zhu Yuanzhang's letter, and made for great temples in the famous mountains of southwest China, in all haste.

There is no written evidence concerning the ultimate whereabouts of Emperor Jianwen, but it is a fact that while he was emperor for four years, Zhu Yunwen had not started building an imperial tomb for himself, as his predecessor had done. Some records say that Emperor Jianwen, silver-haired, dressed in his Buddhist robe and carrying a Buddhist staff, came to Beiping in his late years. After his death, records say, he was buried on the southern slope of the Western Hills. A stone tablet was placed on his grave, inscribed with the words: "The Tomb of the World's Great Master." Probably this was only the good wishes of later generations. However, after Zhu Di became emperor, it is known that he sent many of his trusted men to various parts of the country to search for his nephew.

When Zhu Di ascended the throne, he gave his reign the title of Yongle. This was in 1403. As his troops had been stationed in Beiping for many years, he understood the strategic importance of the location and decided to move the capital there. In the fourth year of the Yongle Reign, he mobilized a million people to build his palace, temples and gardens. The Imperial Palace (the Forbidden City), the Temple of Heaven and the Workers' Cultural Palace today in Beijing were the very buildings constructed in his reign. They are now valuable sites of historic interest for generations to come.

In the fifth year of the Yongle Reign, the emperor's wife, Empress Xu, died. After pondering the matter over and over, Zhu Di did not build a tomb for her in Nanjing, but sent the minister of rites and a geomancer from Jiangxi to Beiping to seek an auspicious site. They covered all the outskirts of the city and after two years had chosen a number of sites for selection. Not until the seventh year of the Yongle Reign, after a personal inspection by Zhu Di, was the present site for the tombs finally decided on. It was to be at the foot of the Huangtu Hills in Changping County.

The location is ideal. Ridges of the Yan Mountains extend from the northwestern highlands, providing a natural barrier for defence; in the centre is a vast plain of scenic beauty, with rivers flowing down from the upper valleys on both sides of the plain. Even more outstanding are two green hills, one on either side of the plain, like two generals guarding the whole area. The tombs were built here not simply because the scenery was superb, but mainly because the mountains provided a protective shield which made the place easy to defend, but difficult to attack. Once troops were stationed there, they could both guard the tombs and defend the capital city. Zhu Di promptly issued his edict: An area of some 120 square kilometres is to be cordoned off for the tombs, access is to be restricted and work will begin building Chang Ling, with troops stationed there to guard it.

In the seventh year of the Yongle Reign, a gigantic project at the foot of the Huangtu Hills was set in motion. More than 400,000 troops and civilians were put to work. According to *Faithful Records of the Ming Dynasty*, a party was given at the Huangtu Hills to celebrate Zhu Di's birthday. In honour of the occasion, the officials called the hills the Heavenly Longevity Hills in order to please him. Zhu Di was delighted and issued an edict authorising the new name.

It took 18 years to build Chang Ling. Empress Xu died in the fifth year of the Yongle Reign and her body was kept in Nanjing for six years until it was moved into the underground palace at Chang Ling, which was completed in the 11th year of Yongle. Thus the empress became the first occupant of the Ming Tombs.

In 1424 Zhu Di commanded the fifth military expedition to the northern wilderness and died of illness on his way back to the capital. The emperor who had played such an active role on the central stage of history for 22 years went to join his wife in his final resting place in the underground palace of Chang Ling.

From the time Emperor Yongle started to build the first tomb for himself at the foot of the Heavenly Longevity Hills to the time the last Ming emperor, Zhu Youjian (Emperor Chongzhen), was buried there, all the emperors of the Ming Dynasty were buried in the vicinity of the hills with the exception of Zhu Qijue (Emperor Jing). There are 13 tombs in all, forming a concentration of tombs for the emperors of the middle and late periods of the Ming Dynasty.

The tombs were enclosed by walls, built at commanding parts of the surrounding hills, which totalled

12 kilometres. The walls were reinforced with ten passes, on which defence towers were built for the tomb guards. The buildings at each of the Ming Tombs constitute an integral architectural ensemble, and the layout, form and structures are the same as those at Xiao Ling for the founding emperor Zhu Yuanzhang in Nanjing. A divine road, a stone bridge and a towering tablet without inscription lead to the gate of each tomb palace. Inside the gate on the same axis are the Gate of Heavenly Favour, the Hall of Heavenly Favour, the Archway That Divides This and the Nether Worlds, the Five Stone Sacrificial Wares (one incense burner, two vases and two candlesticks), the stele pavilion and the Tomb Mound. The mound is surrounded by a thick, solid rampart, on which the stele pavilion stands. The underground palace is beneath the mound. From the far to near distance the land rises step by step, hills loom behind and streams flow by, forming a magnificent and broad panorama. The buildings both above and below the ground are the crystallisation of the extraordinary talents and wisdom of the people of ancient China. They represent the acme of a special civilisation and culture.

The pity is that not all of this wealth, nor even a large portion of it, has been preserved. Following the Tumu Incident* in the 14th year of the Zhengtong Reign (1449), and after the Wala army from the north invaded the Imperial Tombs and set fire to the buildings, the civilisation here began its tragic downhill course. Of the 13 Halls of Heavenly Favour that best

---

*This refers to the capture of Emperor Yingzong by the army of the Wala Tribe in Tumubao.

symbolised the architectural style and ornamentation of the tombs, only that of Chang Ling withstood the repeated ravages of war. This grand building, completed in the second year of the Xuande Reign (1427), has survived relatively intact after 500 years. The Hall of Heavenly Favour is supported by 60 huge, gold inlaid columns of *nanmu* wood, of which the four in the centre are 14.3 metres in height and 1.17 metres in diameter. These huge *nanmu* columns are unmatched anywhere, including the Hall of Supreme Harmony in the Imperial Palace itself. Both in structure and in architectural style, the Hall of Heavenly Favour may be rated as one of the most outstanding models of ancient Chinese architecture. It also reflects the wealth and prosperity of the country at that time.

The wind died down, it stopped snowing and the sun set. The undulating hills were bathed in a silvery evening glow. All was cold and quiet. Zhao Qichang and Zhao Tonghai concluded their first visit to Chang Ling and were about to return to the city. What had they found to take back for consideration?

The third evening after their return, Wu Han's medium-sized study was brightly lit. Photographs, sketches, data and specimens of earth relating to Chang Ling were placed on the floor. Wu Han and Xia Nai were listening to an inspection report from Zhao Qichang: "We walked all over the Chang Ling mound and its rampart for two days, but found no useful clues worth considering. From the two prospecting holes we dug inside the rampart behind the stele pavilion, we took out only filled earth. We found none of the original soil of the site for comparison. Further digging for sample earth was no longer of any significance. Supposition without clues will lead us to failure."

Wu Han lowered his head and tapped the desk with a pencil. Xia Nai kept examining the specimens of earth with a magnifying glass. Silence reigned.

Zhao Qichang, the first to speak, made a new suggestion: "It's cold now and the frozen ground is difficult to dig. Could you spare me two months for consult some historical materials? The emperors and empresses buried in the tombs could not have died at the same time regardless of whether the tombs were built before or after their deaths. Since they could not have been buried at the same time, there had to be the problem of reopening the vaults. How was this problem solved? With these questions in mind, I would like to make further investigations and stay there for a few more days."

Xia Nai had always set great stock in investigation, especially investigation closely linked with written records. He said: "The construction of the Ming Tombs lasted for more than 200 years. There should be some changes in the architectural layouts, forms and structures in the early, middle and late periods. Conduct a general survey and compare the differences. This should give rise to some questions. Analyse the different tombs in connection with the funeral system of the Ming Dynasty, make cross-references and use them to confirm the facts. Something might be achieved. Do all this before the actual work starts, and we will be sure to get somewhere. I agree to your suggestion."

Wu Han also agreed. He told Zhao Qichang: "You want to study the relevant literature? Good idea! I have plenty of books here, take any of them you like; take some with you today." Pointing to the bookshelf he added: "Make a new investigation by all means. But how long will you stay there?" He turned to Xia Nai, "How long do you think would be sufficient?"

Zhao Qichang raised two fingers. "Two months are fine," Xia Nai put in. "A few days for each tomb, two months isn't long."

Wu Han had taken the two fingers to mean two weeks. Since they indicated two months, he let it go at that. The tension broke, and they lapsed into casual conversation.

It may be that Zhao Qichang was finding the load on his shoulders too heavy, for he asked: "Vice-Mayor Wu, Chang Ling is just too big! Why don't we dig a small one as a sort of test?" Wu Han, taken by surprise, turned to Xia Nai: "What does 'dig as a test' mean? What sort of test?" Xia Nai replied with a laugh: "You flunked the test. A test is a test!" Wu Han also laughed: "Then what's the difference between digging as a test, and just digging?"

Xia Nai replied: "A test dig and a dig are the same as to the methods and procedures. There is also little difference when it comes to sorting out the data. Reports are issued all the same. When positive results are rather uncertain, we call it a 'test dig' out of modesty, in a way. There is precedence for this in other countries."

Both Zhao and Xia were unanimous on the question of test digging. As to whether a test would be conducted, the decision could only be made on investigation and approval by a higher authority.

The report over, Wu Han saw them to the door. He said to Zhao Qichang with a smile: "Your trip to Chang Ling must have been hard. It was really cold.

Where in the world did you stay?"

"There are no inns or hotels at the Ming Tombs," Zhao told him. "We had to stay in a small teahouse run by a peasant at the foot of the hills. For two nights the two of us slept huddled on a wooden bench with no room to turn over. We went to bed late and got up early, so we didn't mind the cold so much." Wu Han turned to Xia Nai, "At present, Changping County is not under the Beijing Municipality. It is part of Hebei Province. It might be incorporated into Beijing later. After the work starts, I'll go there to see the local government head. We may need to enlist his help later." Xia Nai smiled: "The field work itself is hard enough. On top of that, you usually can't eat or sleep well. It's like that at the Institute of Archaeology. But you young people can stand a lot...Good luck. At least you will never have a dull moment!"

Spring was on its way. The snow on the ground at the Ming Tombs began to thaw. How would the second trip north to the Ming Tombs turn out?

Chapter Two
PIERCING THE MIASMA OF HISTORY

An Episode at Xian Ling

Zhao Qichang visited almost all the major libraries in Beijing in search of the needed data from among stacks of books. He borrowed a number of classics, including *Faithful Records of the Ming Dynasty*, *Laws and Systems of the Great Ming Dynasty*, *History of the Ming Dynasty*, *Chronicles of the Ming Dynasty*, and *Miscellaneous Records of the Capital City*. These he read carefully. Not even the notes and unofficial history books written by people in the Ming and Qing escaped his scrutiny. He wanted to gain a clear understanding of the emperors, empresses, princes, dukes, concubines and eunuchs of that time. Moreover he needed a clear picture of the layout, form and structure of each of their tombs; the sacrificial rites, burial systems and burial articles; the evolution process of the imperial tombs and funerals, and in particular the form and structure of all the underground buildings. As to this most crucial part of all, little could be found in these records. In order to know exactly what the imperial tombs were like, it was necessary to enter them and make on-the-spot surveys. There was no other way.

The snow melted, exposing patches of withered grass. Walking into the grounds of the imperial tombs, they were at once struck by a feeling of melancholy and desolation. The magnificent pavilions, the halls and the ramparts surrounding the tomb mounds, were now weathered and crumbling, their former glory faded and shabby. Wild grass, broken walls and debris bemoaned the ravages of time. The once splendid architectural ensemble was falling to ruin. Mixed feelings welled up in Zhao's mind. "Where once the imperial tombs dominated the scene, the abandoned graves now look pathetic in the setting sun."

Members of the work team came to the Chang Ling Management Office to begin their visits and investigation. In the daytime they carefully inspected the tombs one by one and in the evening called on local residents. To glean even the slightest bit of information about the 13 imperial tombs was like searching for a needle in the sea.

After days of visits and investigation, they decided to focus their attention on Xian Ling.

Xian Ling is located about half a kilometre west of Chang Ling at the foot of the Huangquansi (Nether World Temple) Hill. Zhu Gaochi, Zhu Di's eldest son, was buried there. The tomb was the closest to Chang Ling, but smaller, and the time of the son's burial was close to the father's. Thus from the angle of excavation, Xian Ling was the most suitable for a test dig. The materials, equipment and personnel could be stationed in the Chang Ling area, where it would be easier to supply food and accommodation. They began work on Xian Ling by first consulting history books, collecting data, making field surveys and looking for leads.

Zhu Di, Emperor Yongle, died of illness at

Yumuchuan in today's Inner Mongolia) while returning in triumph to the capital city from his fifth expedition to the northern wilderness. He had designated the crown prince Zhu Gaochi as successor to the throne.

Zhu Gaochi became the fourth emperor of the Ming Dynasty at the age of 47. His reign was short-lived, for he died within ten months of ascending the throne. "Renzong" was the temple title given to him after his death.

It is very appropriate to call Zhu Gaochi "Renzong". The Chinese character *ren* used here means "benevolence". As a feudal emperor, he was one of the few who were seriously concerned about the welfare of the common people. Early in the 28th year of the Hongwu Reign his grandfather Zhu Yuanzhang personally made him crown prince of the Yan State. At that time most of the princes were sent to the vassal states. Only a few of them were allowed to stay in the capital. However, Zhu Yuanzhang kept his grandsons with him, with the intention of teaching them how to become future leaders of the vassal states. Zhu Gaochi wrote well; no one among the other grandsons could match him. Zhu Yuanzhang often asked him to write remarks or comments on the memorials submitted to him. Most of the memorials Zhu Gaochi selected were about the life of the ordinary people or natural calamities that occurred in different parts of the country. These he would promptly return to Zhu Yuanzhang for further remarks.

Zhu Yuanzhang once asked him: "Why are most of the reports you choose for me to read those about natural calamities?" "Your grandson thinks that food is a basic need of the people. Now there are disasters in some places, and the people are desperate. This is a matter of the greatest urgency. So I beg Your Majesty, my grandfather, to give it priority."

Zhu Yuanzhang nodding, asked again: "When Yao was on the throne, floods prevailed for nine years; during the reign of Tang, droughts lasted for seven years. How did the people survive in those days?"

"They relied on the policies of looking after the people established by the sages of Yao and Tang."

Zhu Yuanzhang was immensely delighted when he heard this. He said: "Although you are a child living in the palace, you are concerned with the hardships of the people. What a fine boy you are!"

After the Ming Dynasty was founded, the economy revived and the state treasury was filled as a result of practising correct policies. However, Zhu Di had a weakness for the grandiose. He mounted many large-scale expeditions; used up huge amounts of manpower and materials in moving the capital to Beijing and dredging the Grand Canal. The very day when Zhu Gaochi ascended the throne, his first decree was to withdraw the fleet commanded by Zheng He on his seventh voyage to the Indian Ocean, recall the envoys who were purchasing pearls in Jiaozhi* and the officials who were buying horses in the Western Regions**; and stop all the costly purchases, castings and supplies for the imperial court. Unfortunately, however, this

---

*Jiaozhi, today's Hanoi, refers to the prefectural capital of Jiaozhou, which encompassed what are now the northern and central parts of Vietnam.

**Western Regions, a Han Dynasty term, includes what is now Xinjiang and parts of Central Asia.

ambitious emperor who was bent on strengthening the country and enriching the people died of illness in the short ten-month period of his rule.

There is one obvious difference between Xian Ling and the other tombs: The Hall of Heavenly Favour and the stele pavilion were separated by a small hill, which divides the tomb area in two. The Hall of Heavenly Favour no longer exists and there are only some ruined buildings behind the hill. Zhao Qichang and his teammates searched for leads around the rampart and the pavilion, carefully studying and analysing all possible traces and marks left at the entrance of the tunnel to the burial vault. Under the tomb system in the Ming Dynasty, the inside of the rampart was filled up with loess and covered with a big tumulus. However, the tumulus of Xian Ling, which looked very simple and shabby, did not reach the rim of the encircling rampart. Zhao Qichang recalled Emperor Renzong's last decree as recorded in the history books: "Economy and frugality must be practised in construction of the tomb, the funeral ceremonies should be held for a matter of days instead of months, all people should take off their mourning apparel in 27 days, and commanders guarding defence posts and ministers with important duties are all permitted to excuse themselves from attending." As his son Zhu Zhanji acted upon his order, the construction of Xian Ling was not extravagant and Emperor Renzong was buried in three months. This record seems to be in accordance with the facts.

They found no clues after two weeks of searching. The work team continued to visit local families. They learned by chance that a "tomb genealogy" had been preserved in a nearby village. It was said to have recorded the tomb construction process and burial rites. Most villages in the vicinity had developed from the defence posts guarding the tombs, so it was highly possible that secret records were in the possession of some of the inhabitants. After three days of inquiries, Zhao Qichang succeeded in borrowing the "tomb genealogy" from a rich peasant. On inspecting it, he could only laugh helplessly. It turned out to be a collection of rumours and guesses with no historical value whatsoever.

Thirty years later we read what was recorded about Xian Ling in the "tomb genealogy". For example:

> ...When Emperor Renzong was crown prince, he loafed about in the palace every day. According to a palace rule, the crown prince could enter an imperial concubine's chamber in the evening if and only if a red lantern hung at her door or on her window. If a green lantern was lit, it meant that a senior member of the family was inside, and so the crown prince should not enter.
>
> One night, when Crown Prince Renzong was idling away his time in the palace, he saw a red lantern hanging on the window lattice of a chamber. He promptly dismissed his attendants and went in. When he took off his clothes, he found his mother's sister on the bed...
>
> This was no secret in the palace. Along with the gossip was a rumour that the crown prince had long shown excessive affection for his aunt, who was several years older than he. That night, he himself had taken the green lantern down from his

aunt's window and replaced it with a red one. Another rumour ran that his aunt, who was in love with him, had taken away the green lantern herself and put the red one up in its place.

After Emperor Renzong died, his son Zhu Zhanji had his father's tomb built behind a small earthen hill, so that the Hall of Heavenly Favour and the stele pavilion were out of sight of each other, implying the use of a hill to cover up the scandal between Emperor Renzong and his aunt. So later, the hill came to be called the 'scandal cover-up hill' ...

The villagers, of course, had no inkling of the true meaning of the hill. According to historical records, the construction of the tomb was in keeping with *fengshui**. The most important principle for the construction of an imperial tomb was to choose the "dragon's ridge"; the undulating hill was a symbol of this. When Xian Ling was built, the hill, shaped like a long table, was left untouched, to serve as the "dragon's ridge". It is called the "Jade Table Hill" in historical records. No one had expected that it would do injustice to the memory of Emperor Renzong.

---

*Fengshui, the direction and surroundings of a house or tomb, supposed to have an influence on the fortune of a family and their offspring.

Visit to a Prison

Little is recorded in the histories about the Ming Tombs. The "tomb genealogy" served only as a topic for idle talk after dinner. Not a single lead could be found for scientific excavation of the huge complex. With the days passing by swiftly, members of the work team were burning with impatience.

To make matters worse they were suddenly approached by two policemen armed to the teeth.

"Some villagers informed us that you've come here to rob the tombs. What's this all about?" the tall one demanded, standing three metres away with a pistol in his right hand.

Seeing the tense, threatening faces of the policemen, Zhao Qichang took a letter of introduction out of his pocket, and said jovially: "We're here on a mission for the government, and we've already informed the Ming Tombs Management Office about the details. It's all above board."

The tall policeman took the letter and read it carefully. A smile spread across his face and he put his pistol down. Offering Zhao a cigarette, he said apologetically, "I'm sorry. The problem is that thieves haunt this place. We heard a report and came here to check it out."

This episode, which should have been dismissed with a laugh, actually gave the work team a new idea: Can we discover some leads from the robbed tombs, or get some inkling of the structure of the underground palace from statements made by tomb robbers? Once the decision was made, they went about their work separately.

Finally, Zhao Qichang obtained some information in Chang Ling Yuan Village. In 1923 a local bandit named Hou Xianwen led a group of 18 people to dig the tomb of De Ling and the tomb of Imperial Concubine Wan, which are located to the east of Chang Ling. They failed because the tombs were strongly built and too big, but for this act Hou Xianwen was thrown into prison where he remained for the rest of his life. In the autumn of 1944 Cheng Laoliu of Chang Ling Yuan Village enlisted more than 100 men and declared himself Lord Cheng Liu, with the area of the Ming Tombs as his base. Once, in the dead of night, he secretly moved his troops to the tomb of Imperial Concubine Wan and began excavating. After three days and nights of shovelling, digging, chiselling and blasting, they succeeded in breaking through the roof of the tomb, went in and took away all the burial objects. Cheng Laoliu needed six horses to carry the gold and silverware to Chang Ling Yuan Village, where he distributed the loot. Each rank-and-filer was given one ounce of gold and 20 pearls, the officers each got a gold pot or its equivalent in gold ware, while Cheng Laoliu kept the lion's share.

On the third day after the tomb robbery, Cheng Laoliu held his wedding. A motorcade of distinguished guests came and a number of animals were slaughtered for the banquet. The ostentation and extravagance of the occasion had never before been seen by the local villagers. At the banquet the bride, wearing the gold headdress of the concubine with an air of elegance, looked as imposing as the empress herself.

His care-free days were numbered, however. Six months later Cheng Laoliu clashed with the garrison forces of the Kuomintang and a fight broke out. Cheng was killed by a stray bullet on the nearby riverbed, and his wife, concubine and property were all taken over by Kuomintang forces.

Once he got this lead, Zhao Qichang made for the site of the tomb of Imperial Concubine Wan to look for further clues.

Concubine Wan from Zhucheng in Shandong Province, was chosen to enter the palace at the age of four and trained as a palace maid. When she grew up, she found favour with the then crown prince Zhu Jianshen and entered into liaisons with him. When Zhu Jianshen ascended the throne at the age of 18, Miss Wan was already 35. However, she still enjoyed the favour of the young emperor because she was a born beauty, sharp-witted and clever at enhancing her charms. In 1466 she was elevated to the status of imperial concubine because she gave birth to a boy.

She died of illness at the age of 59 in the 23rd year of the Chenghua Reign. Emperor Xianzong Zhu Jianshen, deeply grieved, suspended his court duties for seven days. He broke the imperial rule that a person of her status was not permitted to be buried in the imperial tombs. In tribute to his beloved concubine, he had a large tomb built for her at the foot of Su Hill.

However, all that Zhao Qichang found there were piles of rubble and the foundations in ruins. There was only a big mound covered with wild grass and old trees in the deserted hills.

He walked through the ruins, climbed to the top of the mound and looked carefully around, but found no trace of the robbery described. Years of wind and rain had erased all evidence of the criminal actions. Zhao

Qichang bent backward and hammered his aching spine with his fist. Gazing at the distant pavilions and graves in the setting sun he felt frustrated. But in an instant he realised how silly he was. What would be the good of it even if he did find traces of the robbery? he reasoned. The present excavation was entirely different from that of a tomb robbery! The thieves could open the grave anywhere at random and achieve their purpose if they obtained gold, silver and other precious objects. But the excavation of the Ming Tombs had to be based on scientific archaeological methods. The first step was to find the entrance to the underground palace, go in through the tunnel along which the coffins had been carried in, and then find the remains of the deceased...This was what an archaeological dig was all about!

While Zhao Qichang went to the pillaged tomb of Imperial Concubine Wan, Yu Shugong, a member of the work team, paid a visit to the Changping County prison. He explained to the warden why he had come: he wanted to get some clues from one of the prisoners.

A middle-aged convict with a shaved head was led into the interrogation room by two guards. Yu Shugong was sitting at a table.

"Which tombs did you rob?" he demanded in a no-nonsense tone of voice.

The middle-aged man threw himself on his knees, and looking about entreatingly stammered: "Sir, I...I have confessed everything. I know there is leniency if one confesses...and severity if one refuses...I robbed only one tomb."

"Where?" Yu Shugong asked, his eyes lighting up.

"The tomb for a prince...outside the Desheng

Gate."

"How did you get into it?"

"I...I was a mason. The tomb robbers came to me. I helped them take the stones away." Drops of sweat rolled down the forehead of the prisoner; he was obviously a new-comer in the prison.

"How did you find the entrance?" Yu Shugong stood up, a stern look on his face. This was crucial.

"The three of us dug and dug, and we...found the stones. I...I was the first to find the seam. We chiselled...and pried. In about two hours, we opened the top of the tomb." The man's face softened with joy as his mind went back to that unforgettable night.

Yu Shugong knitted his brows. "How large was it inside?" he demanded, glaring.

"It was dark inside...I couldn't see anything." The convict added with a vague gesture: "Probably ...the size of this room."

After listening to him, Yu Shugong sat down again and remained silent for a while. He then signalled the policemen to take the convict away. Two other convicts were brought in, from whom nothing was extracted.

Leaving the prison, Yu Shugong concluded that the visit had been fruitless. How could just a handful of people rob one of these large Ming Tombs? he mused. It couldn't be done, unless it was handled by a warlord like Sun Dianying, who used explosives to blast the tombs of Emperor Qianlong and Empress Dowager Cixi of the Qing Dynasty. But were Sun's methods of any use in archaeological excavations?

So far they had certainly been muddle-headed in carrying out their assignment. In order to find proper clues, they would have to change their "tactics".

An Opening in the Wall

A jeep wound down the mountain road to the Ming Tombs, leaving behind a cloud of dust. In the jeep were Zhao Qichang, Zhao Tonghai and Yu Lianzeng. Peering through the small window, Zhao Qichang could see that the fields were beginning to turn green. He was lost in thought.

The younger Zhao, unable to suppress his curiosity, asked, "What did Vice-Mayor Wu and Director Xia say?"

"Look for clues at Ding Ling first," Zhao Qichang replied.

"Why at Ding Ling first?" Little Yu asked.

"Ding Ling was built in the later years, the ground buildings are in a better state of preservation, and so restoration will be easier."

"What did Vice-Mayor Wu say?" the younger Zhao persisted.

"He said that Emperor Wanli's reign was the longest in the Ming Dynasty. It lasted for 48 years. Maybe there is more historical data about it."

"Then how shall we start?"

Zhao Qichang did not reply. He had not even heard Little Yu's question, because his mind was now immersed in their first survey of Ding Ling and the related historical data about it.

Ding Ling was one of the tombs built later in the Ming Dynasty, a little more than 300 years old. Nevertheless, the ravages of inclement weather as well as of repeated wars had turned this tomb precinct into a scene of devastation. The high, thick, red outer walls were no longer standing, the tomb walls had collapsed in two places, and the magnificent main hall of yellow glazed tiles symbolising the power and dignity of the emperor had been levelled, with only rows of the column-base stones left. All this spoke of its sufferings to anyone who would listen.

According to historical records, Ding Ling was burned in three big fires which caused its ruin and destruction. When troops of the Qing Dynasty came to the area, they inflicted wide-scale destruction on the tombs and set fire to Emperor Wanli's mausoleum Ding Ling, as well as to Emperor Tianqi's, named De Ling.

Not long before, Li Zicheng* had led his army to attack the capital city. Because the general guarding Juyong Pass had surrendered, the peasants' army occupied the Ming Tombs. Li Zicheng ordered his troops to burn the main halls of the Ming Tombs, to destroy the walls and gates of Ding Ling, Qing Ling and De Ling. The whole area of the Ming Tombs was reduced to "bricks and stones, with the flames burning for three days".

After the fourth year of the Shunzhi Reign (1647), the Qing Dynasty took measures to restore and protect the Ming Tombs to alleviate ethnic contradictions. (The Qing Dynasty was set up by the Manchu, whereas the Ming and most other dynasties were ruled by the Han, the largest ethnic group in China.) It set up tomb-protection households, distributed land to them and prohibited the felling of trees for firewood. It also

---

*Li Zicheng was leader of the peasants' army during the late years of the Ming Dynasty.

repaired Si Ling, tomb of the last Ming emperor. In the 50th year of his reign (1785), Emperor Qianlong wrote a long elegy with 13 different rhymes and had it inscribed on the back of the tablet in front of Emperor Yongle's tomb. The front of the tablet bears five Chinese characters praising Yongle as an emperor of "great accomplishments and heavenly virtue". The poem expressed his admiration of the Ming emperors. He also had largescale repairs made at Ding Ling and De Ling.

An inspection of the tombs by the work team revealed that the much-vaunted repairs done to the Ming Tombs by Emperor Qianlong were nothing but a patchwork of old materials. This is reflected most clearly in the ruins of the Hall of Heavenly Favour and the Gate of Heavenly Favour of Ding Ling. Repairs to De Ling for Emperor Tianqi were conscientiously recorded in the historical data, but no work was actually done.

In the early years of the Republic of China (1912-1949), a man by the name of Guo Wu was assigned to take care of and protect the tombs. The government not only exempted him of taxes, but also gave him subsidies every year. An idle man named Wang also wanted to join the tomb-protection household. When he went to Guo Wu and was refused, he flew into a rage. In the dead of night he went to Ding Ling with a pail of kerosene and set fire to the Hall of Heavenly Favour. The flames rose swiftly to the sky, turning the whole tomb area into a raging furnace which could be seen within a circumference of 20 kilometres.

Within three days the Hall of Heavenly Favour was reduced to ashes and charcoal. Wang the idler had intended to shift the blame on Guo Wu, but the plot misfired. In the end he himself was thrown into prison, where he died...

The jeep stopped in front of the entrance to Ding Ling. When they got out, young Zhao and Little Yu stared at Zhao Qichang, not knowing what to do. "We'll start in front of the encircling rampart and proceed backward along the outer side of the wall from both directions," he told them. "I'll start from the south. You two from the north. Remember, never overlook anything suspicious, however trivial. Even if you see one or two bricks that have been moved, check it out carefully." Then he added: "This time, we can't afford to leave here empty-handed. We must make every effort to find something." The two young men were almost out of sight when he called out to them: "If you're hungry, there's food in the jeep!"

Zhao Qichang grabbed a shovel and scraped away the over-lying weeds, bricks, earth and wild grass. He looked around carefully from east to west. The seven-metre-high and four-metre-thick wall still looked magnificent and overpowering, in spite of damage and erosion by the winds and rains of over 300 years.

Since ancient times, certain structures have been imbued with strong political significance. The triumphal arch on the Capitoline hill in ancient Rome doubtlessly reflects the great cause of Augustus Caesar (63 BC — AD 14). The pyramids on the Nile are enduring expressions of eternity and the immortal sway of the divine power and earthly might of the pharaohs. The magnificent Place de la Concorde and its radiating roads in Paris, built during the Ottoman Empire, served to show the unparallelled might of the Napoleonic Empire. The oxblood walls of the Ming

Tombs rising above the viewer inspire a feeling of awe. Like the magnificent Imperial Palace, they have an air of indestructible and eternal authority, making mere mortals shrink at the sight.

Zhao Qichang walked ahead step by step. His neck was numb, his back ached, his legs were stiff. He was completely exhausted. He sat down on a rock and lit a cigarette. Through the smoke coiling up before his eyes, he gazed at the distant hills and the blue sky. His eyes wandered back to the thick rampart. In a flash, a miracle appeared — some wall bricks about three metres up from the ground had caved in and a round opening about half a metre in diameter was revealed.

"What's all this?" Zhao Qichang rubbed his eyes, strained by the sun, and stared at the dark cavity, his heart thumping.

A sudden recollection came to him. The other day a villager had said: "Along the wall of one tomb, I am not sure which, west of Chang Ling, there's a big hole. When bandits or the Japanese invaders came, the villagers used to hide there in the cave..." Could this be the cave? If it was, there must be something in it, he thought.

Bursting with excitement he rushed back, his legs suddenly sparked with energy. "I've found it! I've found it! Come and look, hurry up and come!"

His loud, clear voice carried over the rampart and sounded out farther to the fields.

His two young teammates arrived quickly, and the three of them stared in wonder at the cave opening.

With no ladder, no stones or bricks at hand, how

could they reach high enough? With Zhao Qichang beside himself with excitement, the two young men quickly squatted down and said: "Come on! Climb upon our shoulders and take a look! See what's inside!"

Zhao Qichang stepped on their shoulders and made his way slowly up the wall. The sun at noon shone over the hole, leaving the inside dark. Its upper edge looked like the top of an arched entrance way, and the illuminated part could be recognised as something made of brick, but for the moment it was difficult to confirm the existence of an arched gate. They took turns looking in, but could reach no conclusion about what they actually saw.

"Don't move! You stay here, and I'll go to Chang Ling Yuan Village to phone Professor Xia Nai!" With that, Zhao Qichang set out for the village as fast as he could run.

On receiving the call, Xia Nai hurried to Ding Ling by car, bringing along with him some young archaeologists.

Thirty years after the opening of the Ding Ling underground palace, we read the following passages about Xia Nai in the "Archaeology Volume" of the *Great Encyclopaedia of China*:

> Xia Nai, self-styled Zuoming, was born on December 27, 1909, one of the leading directors and organisers of archaeological work in China.
>
> He graduated from the department of history of Qinghua University.
>
> Attended the University of London, England, in the summer of 1935, and was awarded the degree of Doctor of Egyptian Archaeology.

While studying in England, he took part in the excavation of the ruins of the early Iron Age earth mound Maiden Castle in Dorset, led by Sir Mortimer Wheeler, professor of archaeology, University of London, in 1936.

In 1937 he took part in the excavations in Egypt and Tel Duweir in Palestine together with the British Exploration Team, and learned directly from Sir William Mathew Flinders Petrie. After five years, having finished his studies in England, he returned to China at the end of 1940.

Between 1944 and 1945, he and Xiang Da were charged with archaeological exploration in Gansu Province for the Northwest China Scientific Exploration Group. Through tomb excavations of the Qijia culture at Yangwawan in Ningding County, they confirmed that Yangshao culture preceeded Qijia culture. In his article "New Discoveries of Tombs of the Qijia Period and Revision of Its Years", he corrected the division of the periods of the Neolithic culture in Gansu by Swedish archaeologist Johan Gunnar Andersson, laying the foundation for the establishment of the correct chronology of the Neolithic culture in the Yellow River Basin. This marked a new starting point for China's prehistoric archaeology.

Although he disagreed on the question of excavating the Ming Tombs, he dedicated himself to the work once the decision was made. The urgent matter for the immediate present was to find the entrance to the underground palace through which the emperors and empresses were carried to their final resting places.

Only when the excavation started at the real entrance, would it be possible to reveal what had existed 300 years ago and to distinguish historically between what was true and what was false.

The three members of the excavation team formed a human ladder with their shoulders for Xia Nai to climb up on.

He took a torch from his pocket and searched inside the cave carefully, using his hand-shovel to knock at the bricks and stones from time to time. After 15 minutes he climbed down.

The three drew close to him, their eyes fixed on him in hopes of getting a correct answer to this centuries-old riddle as soon as possible.

Xia Nai pondered for a moment, and turned to them: "According to my observation, these bricks are not the original ones. They are vestiges of relaid bricks. Maybe this was the upper edge of an arched gate."

"The rampart was built so solidly, how could an arched gate be hidden inside?" one of the young men asked.

Xia Nai looked at them and explained, as if to himself: "Ding Ling is more than 300 years old. Maybe because the original tier of bricks and the tier of bricks laid later were not closely connected, the outer tier of bricks, or the later brick wall, collapsed and caved in after years of erosion." He stopped and looked at Zhao Qichang without saying another word.

Zhao Qichang was suddenly struck with a new idea. "It is recorded in the historical data that outside the rampart of Ding Ling and Yong Ling, there was an outer wall," he began. "Although the outer wall was destroyed long ago, the ruins confirm its existence. Can't we assume that if this cavity indicates the passage for the burial, it was inside the outer wall and outside the inner wall, and after the coffins of the emperors and empresses entered the gate, they were carried into the underground palace from here?"

Zhao Qichang looked at Xia Nai after he finished. The others became excited: "Is this correct, Director Xia?"

Xia Nai nodded, without showing his feelings. "You could be right. I'm going back to consult with Vice-Mayor Wu as to what we should do next." He and Zhao Qichang drove back to the city together.

When they arrived, Wu Han looked somewhat impatient. Without waiting for Xia Nai to begin, he asked: "How is the investigation going?"

"I think we have a very promising lead."

"Are you sure?"

Xia Nai looked at the anxious face of his schoolmate and smiled. "I think you are really a layman in archaeology. We can't draw any conclusion before we open it up."

Wu Han flushed, paced up and down, and said sharply, "Give me your word! I need your assurance!"

Xia Nai replied calmly: "We found what looked like the entrance to the underground palace."

Wu Han stopped in his tracks, full of joy. "Have a discussion with the others and submit a report for test digging. Let's get started."

Chapter Three

DING LING, CHOICE OF THE EMPEROR

Wrangling over "Auspicious Land"

Emperor Longqing (Zhu Zaihou), the 12th emperor of the Ming Dynasty, reached the age of 36 on the 25th day of the 5th lunar month of 1572. As far as he knew, his illness was beyond cure, and he would not live much longer. The grand academicians Gao Gong, Zhang Juzheng and Gao Yi were summoned to the Hall of Heavenly Purity to hear his last edict. They arrived in haste to find the emperor lying in bed, his face ghastly pale, breathing his last. At his side were the empress, imperial concubines and the crown prince. The vast hall was a scene of stress and grief. The only anxiety weighing on the mind of Emperor Longqing at this moment concerned his favourite son, Zhu Yijun, the ten-year-old successor to the throne who was standing on his left. To his regret, the empire his son was to inherit was neither peaceful nor prosperous. The emperor's mind was tormented by fear and uncertainty over how his ministers would treat Zhu Yijun and the Zhu family dynasty. He was running out of the time and energy needed to protect his beloved son. Holding Gao Gong and Zhang Juzheng by the hands, his eyes full of tears, he appealed to these ministers in a feeble whisper: "As I leave this world, it is my hope that you will do your best to help the crown prince and ensure that the dynasty will rule the empire forever…"

Emperor Longqing died the following day.

On the 10th day of the 6th lunar month of 1572 Crown Prince Zhu Yijun ascended the throne. The next year (1573) was enumerated as the first year of the Wanli Reign, which was to last 48 years.

In the 3rd month of 1580 Emperor Wanli, still under 18, paid his first homage to the Imperial Tombs at the Heavenly Longevity Hills, at which time he began to think of how to build his own tomb. Fearing that Zhang Juzheng and other ministers would advise against it, he did not openly speak of his intention. A few years later Zhang Juzheng died of illness. Zhang Siwei, who succeeded Zhang Juzheng as chief cabinet minister*, read the emperor's thoughts and suggested that a tomb be prepared for him. This proposal fitted exactly with the emperor's wish and he issued a decree immediately: "I intend to offer the annual spring sacrifices at the Heavenly Longevity Hills in the intercalary second month of the lunar new year, and at the same time, choose a site for my tomb."

To an emperor who was only 21 years old and in the prime of his youth, his seemingly odd decision was by no means because he sensed his days were numbered, but rather that he was conscious of having risen in stature to the height of his illustrious forefathers.

In planning the construction of his tomb, not only

---

*A title for the first grand academician in the Ming Dynasty. The chief cabinet minister was a very important official who handled major cabinet affairs.

was he not dissuaded or obstructed from the task, as he was from some of his other decisions, but was in fact encouraged by his ministers.

As proposed by Zhang Siwei, the construction should follow the precedent for choosing the site for his tomb set in the 15th year of the Jiajing Reign by Emperor Shizong. Ministers, generals, officials in charge of astronomy, astrology, divination and related sciences, and geomancers were ordered to select two or three "auspicious sites" in the Heavenly Longevity Hills for final approval by the emperor himself during his visit to the Imperial Tombs.

On the 4th day of the 2nd lunar month of 1583 Chen Shuling, a high official in charge of sacrificial rites under the Ministry of Rites; Yan Bang, chief official in charge of water supervision under the Ministry of Works; Zhang Bangyuan, deputy chief in charge of astronomy, astrology and divination; and geomancer Lian Shichang, were sent to the Heavenly Longevity Hills to conduct a survey.

They inspected all the hills within the area of the Imperial Tombs as well as the surrounding plain and nearby streams. After careful consideration and comparison, they returned to Beijing on the 14th day. The following day the Ministry of Rites submitted a plan of their selections together with a diagram to the emperor: "From the Ministry of Rites. Chen Shuling, in charge of sacrificial rites, together with Yan Bang, head of water supervision department under the Ministry of Works, and others, paid an advance visit to the Heavenly Longevity Hills and surveyed the whole area. They have chosen Tanyu Hill to the east of Yong Ling, Xiangzi Hill to the north of Zhao Ling and

Lecaowa to the south of Eastern Well as auspicious sites."

After reading the plan and studying the diagram, Emperor Wanli ordered Xu Wenbi, Duke Dingguo; Zhang Siwei, chief cabinet minister; Zhang Hong, eunuch in charge of ceremonies and officials of various ranks who understood *fengshui* to check the selection.

After Xu Wenbi and his entourage arrived at the Imperial Tombs, they first climbed Tanyu Hill, from which they had a clear view of the whole area. Although it was early spring, neither the grass nor the trees had turned green or sprouted. However, when they stood among the hills, they were clearly aware of the advent of spring. At dawn every morning a white fog rose from among the green pines and cypresses. It drifted with the cool breeze and glimmered radiantly like coloured silk in the red glow of morning. The place looked like a fairyland and indeed seemed an excellent place for an imperial tomb.

After visiting Tanyu Hill, they went on to Xiangzi Hill and Lecaowa. Although different from Tanyu Hill, they had their own peculiar characteristics and physical features. On the whole they were found to be equally commendable, equally "auspicious".

At the end of the 2nd lunar month Xu Wenbi and the others returned to Beijing, and submitted their memorandum to the emperor: "All three areas of land are truly auspicious."

Obviously only one could be chosen. This choice had to be made by the emperor himself. Therefore, Emperor Wanli decided to pay a second visit to the Imperial Tombs on the 12th day of the intercalary second month.

On the 16th day of the month, after the sacrificial rites were over, Emperor Wanli and his entourage visited Xiangzi Hill, Tanyu Hill and Lecaowa for further consideration. He expressed reservations concerning all three sites. On the 18th Emperor Wanli returned to his palace and ordered the Ministry of Rites, the Ministry of Works and the chief official in charge of astrology, astronomy and divination, to select two or three additional ones. The Ministry of Rites, chagrined at finding the emperor altogether too particular, submitted a memorandum: "Since we are very ignorant, we beg Your Majesty to allow Zhang Bangyuan to enlist more people to carry out the joint survey. Only in this way will it be possible to choose more auspicious sites for your selection." The emperor fully understood the tenor of this communication. He approved it on the spot. Without revealing any discomposure he issued the order: All officials, regardless of rank, may go to the Heavenly Longevity Hills to take part in the field survey, as long as they are acquainted with the physical features and *fengshui* of the area.

On the 3rd day of the 4th lunar month Xu Xuemo, minister of rites, and Yang Wei, minister of works, after an extensive survey and comparison of all the possible sites, concluded that Xinglong Hill, Dayu Hill and Shimengou Hill were the three "most auspicious sites" and submitted their proposal to the emperor together with a drawing.

On the 6th day of the 9th lunar month Emperor Wanli paid a third visit to the Imperial Tombs together with his empress and concubines in the name of offering autumn sacrifices. On the 9th day the emperor climbed Xinglong Hill and Dayu Hill for a personal inspection. After repeated comparisons, he gave his order: "Use Dayu Hill as the auspicious site for the construction of my tomb."

On the 19th day the Ministry of Rites submitted a memorandum to the effect that since the tomb site had been decided, a date should be fixed for construction to begin. The emperor insisted that this would be decided only after the two empress dowagers had seen it. Imperial Censor Zhu Yinggu suggested that the empress dowagers should not make the trip for the cost of their visit would be prohibitive, but the emperor did not agree.

On the 13th day of the 9th lunar month of 1584 Emperor Wanli accompanied the two empress dowagers, together with his empress and concubines, on his fourth visit to the Imperial Tombs. On the 16th of the same month, the emperor and the empress dowagers climbed the main peak of Dayu Hill for a personal inspection. The empress dowagers both agreed that Dayu Hill was the "most auspicious" site.

With this, wrangling over the "auspicious site" that had raged for almost two years came to an end.

The Magnificence of the Tomb Precinct

On the morning of the 6th day of the 10th lunar month of 1584 the ground was broken for the work on the mausoleum for Zhu Yijun, Emperor Wanli.

Construction of the tomb was a matter of prime importance. A special administration, similar to a committee, was set up. It consisted of three ministers, the eunuch in charge of rites and ceremonies and several generals. Xu Wenbi, Duke Dingguo, and Shen Shixing, chief cabinet minister were major supervisors of the work. Due to the large amount of civil engineering work which would require the physical strength of the troops the administration also included generals. Xu Wenbi was a descendant of Xu Da, one of the founding generals, and all important rites had to be performed with him at the helm, while Shen Shixing would plan and administrate the construction.

The Ministry of Rites had earlier submitted a memorandum to the emperor confirming his wish: The tomb should be built on a similar scale to that of Yong Ling, which "was well thought-out and brings endless blessings to the dynasty."

Under the plan for Yong Ling, the tomb was to occupy a large area; the underground palace to consist of nine halls*; the stele pavilion to be made of carved stones; the crenels of the rampart surrounding the tomb mound, the halls, the stele pavilion and the floor all to be built or veneered with brocatelle (a hard stone with colour veins); the rampart was to be enclosed by an outer wall; and as a matter of course, the huge timbers, stone and bricks were all to be selected strictly according to set standards.

Yong Ling was the tomb of Emperor Jiajing, grandfather of Emperor Wanli. Because his reign lasted for 45 years and his tomb was built before he died, the construction was on a larger scale and the buildings were more magnificent than its predecessors. The tomb precinct is 289.2 metres long and 149 metres wide, the

---
*The underground palace of Ding Ling actually consists of five halls.

grave within the rampart occupies an area of 51,687.2 square metres, the precinct is 41,170.8 square metres, and the total area is 92,858 square metres. The precinct for Ding Ling is 317.5 metres long and 150.3 metres wide, the mound area within the rampart is 41,526.5 square metres, the precinct proper is 42,935.9 square metres, and the total area is 84,462.4 square metres.

The total area of Yong Ling is 8,395.6 square metres larger than that of Ding Ling, but the precinct of Ding Ling is 1,765.1 square metres larger than that of Yong Ling. Therefore, if tourists today make a comparison, they will find Ding Ling larger and deeper than Yong Ling. This fully reflects the ingenuity and originality of the designers of Ding Ling. If we compare Ding Ling with Zhao Ling, the tomb of Emperor Wanli's father, Emperor Longqing, about half a kilometre away, Ding Ling appears large and magnificent whereas Zhao Ling is small and compact. This difference was noticed by ministers and generals at the time when work was first started on Ding Ling. Zhu Geng, imperial instructor, once remonstrated with the emperor: "Ding Ling is within sight of Zhao Ling, and it would be unseemly for Ding Ling to be bigger." The emperor ignored his advice and ordered the Ministry of Works to continue the work as planned.

Except for Yong Ling and Ding Ling, the roofs of the stele pavilions of the Imperial Tombs were all built of wood and therefore were all vulnerable when any misfortune befell the tombs. The Chang Ling, Jing Ling and Xian Ling pavilions which we see today were repaired in the 24th year of the Republic of China. Only the pavilions of Yong Ling and Ding Ling remained intact for the 400 years following their construction because their roofs, including architraves, *dougong**, eaves and corner posts, were all built of carved stone.

Since the tomb was to be built like Yong Ling, brocatelle was indispensable. The stone was a fusion of different coloured cobbles at high temperature, compounded under high pressure as the earth's crust formed. In Emperor Wanli's time it could be obtained only in Xuzhou, Jiangsu Province and Jun County, Henan Province. The brilliantly coloured stone is very hard and so difficult to carve. While mining the stones, only those of maximum size were acceptable. Each was then cut by hand to the desired size and polished. One may well imagine how much time it took to polish one stone. Coloured stones with veins used in the construction of Ding Ling are of fine workmanship. The book *Imperial Tombs with Explanations* describes them as being "so slippery that not a speck of dust may stay on them" and their colours as "dazzlingly brilliant".

No outer walls were built for the Imperial Tombs preceding Yong Ling. Only the tomb precinct was laid out in front and the rampart behind. Upon inspection of Yong Ling after it was finished, Emperor Jiajing was not satisfied with the construction. He asked the minister of works: "Is the tomb finished?" Sensing what the emperor had in mind, the minister replied circumspectly: "There is still the outer wall to be built." After Emperor Jiajing left, the minister ordered the workmen to add a wall outside the rampart. Although this outer wall had not been included in the

---

*Dougong, a system of brackets inserted between the top of a column and a crossbeam.

original plan, it was imitated by his grandson, Emperor Wanli, years later. The outer wall of Ding Ling was built exactly on the same design as that of Yong Ling, being slightly curved in the rear, but straight in front. The wall was high, thick and solid.

The building materials used in the construction of Ding Ling were mainly wall bricks, huge stones, *nanmu* wood and glazed tiles. A tomb of such imposing size required fine workmanship and building materials selected according to the strictest standards.

Most of the building materials used for Ding Ling were large wall bricks, mainly produced in Linqing, Shandong Province. The town is located in the lower reaches of the Yellow River, with the Grand Canal flowing by. The clay in that area was plentiful and of good quality. As transport presented no difficulty, Linqing became an ideal place for brick making. The clay, washed down from the loess highland, was pure, fine, neutral and free of coarse sand after being washed down the river for more than 500 kilometres and deposited in Linqing. The clay was dug out and dried, then filtered, immersed in water, beaten and shaped into bricks before being fired. Each brick measured 49cm long, 24cm wide, 12cm thick and 24 kilogrammes in weight. It was highly pressure-resistant and of excellent quality. Each brick was stamped with the name of the kiln, the name of the workman and the production date. If a brick was found to be below standard, the mark would indicate the kiln and the workman who made it. Because the brick was light grey, or greyish white, it was called white wall brick. In the 4th month of the 2nd year of the Wanli Reign (1574), although there was no big engineering project at the time, an order was issued to all the kilns in Linqing to produce 1.2 million white wall bricks every year for the imperial family.

Apart from Linqing, Wuqing County in Hebei Province was also to produce white wall bricks, starting in the 9th month of 1574. A villager in Wanping County named Wang Yong submitted a memorandum to the emperor: "The clay in Wuqing County is as solid and cohesive as that in Linqing. Wuqing County is only 130 *li* (65 kilometres) from the capital, more than 2,000 *li* nearer than Linqing. Once the source of the product is changed, not only will the food, freight and passenger boats be relieved of much labour but the country can also save money. It is a truly effective way of creating wealth." After a check and discussion, the Ministry of Works ordered Wuqing to produce 300,000 bricks every year. After work was started on Ding Ling, brick production in both places went up sharply.

Apart from white wall bricks, square bricks were needed for the floor of the halls. These were made only in Suzhou, Jiangsu Province. Production and firing techniques were even more complicated than in the case of white wall bricks. The clay had to be immersed in water for several years and strained or filtered several times. The bricks were baked at a mild temperature. The process demanded as much care as collecting gold from the river. Therefore the products were called "gold bricks". The fine quality and glossy surface were rarely found anywhere else. It is a pity that the technique for making these bricks has been lost and that none can be produced today.

The large stones used for Ding Ling were mostly taken from Dashiwo in Fangshan County, some 50 kilometres southwest of Beijing, including greenish stones, white stones and white marble. Of the hundreds of thousands of huge stones used, the heaviest weighed 100 tons or more. They were extremely difficult to transport. As they were mined in hilly areas, they could be transported only by road. When Kang Ling was built, the huge stones were transported in land boats pulled by workmen over slippery roads. The method was onerous: A deep well was dug at intervals of half a kilometre. In winter water taken from the well was splashed on the road surface to make it slippery and the huge stones were dragged along it to the Heavenly Longevity Hills. At that time, it took 20,000 workmen 28 days to haul a huge stone about ten metres long, 3.3 metres wide and 1.7 metres thick to the capital, at the cost of 110,000 taels of silver. Carrying it to the Heavenly Longevity Hills doubled the cost in manpower, money and time.

In the 16th year of the Jiajing Reign (1537), Mao Bowen, minister of works, had an eight-wheeled cart built to save the money, time and manpower spent in the use of land boats, and to overcome the constraints of seasons and temperatures. The cart, drawn by mules instead of human beings, was cheaper, faster, safer and more reliable. A few years later He Shengrui, a department chief of the Ministry of Works, further increased efficiency by building a 16-wheeled cart modeled on the eight-wheeled cart. In spite of all this, the stupendous task of mining and transporting the stones presented difficulties the likes of which have been rarely confronted in the world history of sepulchral architecture.

As Ding Ling was burned several times over the centuries, nothing remains of the main hall. Visitors today can no longer see the much-admired precious wood used in building it. However, from the 60 huge *nanmu* columns that remain standing in the Hall of Heavenly Favour of Chang Ling, one can still imagine what the wood looked like at the time when Ding Ling was at the height of its magnificence.

Most of the wood used in the main hall of Ding Ling was *nanmu*, a tree which grew mainly in Hunan, Hubei, Yunnan, Guizhou and Sichuan provinces. The hard, fragrant and decay-resistant wood was in fact the chief material used for building palaces and temples by the royal family in the Ming Dynasty. *Nanmu* is precious also because it is rare. The slow-growing trees, with their thick, tall trunks, were thinly dispersed in the primeval forests. As more and more were felled, mature big trees could be found only on "cliffs, in steep valleys, or in places inaccessible to human beings". These places were obviously difficult to reach and frequently infested by poisonous snakes, wild beasts, insect pests and miasma. Thus tree felling was extremely hazardous.

During the reign of Wanli, Wang Dewan, a mid-rank official of the Ministry of Works, and Kuang Shangjin, imperial censor, submitted a memorial to the throne describing the hardships suffered by the wood cutters in Sichuan: "Those employed to fell and transport wood risk their lives in crossing the Lu River. Many die of miasma, their corpses lie scattered over the land..." "When lumbermen leave home, their wives and children weep and wail. They fear death as if they were going through fire and water..." "In the areas where miasma is widespread, the tree fellers faint in the gullies and turn stiff when the plague is on them. The corpses block the water flow and the bones pile up in mounds. Those who survive suffer from jaundice or oedema..." "If nearly 1,000 lumbermen die in one county, the number of dead in the province comes to no fewer than 100,000."

More than 20,000 large *nanmu* timbers were needed for Ding Ling, the largest having a diameter of more than 1.4 metres. It is not hard to imagine the cost of preparing just one such huge timber.

According to a folk saying: "One thousand people went to the mountains; only five hundred came back." More than half of the lumbermen died or were injured.

Compared with the production of bricks, stones and wood, the making and transportation of glazed articles was much easier and more economical. More glazed items were used for Ding Ling than for any of the other tombs. Apart from glazed tiles and ridge animals used on the walls and in the halls, major structures, like the tomb gate and the Hall of Heavenly Favour, were all decorated with glazed bricks with designs of landscapes, flowers, dragons, phoenixes, unicorns, sea horses, snakes and tortoises. These added to the magnificence and splendour of the buildings, making them much more outstanding than the other tombs.

The glazed products were chiefly made in the capital city. The potter's clay was first crushed, then screened and mixed with water, and the adobes were made, dried, glazed and finally fired at a high temperature. Liulichang (glazedware kiln), which has now developed into Beijing's antiques shopping centre, was a major location of kilns in the Yuan Dynasty. Kilns were set up again during the Yongle Reign of the Ming

Dynasty especially to make glazedware for the imperial family. Therefore, the name of the kilns and the technique have both been passed down to the present time.

The construction of Ding Ling brought the Chinese nation widespread misery and great disasters, which in turn fused countrywide disorder and social disintegration. An inkling of this was first touched upon in a presentation made by Shen Shixing, chief cabinet minister, and Sun Shizhen, a mid-rank official of the Ministry of Works, as early as 1586 when construction started. These officials pointed out: "The common people are unable to recuperate and prosper, because for many years, the levies and additional taxes in the form of grain or money, originally exempted due to natural calamities, have been re-imposed on them, often at short notice or in one year. Their painful outcries under the birch are heard almost every day. Life of the ordinary people is indeed extremely difficult. Both the state revenues and the people's financial resources are limited. A man who can carry only 50 kilogrammes is unable to carry 60. In recent years taxes have been increased gradually, such as the tax on fodder by the Ministry of Revenue, the tax for construction by the Ministry of Works, and gold and silver supply for the imperial family...The repeated increases in taxation have caused a state financial deficit and led to poverty among the people. How can the common people pay additional taxes when they are unable to pay the normal taxes? Recently the judicial officials, misusing their power, have filed lawsuits based on false charges against the common people. One suit led to the breakup of several families, another involved several dozen people. Many innocent people have been beaten to death or died of hunger and illness in prison. Moreover, this year floods have been unusually serious, forcing many people to flee their homes. Droughts have occurred in Shanxi, Shaanxi and Henan, where huts and houses were submerged under water. Once the people become poverty-stricken, disorder is inevitable. Today, in Shaanxi the borders have been repeatedly harassed by four neighbouring tribes; in Shanxi miners are getting together to make trouble; in Henan hungry peasants seized the wheat which should go to the state; and in Zhili (today's Hebei Province), some people raised a banner and went on a looting spree. Therefore, people have gathered and risen in rebellion under the slogan: Famine haunts; die as rebel not victim."

In this situation, Emperor Wanli, instead of ordering the work stopped, issued a decree requiring all ministers and generals to make contributions: "The tomb construction is a huge project, and there is still extensive work to be done. I am told that during the reign of Jiajing, all officials made contributions to help construct the imperial buildings. I ask the Ministry Works to consider if this is feasible."

On receiving the decree, officials of the Ministry Works, who used to be submissive and obedient to the emperor, could not agree in the face of the countrywide misery of the people. When he found that this was not feasible, Emperor Wanli introduced a new regulation for raising funds by selling official titles. All those who were willing to pay the high prices stipulated, regardless of family background, record of service or education, could buy titles corresponding to official posts. Most of these official posts were bought by squires, local tyrants and rogues. When they took up their official posts, they oppressed the local people and rampantly plundered the country's wealth. As a result officialdom in the late years of the Ming Dynasty was thoroughly corrupt. With widespread bribery and perversion of the law, the normal operation of the state machine was seriously impeded.

Money extorted from the people by Emperor Wanli and contributions from the ministers and generals enabled the work on Ding Ling to be carried at length to a conclusion in the 6th month of 1590. The total cost of the tomb was 8 million taels of silver, equivalent to the total state revenue of two years.

When Emperor Wanli gave a sumptuous feast in the underground palace and conferred higher titles upon his loyal officials, he did not and could not realise that the world had undergone tremendous changes and that the history of the vast empire of the Great Ming Dynasty was soon to suffer a reversal.

Death of Two Emperors and an Empress

The year 1583 had brought portentous changes. In low spirits Emperor Wanli went to the Heavenly Longevity Hills to seek his paradise after death. At that time, Nurhachi, who was four years older than the emperor, was in command of the cavalry of the ethnic Nuzhen group. He began by annexing the neighbouring tribes inhabiting the snow-covered northern wilderness. At the age of 25 he had shown remarkable military talent. Now he was spurred on to seek revenge against Li Chengliang, general commander in Liaodong (today's northeastern provinces), and Nikan

Wailan, who had used stratagems to kill his grandfather and father. Nurhachi and his clansmen, who between them had only 13 suits of armour inherited from his ancestors with which to defend themselves, defeated Nikan Wailan. When Emperor Wanli received the official dispatch from Nurhachi reporting the arrest of Nikan Wailan and demanding the return of the bodies of his grandfather and father, he could not foresee or even imagine that this Nurhachi would face him as an equal in the not too distant future. With the utmost serenity, he appointed Nurhachi commander of the troops stationed in Jianzhou and conferred on him the title of Dragon and Tiger General. This new appointment gave Nurhachi increased might, adding wings to the tiger. He annexed the surrounding tribes one after another and during these expeditions built up and improved his military organisation. Meanwhile he ordered his people to mine gold, silver and copper and to build refineries. He encouraged peasants to raise silk worms and develop handicrafts. In time his role as a subject of the Ming Dynasty no longer satisfied him. Between 1583 and 1618, while Emperor Wanli became more muddle-headed, indulging his fondness for drink, sensual pleasures, collecting pearls and amassing jewellery, Nurhachi built up a formidable army capable of challenging the Ming Dynasty for control of the empire. Moreover, while the eastern part of Liaoning Peninsula was weakly defended, he took the opportunity to expand his own private forces. He skilfully practised a double-faced policy of superficial submission to the Ming Empire but secret assumption of the title king or khan while actively developing his power.

In 1618 Nurhachi commanded 20,000 mounted troops in an attack on the important fortress of Fushun, forced its defending general Li Yongfang to surrender, and killed General Zhang Chengyin and others who came to Li's rescue. After taking the Yagu Pass southeast of Fushun, he went on to capture Qinghe. His troops advanced victoriously like a knife through butter, sweeping across the northern areas, and quickly pressed forward towards the Great Wall.

His own armies unable to withstand the advance of Nurhachi's mounted troops, Emperor Wanli called in a practitioner of geomancy named Wang Laoqi in a last effort to turn the tide. After divination, Wang Laoqi knelt before the Emperor and declared: "The rise of the Nuzhen is due to the geomancy of the tombs of its ancestors. If the tombs of the Jin emperors* in Fangshan are destroyed to dispel its magic luck, the army of the Ming Dynasty will turn defeat into victory." Overjoyed, Emperor Wanli ordered the Ministry of Defence to send troops immediately to Fangshan to carry out the job. This served as the ultimate provocation to Nurhachi, who deemed himself a descendant of the Jin.

When the Ming troops went to Fangshan, they set fire to the buildings and robbed the tombs. Flames, smoke and dust consumed the tomb area. In a matter of two months the imperial Jin tombs, which were by no means inferior to those of the Ming in architecture as well as in historical and artistic value, were levelled to the ground.

---

*The Jin Dynasty (1115-1234) was established by the Nuzhen tribe which inhabited the Changbai Mountains and the Heilongjiang River basin.

The armies of Nurhachi advanced southward, entering northern China over the Great Wall. General Dorgon ordered his troops to destroy the Ming Tombs in retaliation for the destruction of the Jin tombs. Ding Ling suffered the most serious devastation of all. The crenels of the rampart, the coloured floor stones of the stele pavilion and the outer wall were all smashed up or burnt down. Only the lone stele pavilion was left in the magnificent tomb precinct of Ding Ling. This retaliatory destruction was not perpetrated until 24 years following the death of Emperor Wanli.

Seriously ill, the emperor knew that his ancient empire was listing dangerously like a sinking boat and that he would no longer be aboard in the final maelstrom. Although shouts and signals for help from the deck were clearly noted on all sides, he only hindered the rescue operation.

On the 6th day of the 4th lunar month of 1620 Empress Wang died.

On the 21st day of the 7th month Emperor Wanli became bed-ridden. The monarch of the empire, who had hidden himself deep in the palace for more than 20 years, had no wish to see his crown prince Changluo, nor did he permit his ministers and generals to pay their last respects when he was about to leave the world. He only wanted Concubine Zheng to be with him, the imperial lady who had brought him both happiness and distress.

By the time Fang Congzhe and other ministers were called into the Hall of Heavenly Purity, the emperor's face was ashen, and each gasp seemed his last. They knelt down and wept unrestrainedly. Wanli raised his hand slightly, signalling Fang Congzhe to come forward.

With tears in his eyes, he took Fang's hand tremblingly and whispered in a feeble voice: "In view of her great kindness to me, I make Concubine Zheng an empress. After her death bury her together with me in the underground palace of Ding Ling..." These, his last words, were uttered with his last breath.

After Wanli died, his eldest son Zhu Changluo ascended the throne and changed the reign name to Taichang. The reign was short-lived as was the emperor, who died within a month. Between the 6th day of the 4th lunar month and the 1st of the 9th in 1620, one empress and two emperors of the Ming Empire passed away, events rarely found in the court annals of Chinese dynasties.

Zhu Yijun (Emperor Wanli), who ruled for 48 years, should have felt ashamed before his ancestors in the nether world. Although the Ming Dynasty was destroyed in the end by a peasant army and the Great Qing army 24 years after his death, politicians and historians of the later generations all agree that it was not Emperor Chongzhen, but Emperor Wanli who was responsible for the final demise of the Ming. Its irreversible dive into extinction was first set in motion during his reign.

Chapter Four
EXCAVATION OF DING LING

Underground Palace Entrance and the Tunnel Gate

On May 18, 1956 a truck arrived at Zhao Ling Village, 500 metres south of Ding Ling. Besides the team members, it was carrying luggage, beds, desks, chairs, kitchen utensils, dishes, stoves, shovels, picks, bamboo baskets, shoulder poles and rope. The new-comers settled down in the courtyard of a resident named Chen. In the group together with Zhao Qichang was a man in his late fifties, his hair greying at the temples. This was Bai Wanyu from the Institute of Archaeology, a specialist in sorting out and restoring unearthed artifacts. Bai was a member of the excavation team, but he had been too busy with his daily work to join in the early part of the survey. After the decision was made to test-dig Ding Ling, Zhao Qichang went to Xia Nai and said: "Professor Xia, this is a huge tomb, as you know. If I'm to be in charge all by myself..." What he really meant was, he wished to have Bai Wanyu join his team as early as possible. Xia Nai assured him: "Once the digging is started at Ding Ling, I'll send Bai Wanyu over right away."

In the prime of his youth, the old man had followed Andersson and Sven Hedin to the Western

Regions, and worked with them at length. Zhao Qichang and his team members were full of confidence as they embarked on the first archaeological excavation of an imperial tomb. On the afternoon of their arrival, the team decided to open a ditch inside the rampart, starting at a place corresponding to where wall bricks had collapsed. They chose the location behind the stele pavilion, drove in wooden stakes and tied a cord on them to outline the ground to be dug. A wooden plate was placed on it, with the word "T1" written in fresh black ink to mark the first prospecting ditch. With everything ready, work was to begin the next day.

In the early morning of the following day, Zhao Qichang and Bai Wanyu went to the worksite, together with 38 workers chosen from neighbouring villages. Bai Wanyu told them the purpose of the excavation, explained how they should work, and asked them to maintain secrecy before the underground palace was opened. This request not only cast a shadow of mystery on the minds of the peasants, who had always held the Imperial Ming Tombs in awe and veneration, but later led to an unexpected commotion.

At seven o'clock the 38 peasant workers and the excavation team members stood at attention, shovels and picks in hand. A 32-year-old peasant named Wang Qifa volunteered to act as leader of the peasants' group. Before they started, Zhao Qichang took the first picture of the team with his camera. Bai Wanyu gave the order: "Start!" Wang Qifa bent over and dug out the first shovel of earth. This marked the formal beginning of China's first scientific excavation of an imperial tomb in an organised way and with archaeological methods. It was May 19, 1956, a day that would surely go down in the history of New China's archaeology.

Guided by the marks shown by the cord, the peasants dug the earth shovel by shovel, loaded it carefully into baskets and carried it away. Although it was the first day, the peasants were keeping well in mind what Bai Wanyu had said: "We are not working on a building project, nor are we digging a reservoir for a big dam. We do not require speed; we want meticulous observation and careful handling..." The peasants knew little about archaeology, and had never heard of digging an imperial tomb in a scientific, archaeological way. Through their minds ran reminiscences of the warlord Sun Dianying's plunder and the bandit leader Cheng Laoliu's robbery of tombs in the dead of night. The present situation alerted them to the fact that this project was totally different from anything they had heard of before. Each basket of earth had to be carefully inspected, and very often they had to level the ground surface and scrape the earth with a small spade, bit by bit, to search for dubious leads.

Zhao Qichang and Bai Wanyu supervised the work closely. Bai Wanyu scrutinised practically every basket of earth as it was dug and noted changes in soil texture. In two hours they had dug a prospecting ditch one metre deep and three metres wide. Stone slabs laid laterally inside the rampart were exposed. A peasant suddenly cried out in surprise: "Hey, look here! There are words on this slab!"

Zhao Qichang and Bai Wanyu were there in a flash. Sure enough, there were some indistinct characters chiselled on a small slab which was lying laterally in the wall. Zhao Qichang took a brush, squatted and cleared the slab of soil. It was a miracle: three roughly-inscribed characters emerged. Zhao and Bai shouted in one voice: "Tunnel gate!"

Zhao Qichang almost brushed his face against the slab. He said, as if to himself: "We're right, we're right! These are the three characters for the tunnel gate!" Bai Wanyu, unable to suppress his excitement, echoed him: "Right! Right! This marks the tunnel gate!" The shouting and excitement of the two leaders conveyed little to the peasants about the true meaning of "tunnel gate". From the flushed and smiling faces they had a premonition that success of some kind was in the offing.

After this spate of excitement, the two leaders of the work team stared blankly at the slab, pondering over its origin and intention. Strict requirements had been made for the construction of the imperial tombs, and the work had to be done according to set procedures. What was the tunnel like? What was the underground palace gate like? Where had the decorations and marks been set up? This was the first excavation of an imperial tomb in New China. There were no historical records describing the inside of the tomb. They could only draw up an analysis and use their own judgement on the basis of unearthed artifacts.

Zhao Qichang gazed at the three characters in fascination while Bai Wanyu squatted by his side in silence, smoking a cigarette. The inscription appeared to be shallow and not neatly done. It did not look like a practice customary to the construction of tombs. So why the slab with its three characters? Could it be a false signal created deliberately to mislead tomb robbers? They had heard a folk story about "the misleading stone" buried in imperial tombs; could this be the slab? Zhao Qichang thought for a long time and concluded that such an inference was absurd. Since all the tombs were heavily guarded by troops, the emperors and ministers at that time could not have believed that there would be robbers. Still less could they have conceived that the tombs would be excavated for scientific study several hundred years later. Talk of a "misleading stone" could be no more than a fairy tale.

Then, what did these three rough characters mean? By recalling the historical data, they made the following inference: Thirty years elapsed between completion of the tomb in the 18th year of the Wanli Reign (1590) and the emperor's death in the 48th year of his reign (1620). After the tomb was finished, it had to be closed up and protected by an earthen covering until it was to be opened for the emperor's burial. Since the date of his death could not be predicted, once he died, the tomb had to be opened without delay for the coffin to be moved in. Failure to find the entrance immediately would delay the burial and surely jeopardise the lives of the workmen. The entrance, left tightly shut for many long years, would be very difficult to find when the urgent situation arose. Therefore it was necessary to leave a mark at a certain place near the entrance. Wrapped in thought, Zhao Qichang turned to look at Bai Wanyu and said in a low voice: "Am I right if I say that the slab was laid secretly in an inconspicuous place near the rampart by the tomb builders?"

Bai Wanyu blew a long puff of smoke and said: "I was also thinking that the words on the slab may have been left on the instructions of the Ministry of Works, or secretly by the workmen themselves. After the emperor died, it fell to the Ministry of Rites to set the burial date. Once the date was set, if the Ministry of Works could not open the underground palace promptly, both the officials at the Ministry of Works and the workmen in charge would be severely punished. This explains why the mark was left here. Beyond all doubt, this marks the tunnel leading to the underground palace."

Great minds think alike. Each looked at the other with a knowing smile.

Bai Wanyu, remaining at the worksite, instructed the peasants to continue digging, while Zhao Qichang returned to Beijing to inform Xia Nai of their discovery and its implication. Xia Nai listened in silence and then nodded: "I think your inference is well-founded. Apparently you two are entirely capable of seeing this job through."

Xia Nai and Wu Han came to the worksite one after the other. After carefully studying the inscribed characters ''tunnel gate'' they also reached the conclusion that it indicated ''the entrance of the tunnel leading to the underground palace''.

As expected, after digging for about ten days, they reached a depth of 4.2 metres below ground level. There they found neatly-laid, parallel brick walls at a distance of eight metres apart, forming a curved lane running south to north. This discovery confirmed the idea that the coffins of the emperor and empresses had been moved in through this tunnel. The characters "tunnel gate" faced the central part of the tunnel, which afterwards came to be referred to as the "brick tunnel" by the excavators.

After Lightning

The rainy season began in July. With frequent downpours the excavation was often interrupted.

Following the opening of the first prospecting ditch inside the rampart, work progressed smoothly. The peasants carried bricks, earth, sand, stones and pebbles out of the ditch basket by basket. In little more than a month, after the ditch had been meticulously cleared, as expected, a large arched brick gate was revealed under the inscribed slab. This proved that the caved-in opening which Zhao Qichang had first discovered was indeed the upper edge of the outer side of the gate, the first gate of the tunnel leading to the underground palace. After the coffins of the emperor and empresses were buried, the gate had been skilfully filled in with wall bricks indistinguishable from those forming the wall. Little did the emperor, ministers and workmen imagine that the clever disguise they had contrived would fail to pull wool over the eyes of the archaeologists.

Since the surrounding area outside the gate was but a stretch of wilderness, once the gate was opened, no one could ensure the safety of the area inside the tomb. Therefore the excavators did not open the gate. As a result, a small stone tablet buried inside the arched gate which would have shown them the direction in which the excavation should progress, escaped the scrutiny of the team. Inscribed clearly on the stone tablet were the words:

Inside the arched gate of the rampart is a stone tablet, and one *zhang* (about ten feet) inward from the earth lining of the wall is the coir rope of the tunnel. The rope is 34 *zhang* and two *chi* (about 342 feet) long. At the end of the rope is the front lining of the diamond wall.

This passage could be called the first key to opening the underground palace. It touches on two subjects: The first is the location of the stone tablet, from which the tunnel leading to the underground palace could be located. The second tells the exact distance between this place and the front lining of the diamond wall. It was only after the palace was opened, cleared and restored that the stone tablet was found and taken out of the wall. No vestige of the coir rope was ever found.

Since this heaven-sent tip was not uncovered in good time, it was unavoidable that the excavators should fall into a quandary and go astray, and that their path should likewise be strewn with mishaps and stumbling blocks.

The brick tunnel inside the gate did not extend directly to the back of the stele pavilion. There was still a long distance to go to reach the pavilion. Moreover, since the tunnel followed a winding course, excavating it, apart from involving the removal of large amounts of earth, would result in the destruction of many centuries-old pines. Another approach was to open a second ditch, starting at a point on the line that linked the tunnel, the pavilion and the tumulus. After careful consideration, the work team decided to open the second ditch at some distance from the first. Xia Nai approved the proposal and on July 6 the ground was broken for the second ditch, also behind the pavilion, along the extension line of the first one. A wooden plate marked "T2" was put up at the site.

To speed up excavation of the second ditch, manpower was replaced by a pulley for hauling earth up to ground level and dumping it into handcarts to be wheeled away. More than a month passed. Not only were there no new signs or leads, but even the traces of the brick tunnel they had observed were lost. Here yawning up at them was a ditch seven metres deep, six metres wide and more than 20 metres long.

The excavators began to worry. Doubts grew as to the accuracy of their scheme. Enthusiasm plummeted. Zhao Qichang, as leader of the work team, kept to his quarters perusing mounds of historical data for possible insight, or paced up and down the prospecting ditch silently. His previous loquacious remarks, cheerful comments and witty observations were no longer heard.

Bai Wanyu squatted by the ditch every day smoking his pipe calmly, as if he had a well-thought-out plan and success was in sight. However, it was only after the underground palace was opened that the white-haired old man admitted his true feelings as he recalled the situation: "When everyone was upset, if I, as the veteran on the team, did not keep my cool, failure would have been certain. In fact, I was just as frustrated as everyone else." He proved worthy of his status as an honoured veteran in the field. In the commotion that arose soon after, he showed his resourcefulness and talent. When the excavation team was in this difficult position, some members of the older generation of archaeologists who were concerned about the impasse came to the worksite. After strolling up and down by the ditch, they approached Zhao Qichang and Bai Wanyu. Pointing to the crown of his own head, one of the "specialists" said: "The ditch is too shallow. You're dreaming if you expect to find the underground palace through a ditch only as deep the height of a man!" Hearing his off-hand remarks, Zhao Qichang said nothing. He understood that they simply expressed some sort of regret, hope and concern.

From the very start, when they had begun to look for the entrance to the tunnel, people interested in the project had proposed alternative approaches. The excavation, they held, should start at the stone altar in front of the stele pavilion, digging should continue under the pavilion and straight ahead beneath the tumulus. Some of these people were leaders, some were scholars. Their sincerity was praiseworthy, but archaeology had its own methodology. All unfounded suppositions were no better than mere guesswork. Even without reading the historical data and literature, they could see macroscopically that the pavilion of Ding Ling was structurally different from that of the other tombs. Built entirely of stone and brick, its weight and solidity exceeded those of any of the other Imperial Ming Tombs. According to historical records, in building the stele pavilion of Ding Ling, molten iron was poured into the foundation to fuse the pavilion with the underground rock into an integral whole. It was precisely because of this that after Ding Ling was devastated by the Dashun troops under Li Zicheng, by the Qing troops commanded by Dorgon, and by bandits, the pavilion alone stood intact. Therefore the excavation team firmly opposed the proposal, and stated plainly: "It was absolutely impossible for the coffins of the emperor and empresses to enter the underground palace from here, because it would surely have been a very arduous and difficult undertaking to build a tunnel under the pavilion. Moreover, it was not necessary to build such a tunnel; the officials and people in charge of the work could not have been so stupid." So Zhao Qichang heard out those well-meant suggestions with a helpless smile while Xia Nai kept silent.

It was a pitch-dark night. The team members fell asleep after an exhausting day of toil. Silence brooded over the whole deserted tomb area, the stillness broken only by a bird call or the barking of a dog.

Restlessness and sultriness kept Zhao Qichang awake. He lay on his bed, feeling oppressed in the dark as if there was a heavy weight on his mind. More than one month had passed; the second prospecting ditch grew wider, longer and deeper, but yielded no new clues. He recalled his college days. His teachers had lectured on how to differentiate earth formations, discriminate colour and texture of soil, and how to determine the relations between the different formations and strata. During archaeological field work in Xi'an, Luoyang and Zhengzhou, and while participating in various excavations on the outskirts of Beijing, he had always kept in mind his teachers' instructions. He did the same this time. Carefully observing the soil formations in the prospecting ditch, he had found vestiges of tamped soil. It showed that the place had been dug before. It also indicated that they had been correct in choosing the location for the second prospecting ditch. So why couldn't they find signs of the brick tunnel? Was it because that the ditch "was too shallow"? He kept turning over in his mind the remarks made by the visitors at the worksite, and felt that they were unfounded. If there was anything wrong with the ditch it was not lack of depth, it was a problem of width. Their ditch was only six metres wide, whereas the tunnel they had found at the wall gate was eight metres wide. Zhao Qichang mulled this over. Outside a steady patter announced it had begun to rain again.

The patter-patter increased his anxiety. He flung on his jacket and stepped outside. He stood in the rain, the drops falling on him and rolling down. They cooled his face and moistened his hair which was matted with mud. This baptism of Nature helped dissipate his uneasiness and he pulled himself together. Brushing the rain water off his face, he straightened his back and took a deep breath, as if he had seen a gleam of light in the darkness.

A heavy rain set in. Cracks of thunder rent the air. Flashes of lightning illuminated wide screens of fleeting raindrops and turned them to gold. The storm enveloped the wilderness, merging the sky and earth into one. All his surroundings of minutes before were transformed.

Suddenly a flash of lightning split the darkened sky in two, immediately followed by a deafening thunderbolt. An avalanch of water poured down, sending the universe into a swirl. With a bound, Zhao Qichang re-entered the room, shouting to his startled team members: "What a mess! The last thing our ditch needs is water..."

The next morning the storm was over and the skies cleared. Hovering over the ditch, the team members and peasants stared into the muddy water wondering what to do next. Just then a man came running from a distance and shouted to them: "Quick! Go and see — a tile animal on the pavilion was struck by lightning!"

Surprise, consternation, shock. They ran to the pavilion and looked up. The glazed tile animal that had sat on the right corner of the front eave was no longer there. It had indeed been struck down and was now lying on the ground.

The sight shook them. A commotion arose. The peasants became nervous. Seeing the sitting animal's head cut off, they whispered: "It's an ill omen! The animal guards the emperor's tomb! It did not guard it well, so the emperor became angry and had its head cut off." This prompted others to exclaim: "It must be the emperor's warning to us!"

"The emperor's spirit punished the animal as a warning to us. Who knows what'll happen next?" Some saw this as an opportunity to stir up trouble.

"We can't dig up and rob the Imperial Tombs just like that! We've got to stop right now and think it over." Once the scientific archaeological excavation was suddenly termed "robbery", naturally some had to think it over.

An elderly peasant knelt down before the pavilion, and kowtowed again and again repenting for his "sin".

The same morning, more shocking news reached the worksite. A villager named Gu Yongzhong who had been guarding Ding Ling had been killed by lightning; Zhang Li, also struck, was seriously injured and sent to hospital.

The peasants burst into uproar. Whispers turned into public outcries, discussions, debates and even curses. It became impossible to continue the work. Both Zhao Qichang and Bai Wanyu looked as if they had been trapped and did not know how to handle the situation.

Other incidents followed, some quite ridiculous. A middle-aged woman in Yu Ling Village suddenly fell to the ground, foaming at the mouth; she had lost consciousness while picking hay from a haystack. Her husband promptly brought in a witch doctor to treat her. The practitioner appeared not in the least alarmed. She took out a silver needle about an inch long from her pocket, wet it with saliva, and inserted it deftly into the groove of the woman's upper lip. In a flash, the patient uttered a strange cry, jumped up and ran into the village street, shouting: "It's no fault of mine! Some people have come to Ding Ling. They're about to dig up my resting place. I can't stay there any longer. Help me! Help me!" The villagers said that she had been bewitched by the emperor's ghost.

Two days later, a demented old woman came to the worksite, her white hair dishevelled and her face covered with dirt. She wore a long ragged pink garment and looked like a goblin. She strolled hither and thither about the worksite like a lunatic, and bowed low to anyone she met: "Have mercy on me! Please forgive me! I won't harm anyone again; I don't dare. Never again..." All who saw her were terrified. The peasants whispered: She's bewitched by the fox spirit. Seeing their work interrupted by the old woman, Zhao Qichang asked four peasants workers to take her back to her village, but she lay on the ground and refused to leave. Her eerie cries were frightful. Since their soft tactics were to no avail, they picked her up and carried her out of the tomb precinct by force, leaving her in the adjacent fields. Two men were posted at the gate to prevent her returning. Her relatives were sent for.

In no time, astonishing stories of women bewitched by the fox spirit or ghosts swept in from the surrounding area. The phenomenon was much talked about among the villagers, while the peasant workers languished in low spirits. One of them, from Zhao Ling Village, came to Zhao Qichang and entreated him: "Please, Mr Zhao, my wife is at home, completely bewitched. She has smashed all the kitchen utensils and dishes to pieces. You have a good fate. Please come and help me to banish the spirit! We need to hurry…"

On hearing this, Zhao Qichang's blood boiled; his heart was ready to burst with frustration. The fiascos of the last few days had made a farce of all his hard work, and this was the climax. He was terribly upset. He felt he had to stand up and battle against these setbacks even if it meant quelling an "evil spirit"; there was no other way. With this in mind, he put his shovel aside and said: "All right, I'll come."

The peasant woman was still shouting and hurling things about. Zhao Qichang picked up a brick, made his way through the crowd, and went toward her shouting loudly: "I've come! My name is Zhao. What on earth are you trying to do?" His thunderous voice startled everyone. The woman quickly put down the jar she was about to smash and stood still, staring blankly at the big new-comer towering over her. Someone came forward to take the jar and put it in a safe place; others led the woman into one of the inner rooms. She huffed a few times, plumped herself down on the bed and fell silent. The farce was over.

Bai Wanyu organised the peasants to drain the water from the ditch. One of them asked for leave to fetch some tools from home and failed to return. Another wanted time off because he was busy at home. Those who remained at the worksite moved listlessly and accomplished little. Someone had told the peasants: ''You know, we countryfolk can't afford to offend the Son of Heaven, the true dragon seed. Not even the spirits and devils living in the tomb area can stand it here any longer. If we go on digging, we'll all be struck dead for sure, like the old man who was guarding the tomb. As for these townspeople, they're blessed with a good fate and we'd better not be so foolish as to take part in their reckless adventures.''

In the face of all this commotion, some members of the excavation team could no longer control themselves. Liu Jingyi went to Bai Wanyu, and insisted angrily: "Elder Bai, just explain to them that thunder and lightning are normal natural phenomena. Their talk of devils and spirits is pure superstitious nonsense!"

Liu's face was contorted with suppressed outrage. Bai Wanyu shook his head gently: "I'm afraid we can't do that. You don't understand their psychology. These peasants have lived in the Imperial Tombs area for generations; many of them are descendants of the early tomb guards. They have always blindly worshipped the emperors. We just have to be patient."

Storm Over a Stone Tablet

More and more earth piled up on either side as the ditch was widened.

On September 2 Luan Shihai, a peasant from Qing Ling Village began his day at the worksite and as he started digging, he happened to strike something which emitted a metallic sound. Using his pick he moved the earth aside bit by bit and before long a small stone was exposed.

"Come and see this!" he called out loudly. Those at the bottom of the ditch gathered round. Bai Wanyu cried hastily: "Be careful, don't break it!"

They used their shovels to move the earth away and in ten minutes a small stone tablet was uncovered. One of the peasants cried out: "There are characters on it!" Wang Qifa promptly took a small piece of bamboo and scraped the soil away from the characters. Bai Wanyu took a brush and went down into the ditch. While he was climbing down, he told a peasant nearby: "Call Zhao Qichang over! Tell him to hurry!"

Fifteen minutes later Zhao Qichang came running breathlessly. He jumped into the ditch and made his way through the crowd to see the tablet. Bai Wanyu was kneeling on the ground; the hand that held the brush was shaking; his voice trembled: "This time we've got a treasure!" Zhao Qichang scrutinised the tablet, which was more than a foot long and six inches wide, identified the words and read aloud: "The distance from this stone to the front lining of the diamond wall is 16 *zhang* (about 160 feet) and the depth is 35 *chi* (about 35 feet)."

Hardly had he finished when the crowd burst into

loud cheers of joy. They threw down their tools and milled around the tablet. The morning rays lit up their rapt faces.

This wave of excitement was followed by a heated debate. "The distance given on the tablet must indicate the distance to the underground palace," said Wang Qifa, leader of the peasants' group.

"Then, that is the key to opening the underground palace," someone echoed in agreement.

"You are wrong," a robust young man put in. "How could the emperor be so stupid? Did he want it to be so clearly indicated that people could easily open up his tomb later on? Maybe the ministers had some tricks up their sleeves. They buried this stone here just to mislead people. It's a ruse!"

His remarks seemed to awaken more random suspicions. Someone suddenly came up with a horrendous supposition: "What is this diamond wall anyhow? Seems to me it's a trap of some kind. If you go there as indicated on the tablet, you will surely be killed by poisonous arrows shot from a hidden mechanism!"

Zhao Qichang found that the longer the discussion continued, the more mysterious and eerie it became. To avoid any incidents similar to those which had occurred previously, after talking it over with Bai Wanyu, he decided that all the peasants should be given a day off.

In the course of the Ding Ling excavation, the team had always found time to read the relevant historical data whenever necessary. According to their division of labour, Zhao Qichang was the chief supervisor of the excavation; his work included drawing sketches, compiling notes, taking photos and preparing plans.

Bai Wanyu supervised the worksite and issued specific instructions to the workers. Reading the relevant literature and collecting data was Liu Jingyi's job.

The vast sea of historical data relating to the Ming Dynasty yielded only general information about the tomb, such as the date of its construction, its scale, the amount of manpower and materials used, and the cost of its construction. Nothing was revealed of the shape, composition and structure — this was an extremely strict system in the Ming Dynasty. However, since such a system existed, some traces of it must exist. The role played by the small stone tablet could be recognised in the burial system for the empresses, as was later discovered.

After the peasant left for home, members of the excavation team surrounded the tablet and studied it carefully. In fact they were even more excited than the peasants. The fiascos that had occurred one after another in the last three months and the ensuing stories had left them somewhat frustrated. The sight of the tablet gave them hope again. The vast, quiet wilderness in which they had been groping at last yielded this thread of light emanating from the mysterious tomb. How could they not be overwhelmed with joy!

The noonday sun spilled into the ditch and lit up the tablet. The characters inscribed on it became even more distinct. Bai Wanyu put down his brush and, with a grave look at his team members, announced slowly: "I think it indicates the right direction."

Liu Jingyi cast a surprised look at the old man and then turned to Zhao Qichang: "If so, was this a mark left by the workmen?" Bai Wanyu did not reply. He took a cigarette from his pocket. Zhao Qichang paced up and down for a while, stopped abruptly, took a cigarette from Bai Wanyu, lit it and smoked in silence before he began: "You are right! Whether emperor or empress, they were human beings. All human beings must die. Unless it was a special situation, they would not die simultaneously. Such being the case, the question arises: First to die buried first? Or the first to die waits until the other dies and is buried at the same time?"

He continued his inference slowly: "As recorded in the historical data, the procedure for burial of emperors and empresses in the Ming Dynasty followed the first practice. Take Chang Ling for example, Empress Xu died years before Emperor Yongle. Her remains were moved from Nanjing for burial after the underground palace of Chang Ling was built. When Yongle died later, the tomb was re-opened for him to be buried together with the empress. The other emperors and empresses were also buried in the same way. Ding Ling was built long before Emperor Wanli's death. His tomb had to be closed and covered with earth. It was re-opened only after he died. This is just hypothesis; the facts may turn out to be different. This can at least be confirmed by the texture of the soil we dug. This tablet was buried by workmen secretly as a sign to aid re-opening the tomb when the emperor or the empresses died. The words on the tablet are straightforward and credible. It is not a ruse to mislead marauders, but a genuine key to opening the underground palace."

Zhao Qichang turned to Bai Wanyu, who nodded his agreement with a smile.

The next day the peasants made a wooden case to

cover the small tablet; it had given them hope at a crucial moment. Forty years later this marvellous "guidestone", which performed such a meritorious function in the excavation of Ding Ling, lies intact in a display window of Ding Ling Museum. It was the first valuable relic to be unearthed after the excavation of Ding Ling began.

To celebrate the various "victorious exploits" during the digging, the excavation team decided to give a small towel to each of the peasant workers who served earlier and a cake of soap to each of the new-comers as a reward. They were precious prizes in the China of 1956.

On hearing the report, Xia Nai concluded without hesitation: "This is obviously a key to the underground palace." One question remained: Why had the direction leading to the brick tunnel been lost during excavation of the second ditch? Although it was widened to nine metres, there was still no trace of the brick tunnel.

With further digging the answer emerged. As it turned out, the second prospecting ditch was being dug at the end of the brick tunnel. The small tablet had been placed at a point where the brick tunnel ended. At some distance away a stone tunnel leading to the underground palace began. As the two tunnels were neither linked, nor met or crossed each other, it was unavoidable that the excavators should have lost their bearings at this spot. Looking back years later, this reminded them of the stone tablet hidden inside the tunnel gate of the rampart. It was just because they did not open the arched gate of the rampart that they lost their way and met with so many ridiculous incidents.

The excavation team also remembered that one night during those depressing days, Liu Jingyi had woken suddenly from a dream, looked over at Bai Wanyu, who was still awake, and said soberly: "I just dreamed about a stone tablet lying at the bottom of the ditch! It had characters written all over it! The words were covered with mud, so I couldn't read them."

Bai Wanyu dismissed his somniloquence with a laugh. He assumed Liu was talking nonsense. They never expected that in half a month his dream would come true. Then was it a spiritual revelation, or perhaps a supernatural message? Quite likely, as a Western philosopher said: "A dream is not an illusion, but a premonition of the future."

Chapter Five
LOVE IN THE IMPERIAL TOMB PRECINCT

A Bone Needle

A few days later Wu Han and Xia Nai arrived separately at the excavation site. After inspecting the shape and location of the small stone tablet carefully they joined the excavation team in drawing up a plan for their next action. They decided to open up a third ditch, running east to west, two metres to the west of the second one, which ran from north to south. The third ditch was to run to the underground centre of the tumulus. In this way they could take a shortcut to locate the tunnel leading to the underground palace.

With the appearance of the small stone tablet, the peasants were no longer as lax as before. The summer heat had receded and autumn breezes blew in the precinct. They went about their work in high spirits.

Just when the third ditch was dug to a depth of two metres, one of the peasants found a thin probe-like object about five centimetres long. It was somewhat thinner than a pencil and looked to him exactly like a jade hairpin worn by an empress. He brushed off the soil and debris with his hand, rushed over and shouted: "Mr Zhao, I've dug up the empress's jade hairpin! Look!"

Happily surprised, Zhao Qichang took it and studied it carefully. He opened his mouth to say something, but withheld his comment. Finally, he said a few words of encouragement to the peasant and went to find his colleague and mentor, Bai Wanyu.

"What do you make of this?" Zhao Qichang handed "the hairpin" over to him. "To me, it looks like a bone needle, an artifact of the Neolithic Age."

Bai Wanyu held it with wrapt attention, weighed it in his hand as a jeweller would a piece of gold, blew some dust off it and nodded: "You're right. It's a bone needle, thousands of years old. How does it happen to be found here?"

According to accepted classification, a bone needle like this belongs to the later period of primitive society dated at least 3,000 or 4,000 years ago. Why should it pop up in this 300-year old ditch? Where did it come from? What's the connection between this mysterious bone needle and the emperor's tomb anyhow?

Their intense probing of these questions was interrupted by the arrival of Xia Nai. Zhao Qichang passed the bone needle to him and said in mock earnest: "Director Xia, we found this 'jade hairpin' lying in the ditch. What do you think of it?"

Xia Nai glanced at it with a faint smile: "Ah yes! It's really a fine 'jade hairpin'!" He paused for a moment, pondering awhile and said: "This bone needle was brought here from some distant place. It came mixed up in the earth that was moved here to fill the tunnel. There must be ruins of the New Stone Age in the vicinity. Try to look into this when you have time."

The local people said that the loess soil covering the

tumulus within the ramparts of all the Imperial Tombs had not been gathered in the vicinity but brought from several kilometres away. This was related to the extreme importance which the emperors attached to geomancy and the dragon's ridge. The workmen were not allowed to take the local soil, nor could they use carts to transport the earth from a distance. Soldiers and civilians had to form a long line and pass the earth basket by basket from one to the other. According to historical sources, this method was first used in the Jin Dynasty: When the capital Zhongdu (today's Beijing) was built, earth was moved from Zhuozhou, a distance of 50 kilometres away. Records of this practice can also be found in the literature of the Ming Dynasty. If earth was dug from the hills, it would slash the dragon's ridge. There seemed to be some foundation to the story. But how far did the dragon's ridge extend? The small bone needle led the excavation team about eight kilometres southwest of Ding Ling, where there was a clean tract of loess. In the centre was a large depression more than 20,000 square metres in area. This hollow used to be filled with water, but was now dry. The villagers nearby called it the "yellow soil pond". From around the edges of the pond, the team collected some pottery shards belonging to the same archaeological period as the bone needle. A soil sample was taken and compared with the filled earth at Ding Ling. They were the same. It was certain that the filled earth at Ding Ling had been taken from "the pond", thus creating the hollow. The remains of a people from 3,000 years before had become loess on the imperial tombs.

The small bone needle led the team to another place

called Bao Hill northeast of the Great Red Gate of the tomb area. At the foot of the hill they found a stone axe, some shards of earthen vessels and the legs of ancient cooking tripods. They also discovered some broken tiles of later periods. When Zhao Qichang, Bai Wanyu and several colleagues from the Institute of Archaeology inspected the hill, everyone found relics of one kind or another. Professor Su Bingqi, chief of the Beijing University teaching and research section of archaeology, asked Zhao Qichang in the presence of the team: "What do you think of this site?"

Bai Wanyu came over and interrupted: "Professor Su is giving you an exam. This is a make-up test in field work. Answer to the point, so you'll get full marks!" Zhao Qichang smiled and then answered seriously: "This was an ideal living place for these prehistoric people. First, the northern side of the small hill was steep and at its foot was a river. So it was convenient for them to fetch water. Second, the southern side of the hill was a gentle incline suitable for farming. The upper slope was sunny, a good place to put up straw huts. As to the time, the relics seem to date back to the later period of the Neolithic Age. But judging from the tiles bearing the impression of woven material, human beings may have been living here right up until the Han Dynasty or even later." This caused a hubbub, with everyone talking at once: "That's good enough for a pass, but not for full marks. How could the people guard against wild beasts?" Zhao Qichang said: "The big river to the north was a natural protective barrier. How could wild animals get here?" Pang Zhongwei of the work team gave a prompt response! "To tell you the truth, there were wild animals here. A wolf's den was found at the foot of the hill. Not long ago a young man at Tai Ling caught three cubs in a cave, and the mother wolf howled for several nights. If the cubs had not been caught beforehand, even the old wolf could have been caught together with them." Su Bingqi laughed: "I am not worried about the northern defence; I'm speaking of the defence to the south."

Zhao Qichang caught on: Professor Su was joking with him. Changing the subject, Zhao said, "The village in the south is called Longmu (Dragon's Mother) Village, the birthplace of Cheng Laoliu of Chang Ling Yuan Village. When this bandit robbed the tomb of Concubine Wan, he took her headdress. His bride wore it at the wedding, really disgraceful. It is also recorded in history that Yao Guangxiao dressed himself up as a geomancer in Longmu Village to help choose the location for Emperor Yongle's tomb."

Director Xia remained silent for a while and then said with a smile: "It seems to me that a new entry should be added on the archaeological map of Beijing to indicate the ruins of Bao Hill. After you finish your work on Ding Ling, I'd like you to go on to Bao Hill." Bai Wanyu laughed: "I'm too old! Qichang is still young, with many promising years ahead of him!"

From the ancient people of 3,000 years ago to the builders of the Imperial Tombs of 300 years ago, no one would have dreamed that time would bring such great changes to this area. Yet in the last 30 years hotels and tall buildings have gone up. The ancient and the modern coexist in juxtaposition. The two long threads drawn by the bone needle were cut short in this way.

Collapse of a Wooden shack

Excavation was speeded up. Some construction workers were brought in to build over a dozen simple huts of wood planks and bamboo under the wall of the northern side of the tomb precinct. In mid-November the excavation team moved from Zhao Ling Village to settle into these shacks surrounded by centuries-old pine trees and grass.

The dwellings were simple and unique. The interiors were lined with shaving boards and the roofs were covered with asbestos shingles. They stood out prominently in this ancient, decaying tomb precinct, and added a modern touch to it. The living quarters were distributed according to age and work requirements, with each room shared by two people. Two extra rooms were reserved for reception and storage.

After they moved into the temporary shacks, Zhao Qichang and Liu Jingyi began to fix up their room with meticulous care. A bed board was put up to serve as a desk, on which to keep their books, data cards and reference material, plus some foreign and Chinese classics. If a friend or schoolmate dropped in for a visit, the books were piled on the floor and the board turned back to use as a bed. Big timber stakes were driven into the ground to make fixed stools. Some wooden boxes were piled up to serve as shelves for ceramic tiles, glazed animals, a stone axe, the precious bone needle, earthenware shards and big bricks with inscriptions on them. They felt at home living in this miniature museum. The walls were covered with charts, graphs and diagrams. The moment anyone entered, they could see the locations of the Imperial Ming

Tombs, their architectural shapes, and the sites of the three prospecting ditches. When it was all finished, the two young men invited Bai Wanyu to come in. "What do you think of our room?"

Bai Wanyu looked around, beaming. "This is a very good command headquarters," he said, sitting down on the bed sociably. With a crack, his whole body bumped on the floor, his head nearly hitting the wall. The two young men burst into loud laughter.

"What's all this about?" Bai Wanyu struggled to his feet again. He lifted the mattress up: underneath the four bed legs were made of wooden stakes driven into the ground. The head, foot and sides of the bed were wooden planks, and within this enclosure were jujube branches and dried grass. A layer of straw was spread over it all, and finally a cotton-padded mattress was laid on top with a white cloth spread on for a sheet. Bai Wanyu turned and, pointing to Zhao Qichang's nose, said: A prankster like you can never resist playing tricks!"

"How about the bed? If you like, we can make one for you, too. See how soft and warm it is, and also beautiful," Liu Jingyi said with a laugh.

Bai Wanyu shook his head. "I'm not so lucky. If I turn over in the night and jujube twigs stick in me, my bones might also end up in the underground palace."

One night ten days later, Zhao Qichang and Liu Jingyi were sleeping soundly on their soft beds, when the ceiling collapsed and fell on them. Following a loud crack, their bodies sank in the beds. Hearing their cries, Bai Wanyu and some team members got up and rushed into their room. They lit a candle and saw the ceiling still shaking, with Liu Jingyi screaming with pain under it. Bai Wanyu directed the young men to remove the ceiling at once. Liu Jingyi got up quickly and breathed a long sigh: "Damn it! What next! That was a miserable scare."

Early next morning the peasant workers came around to see Liu Jingyi. They asked him why the ceiling had collapsed. Liu answered casually: "If it wasn't because the hut was built in such an amateurish unscientific way, it must have been ghosts from the spirit world making trouble again!" This comment aroused general laughter. They said: "Spirits are unreal, science is real! Or how else could we have found the small stone tablet? With the tablet as a guide, how can we fail to find Emperor Wanli?"

Winter came. It brought more difficulties in both working and living conditions. Every morning the peasants had a hard time opening up the frozen top layer of earth, and the howling north wind pricked their faces like the thorns of the jujube tree, causing unbearable pain. Working in the damp soil the whole day made both their hands and feet begin to chap and progress slowed down perceptibly. In the evenings the six or seven members of the excavation team were left shivering and alone in their draughty wooden shacks as the peasants all went home. The small heating stove was not adequate against the bitter cold. At best the fire gave them only temporary warmth. Once it went out, the cold winds sweeping across the wilderness launched repeated attacks against their shacks. The howling winds, the soughing of the withered tree branches, and the plaintive cries of wild beasts and birds combined with the mysteries of the ancient imperial tomb precinct to create a bleak cacophony. This was a place where the living mingled with the dead, where this world merged with the nether regions. The tiny cluster of secluded shacks, peculiarly at odds with their surroundings, appeared dimly like a supernatural apparition. Survival instincts were tested to the utmost. In this place almost every member of the excavation team clenched his teeth and only managed to fulfil the day's demands with difficulty. However, there was one exception. In the face of all the inconveniences and discomforts, he talked cheerfully and humorously as usual and went about his business with ease. This was the veteran Bai Wanyu.

The Imperial Ming Tombs could not be mentioned here in the same breath as the desert of the Western Regions. In that much harsher environment, Bai Wanyu had stood the test of Nature at the cost of two fingers, displayed a stubborn vitality and tramped on determindly through the great deserts.

In 1914 the Swedish geologist Johan Gunnar Andersson came to the western part of China to conduct a survey and exploration of mineral resources in the region. When he arrived in Longguan County, Chahar, he was short of assistants and decided to recruit some of the local young men to assist him.

Bai Wanyu had lived a poor life as a child. When his father, who was hired by foreigners to do odd jobs in a local church, learned the news, he asked his 15-year-old son to apply for the job. The experienced Swedish explorer set an unusual test for the group of skinny children from poor families. He asked them each to plant a small pennant on a designated hilltop. When everyone was ready, Andersson shouted

"Start!", and the children raced up the hill. Bai Wanyu was the first to plant his pennant on the top. Andersson nodded with satisfaction and recruited him along with two other boys of 16 or 17.

From then on Bai Wanyu underwent rigorous and variegated training. He learned tailoring, cooking, to cut hair, to bake bread, to ride, to shoot and collect samples of ancient relics in the field. Then he accompanied Andersson to the Western Regions across the Gobi Desert and thus began his long trek throughout these distant areas. When they travelled through the Lawak Desert to ancient Loulan, they entered a grotesque world where natural castles, tortuous passages and deep sunken pits formed a mysterious labyrinth. The topography there was called *yadan* by the local people, or "wind-eroded terraces" in geographical terminology.

Bai Wanyu trudged through this bewildering, complicated *yadan* region together with Andersson and his group. They came upon grey layers of salt crust covering the ground. When they trampled upon it, the crust crackled, and sometimes gave way, so that their feet plunged through. The heavily-loaded camels and horses also had difficulties making their way over the hard alkaline soil. From time to time their hoofs bled and developed painful ulcers. Andersson was at last forced to leave the animals behind and to reorganise the group to continue their course through the desert on foot.

It was already October, when biting winds and raging sandstorms might arise unannounced at any moment. At night the temperature dropped to below minus 30 degrees Celsius. The team members had to grit their teeth and persist on a forced march for more than two weeks before they finally emerged from the *yadan* region, much the worse for wear. By this time two of Bai Wanyu's frostbitten fingers were beyond saving and it was necessary to amputate them in order to save the others.

The three years in the desert helped Bai Wanyu deepen his knowledge of archaeology. He became familiar with the methods of survey and the essential principles of excavation. He developed the skills needed for preserving and restoring disinterred relics. At the same time the fierce desert sandstorms steeled him into a man of indomitable character. In 1927 a joint northwest China scientific exploration group was formed between Chinese academic societies and associations, and the Swedish explorer Sven Hedin. Xu Bingchang, veteran archaeologist, was its leader on the Chinese side. Bai Wanyu went with the group on this exploration of the Western Regions, the second time for him. By this time, having matured in the course of his work, he was able to play a tremendous role in the survey and excavations. From this time on, he was destined to be cited in the "Archaeology Volume" of the *Great Encyclopaedia of China* as one of the first Chinese archaeologists.

It was precisely because of the extraordinary experiences of his childhood and the prime of his youth that the work at Ding Ling proceeded in an orderly way without a single death or major injury occuring as a result of the excavation; bolts of lightning being the exception.

In the three prospecting ditches opened at the worksite of Ding Ling, both walls of each ditch were sloped at a gradient of 70 degrees according to his orders, and were terraced every two metres and crenelled every five or six metres. This method was based on the experience and lessons he had drawn in his youth.

In 1934 he worked with Professor Su Bingqi in digging a prince's tomb near Baoji, Shaanxi Province. The gradient of the slopes was too steep and the distance between the steps upon them was too large. The slopes collapsed burying a dozen or so peasant workers in the ditch. By the time they were rescued one or two of them had already stopped breathing. It was a small tomb; the amount of earth dug out could not be compared with that of Ding Ling. It was because of this tragedy that Bai Wanyu was especially cautious and checked the soil layer very carefully every day to eliminate any danger of a similar occurrence.

New Year's Day

In the morning of New Year's Day, 1957, when the members of the excavation team went out, they were surprised to see the whole tomb precinct covered with a thick layer of snow. The old pines and cypresses, the stele pavilion, halls, and rampart were all dressed up in silvery sheen. The sun rose quietly above Huyu Hill in the east. It pierced the dense pine woods, spreading its golden rays over the snow-covered ground.

The peasant workers walked on the crunchy snow to the precinct in twos or threes, and gathered in front of the wooden shacks. Their honest, weather-beaten faces were beaming with excitement and delight. The excavation team decided that everyone could have a day off;

the morning would be spent at a banquet for all, and the afternoon would be free. This was the first time in their lives that these peasants, who had worked on their farmland year in and year out, spent a New Year's holiday like this.

Wang Qifa made the first move. He had dug the first shovel of earth from the ground in the excavation of Ding Ling, and now, with a natural instinct for taking the lead, he picked up a carrying pole with two buckets dangling on it to fetch water from Jiulong (Nine Dragon) Pool one kilometre away for the kitchen. He was wearing an old cotton-padded jacket, with a straw rope tied around his waist and a hemp string around the trouser legs. When he returned, sweat running down his face, the two water pails, one in front and one in back, moved up and down in harmony with his steady gait while on his padded hat, two rabbit-skin earflaps tossed rhythmically. He looked like a tight-rope walker negotiating a steel cable. This provoked great laughter among the excavation team members and the peasants.

The noon sunshine over the snow-covered ground was dazzlingly bright, and a warm stream of happiness flowed through the heart of everyone present. Before long the meal was spread. Near the kitchen on a long stone slab, which served as a table, appeared cold delicacies and hot food of various kinds. In the clean air hung an inviting fragrance of delicious food. Even before drinks were served, everyone seemed a little bit drunk. Zhao Qichang, raising a bowl of wine and sweeping a glance over the excited and rough faces of his team members and the peasants, spoke in a loud voice: "My elders and brothers, we have come together to excavate Ding Ling. For six months, we have worked here day in and day out in the muddy water, and surmounted many difficulties, both technically and in our daily lives..." Here he suddenly became choked with emotion, unable to continue. Puzzled at this inexplicable behaviour, they looked at him. They did not realise that Zhao Qichang had already become immersed in thoughts of the recent past and was now overcome by the memories.

As he was lost to recollection, at noon the peasants lunched on food brought from home in the morning. The bamboo food steamer was opened, revealing the content of their daily fare: balls made from sweet-potato leaves, shreds of turnip and bean leaves, mixed with a little corn flour and sweet-potato starch. Whenever he saw the peasants dragging their tired legs to the steamer, their faces daubed with mud, Zhao felt a pang of anguish. As they devoured their simple meals uncomplainingly, he became depressed. The People's Republic was already seven or eight years old, but these peasants were still living on mixtures of chaff and inedible vegetables to keep going. This could not be regarded as other than a sad oversight. He became even more upset at the idea of all these ragged peasants working with full devotion, whatever the weather in New China's first excavation of an imperial tomb, although they did not know the real importance or value of the project.

Seeing Zhao Qichang choked with emotion, Bai Wanyu raised his bowl of wine. "Thanks to your support, we are beginning to see some results from our efforts. The difficulties ahead of us will be even greater. It is my hope that we will grit our teeth and surmount all obstacles. I propose a toast! Bottoms up, everybody!"

All stood up, lifted their bowls to shoulder height, gazed at one another for a moment, tossed their heads and drank down the white "fire-water".

Wang Qifa blushed a little. The amusement was gone from his face. Filling a second bowl of spirit all around, he rose slowly to speak. He was solemn and a bit nervous. "We peasant workers, including myself, were once misled by some nonsense about ghosts and spirits; we did some things we shouldn't have done, caused a lot of trouble for the comrades of the excavation team, and delayed the work. When it was all over, everyone of us felt bad. We wanted to talk it over with Team Leader Zhao and Mr Bai, but we felt ashamed to bring it up. Today, I mention it on behalf of all of us, and promise that hereafter, we'll fulfil all the tasks given to us, no matter what happens…"

His sincere words inspired a round of applause, with Zhao Qichang taking the lead. He had not expected that the get-together would turn out to be so convivial, that the peasants would be so communicative and that all along, a latent mutual affinity had existed among all participants in the excavation. That day, together with sorghum spirit, they drank in renewed strength, conviction and contentment blended with hearty and sentiments of good will…

The sun set, and darkness began to creep over the land. The peasants all returned home, and the precinct was once again deserted and silent.

The team members returned to their room and sat around the stove for warmth. Their excitement remained at a high pitch, and Liu Jingyi ventured to ask Bai Wanyu to tell them some stories.

He did not decline the invitation, taking the opportunity to tell of his unusual experiences during his exploration of the Western Regions. This was the most brilliant period of his life and also his own personal contribution when called upon to entertain.

"When I came to Lop Nur with Andersson, this famous lake had already dried up. The lake bed was covered with a layer of white alkaline, and was dry as a bone. Everyone felt rather despondent. Prior to this, we had travelled through the Taklimakan Desert, then heading north from Yingkule crossed the Peacock River where we took in a supply of water, and continued along the dry bed of the Kuluk River to Lop Nur. By the time we arrived, our water supply was depleted, and we were all overcome by thirst and exhaustion. Suddenly, we caught sight of a man lying by a sand dune a short distance away. Hurrying there, we saw his arms were thrust deeply into the river mud. The whole body was as stiff as a mummy. This frightened us all into a cold sweat. We stood there silently for a long time before we could gather our strength to bury him in the sand. At the time, we could not help but heed a loud reminder from this silent mummy: Your destiny may well be no different..."

"Hey, this is New Year's, don't talk so much about corpses! We want to hear something more entertaining!" Liu Jingyi shouted, without allowing Bai Wanyu to bring his story to a fitting climax.

With a glance at Liu Jingyi and a puff on his pipe he nodded agreeably: "You're right, today we celebrate, so I'll tell you a more amusing story. This is also when I was working with Andersson. We were staying at a village near Jiuquan, in Gansu. As it turned out, we had as a neighbour a young widow. She was not only beautiful, but also kind-hearted. When she saw the thin lined jacket which was my chief defence against the cold winter, she secretly made me a cotton-padded jacket and cotton-padded trousers. Out of gratitude, I gave her some small, rare objects which I had found at an excavation site and sometimes, some money. We liked to talk together, and did so more and more often. As time went on, we fell in love. The more we loved each other, the harder it became for us to part, even for a few hours. However, finally we did part. We had to, because I was committed to continuing exploration westward with Andersson. The day I left, it was drizzling. She stood at her door, reluctant to say good-bye, tears running down her cheeks..." At this point, Bai's own eyes were wet with tears. He sighed deeply: "Ah, it's been several dozen years. I don't know how this young widow is now. She may be already in heaven for all I know..." Memory of love is always a rosy cloud.

The room had become quiet again. They were immersed in the two stories just as if they had been together with Bai Wanyu back in the days of his westward journey across the desert, and were now chewing over his unforgettable regret and sweetness.

Chapter Six
THE DIAMOND WALL

Message in the Stone Tunnel

The excavation of Ding Ling was speeded up after the New Year. In order to reach the tunnel gate to the underground palace, the excavation committee decided to use machines instead of human labour for removing the earth. Moreover, a highway was built between Beijing and Changping by the Beijing Municipal Highway Bureau with permission from the Ministry of Communications.

Using machines for transportation multiplied the quantity of earth that could be dug out many times over. In a month after the third ditch was opened, they found traces of walls, laid with large rectangular stone slabs, on both sides. Gradually two large complete walls emerged. The archaeological team made a timely judgement: This was the final section of a paved path used for the burials of the emperor and empresses, or what was referred to as the "stone tunnel". The use of stone instead of bricks was an obvious improvement. Although the tunnel was slightly curved, there were no detours. The underground palace lay ahead! The protracted tension may now have relaxed slightly, yet, as all realised, the work of opening and entering the underground palace, to say nothing of sorting out the relics, would prove much more difficult and multifarious. The work team had to devise all kinds of tentative plans, make analyses and draw inferences: What action would be appropriate to the state of preservation or decomposition of the corpses? What immediate repairs should be made to preserve relics which had only partially disintegrated? How should transient signs be recorded and photographed? These questions were not only a test for the young archaeological team, but also a test for the level of archaeological work in China. The main threads had to be sorted out of the mess, and each one of them required its own particular preparation, meetings, personnel, tools and chemicals...For the time being, hoists, diesel engines and small mining cars were roaring in the daytime, while throughout the night in the shacks candles burned quietly.

Within a few months the stone tunnel was completely open to view. It was composed of two large walls running from east to west. The eastern end curved southward; it was close to the brick tunnel, but neither connected, nor opposite to it. Brocatelle was used to construct the walls except for the top parts and the western end close to the diamond wall, where a small number of bricks had been laid instead. The stone had been carefully polished and processed, appearing glossy and smooth, and containing many beautiful colours. The whole tunnel sloped gradually from east to west, running shallow to deep. The layers of coloured stones making up the walls increased progressively from one to 17, with the total length of the walls being 40 metres. The distance between them was eight metres. The tunnel had been filled with tamped loess and the top covered with a thin layer of lime. After the tunnel had been filled, the tamped loess rose higher than the walls and reached ground level. In the course of the excavation, vestiges of timber pillars were found on the two sides of the tunnel, which were believed to have been the temporary facilities used for the burials of the coffins.

When first proposed, the use of machines for the excavation had aroused censure from all sides. Even the leading scholars in academic circles became divided into two camps. The opposition, at first, seemed to hold the fort. Picks, spades and shovels, they contended, had always been used in excavations of ancient tombs and ruins for scientific archaeological purposes throughout the world. From the excavations of the Yin ruins, the unearthing of the Upper Cave Man's skull and the triangular-shaped divine animal mirror in China, to the great excavation of the Pazyryk Barrows on the northern side of the Altai Mountains, and that of the Babylon Empire, all depended on human labour, hand tools and instruments. Wouldn't the use of mechanical equipment in the excavation of Ding Ling damage the ruins of the tomb tunnel? Would it represent an advance in creation or the destruction of culture? After much heated discussion, Xia Nai made the final decision: mechanical equipment would be used only for transporting earth, dug by hand, to the outside, and would not damage or harm the ruins and buried objects.

Events proved that this was the correct decision. The digging of the third ditch did win time for an early opening of the underground palace without damaging the remains of the tomb passage. It was only years later that people came to understand the principal reason why the team introduced machines at that time. There was a secret hidden behind their thinking: Like fighters on the battlefield, they had to make sure they were ready for the humid season — which was not too hot or too cold. Then they would be engaged in the most important work of all — that of sorting out the burial objects after the palace was opened. Such climatic conditions would be favourable to the preservation and protection of the unearthed objects. However, there was one point they had not taken into consideration — there had been a sharp change in the political situation. If the underground palace could not be opened in time, the next year they would not be allowed to stay there for a moment longer than the term of contract already fixed. No matter how reluctant or even bitter they would be to leave, it was inevitable that work at the underground palace would be handed over to another group of people. Come what may, this group was determined to make the best of their present opportunity.

The stone tunnel yielded rich material for study. It was now 40 metres long and 20 metres deep. About two metres from the bottom stone, slabs were found with characters written on them in black ink. After they brushed the soil off the slabs, the words became legible. Most of them were records of years, months, names, birthplaces, official titles and the quality of the stone. Notes taken down during the excavation included such details as:

26th day, 4th lunar month, Jin Hu
26th, Liu Jing
Hu Xi'er, Shandong
Wang Bao, below, Second Team, Third Brigade, Eighth Battalion, Fifth Army, 7th day, 4th lunar month

The arrangement and structure of the characters lacked regularity and neatness. Some were little better than doodles. In some cases, a person had simply made a cross as his signature. The archaeological team analysed these scribbles as marks made by inspectors of the stone materials, who were mostly military officers. It was recorded in the reference literature: "On the Ox Day of the 10th Heavenly Stem in the 1st month of the 18th year of the Wanli Reign, Hong Youfu, inspector of military barracks in the capital, and others submitted a memorial to the effect that the number of troops involved in the building of the tomb far exceeded the scanty amount of work done..." Evidently most of the tomb builders at that time were troops. This is confirmed by the scribbles. The literature and the relics corroborate each other.

Inverted-V Opening Discovered

For an archaeologist, research ability is important, but the most treasured qualifications in field work are rich experience in survey and excavations, and a high sense of responsibility. Field surveys and excavations must follow a strict, systematic methodology. Only when they are conducted in keeping with rigorous scientific methods, can they embody true archaeological work. "The stature and achievements of an archaeological worker are decided in the main not by what he has exhumed, but by how he carried out the excavation." This was a celebrated dictum of Xia Nai, also a constant doctrine he followed closely throughout his life. In 1944 in excavating a tomb supposedly belonging to the Qijia culture at Yangwawan in Ningding, Gansu Province, he squatted all day long in the open pit like a marmot, using a small spade to carefully move away the filled earth. He finally uncovered some painted pottery shards representing the Yangshao culture. The stratigraphy of the site confirmed that the Yangshao culture was earlier than the Qijia culture — a finding which corrected the erroneous conclusion reached by Andersson regarding the division of cultural periods of the Neolithic Age in Gansu. When Xia Nai's essay "New Discoveries of Tombs of the Qijia Period and Revision of Its Years" was published in the journal of the British Royal Anthropological Society, it aroused much interest in British and other European academic circles. The first ray of morning glow rising from Yangwawan marked not only the end of the time when foreign scholars dominated Chinese archaeology, but also a new starting point of China's prehistoric archaeology. In the winter of 1950 Xia Nai directed the excavation of the chariot and horse pit of the Warring States Period at Liulige in Hui County, Henan Province. He dug everyday, manipulating a small spade in the teeth of wind and snow, and at last unearthed the remains of 19 large wooden chariots. The successful excavation at Liulige demonstrated for the first time the superb skills and high level of New China's archaeological field work. His exacting work and his spirit of seeking truth from facts put him on a par with great masters like Sven Anders Hedin, Johan Gunnar Andersson, Daniel Green and others. The famous Japanese archaeologist Takayasu Higuchi published a high appraisal of him in his book *Xia Nai and Chinese Archaeology*:

> Xia Nai was director of the Chinese Institute of Archaeology for 20 years. Although he underwent the test of the "cultural revolution" during this period, he retained the top position in Chinese archaeological circles. This was because of his noble character and his single-hearted devotion to the search for knowledge. He has a wide knowledge not only of domestic but also international archaeology. His wide range of archaeological studies is unmatched in the field. Important among them are his studies in the Western Regions. For one who studies the Western Regions, knowledge of Chinese archaeology is not enough. He must also thoroughly understand the West. This includes, for example, research of the silk fabrics made in Xinjiang, gold coins from Eastern Rome and silver coins of the Sassanids unearthed in China. In my opinion, probably no one but he could prove equal to the task. He not only enjoys the highest prestige among Chinese archaeologists, but also internationally ranks among the few archaeologists accorded such an outstanding reputation.

Just because there was a director of wide knowledge and mature experience, the young archaeological team managed to avoid making a detour in New China's first excavation of an imperial tomb. Very soon Zhao Qichang's prospecting spade uncovered the upper part of the diamond wall under the tumulus in the western part of the stone tunnel. The diamond wall was buried to a depth of 13 metres below ground level and 1.2 metres above the stone tunnel. Although it was still buried deep underground, change in the soil texture helped to ascertain its exact position and its relations to the stone tunnel. After a year's excavation, the peasant workers had learnt how to do their job and to distinguish suspicious signs according to archaeological standards. Their excavation skills also matured. When they were told about the position of the wall and its link with the stone tunnel, they were all eager to see it as soon as possible. Somewhere just ahead was a mysterious wall that had been buried for centuries! They worked longer and longer every day; the amount of earth dug from the ditch doubled and even tripled. Finally, having moved away all the filled earth from the stone tunnel, they reached it. The diamond wall (also called Buddha's warrior wall) was 8.8 metres high, and 1.6 metres thick. It looked indeed like Buddha's stalwart warrior guarding the gate of the underground palace. Its thick wall foundation consists of four layers of long stone slabs, above which were 56 layers of wall bricks filled with mortar. At the top were solid upturned eaves of yellow glazed tiles, which looked like a helmet cast in gold. Illuminated by the setting sun, the whole wall radiated brilliant rays of gold. The simple but vigorous artistic design of the wall was undoubtedly a demonstration of a powerful and indestructible force.

On careful inspection, a new miracle was revealed. There was an obscure opening on the wall, which was narrow above, wide below and shaped like an inverted V. The opening was originally sealed with 23 layers of wall bricks lined with mortar, with no vestige of the seal left. Due to the pressure exerted over a long period of time by the filled earth in the tunnel, the sealed bricks became inclined inward slightly and the seal was gradually exposed. They concluded that the sealed opening must lead to the gate of the underground palace where the emperor and empresses were buried. The day was May 19, 1957.

"We've found it, we have finally found it!" Zhao Qichang shouted loudly in his excitement. The peasant workers gathered around him to see the mysterious sealed opening. At the depth of 20 metres there were sudden noises of jubilation. Looking at the seal, Liu Jingyi turned around abruptly, threw himself on the back of Bai Wanyu, and cried: "We — have succeeded!" Hardly had he finished when the old man fell to the ground with a flop. Liu Jingyi made off at once. Bai Wanyu climbed out of the ditch and sat on the ground; without knowing whether to laugh or to cry he complained: "You scamp, you silly little boy..." There was another burst of laughter in the ditch.

Gazing at the sealed opening in the diamond wall, Zhao Qichang instantly recalled the words inscribed on the small tablet found earlier on in the second ditch: "16 *zhang* (about 160 feet) from this stone to the front lining of the diamond wall, 35 *chi* (about 35 feet deep)." He snatched up a tape measure to ascertain the distance from the wall to where the small stone tablet was found, and converted the result into the units of measurement used in the Ming Dynasty. It was exactly 16 *zhang* as recorded on the tablet. Zhao Qichang nodded, looked at the solid wall and murmured, "Thank Heaven!"

From May 19, 1956, when the first shovel of earth was tossed up, to May 19, 1957, when the sealed opening of the diamond wall was revealed, it had been exactly one year. Was this a historical coincidence or one of Heaven's whims?

The discovery of the diamond wall created a sensation in cultural circles. A large and steady stream of historians, archaeologists, scholars and political VIPs went to Ding Ling in a steady stream to see the magnificent diamond wall. The sensitive press organisations lost no time in sending journalists and photographers to cover the event. In view of the situation, the Chang Ling Excavation Committee made the following decision: "Except for the Central Newsreels and Documentary Film Studio which is allowed to shoot on the spot, the excavation of Ding Ling is closed to all media. All relevant information is highly confidential." In view of this decision and the political situation in China at that time, it was not until September 6, 1958 that news of the excavation of Ding Ling was first published at home and abroad by Xinhua News Agency.

The specially entrusted Central Newsreels and Documentary Film Studio promptly sent three power-generating trucks, cinecameras and two trucks of film-shooting equipment to the site, and assigned three specialists — Zhang Qinghong, Shen Jie and Mou Sen to tape the excavation. From then on the film workers settled down at the excavation site and photographed the whole process of the opening of the underground palace. The documentary "Excavating the Underground Palace of Ding Ling" that is now shown in the main hall of Chang Ling is compiled of what they filmed almost 40 years ago.

On the afternoon of May 21, a gathering was held under the pines and cypresses in front of the stele pavilion of Ding Ling to celebrate the first anniversary of the excavation. The awarding of prizes to the peasant workers formed part of the ceremony.

There were ten winners of the first prize, each being awarded a pair of gym shoes; 20 winners of the second prize, each receiving a white towel; and 36 winners of the third prize, each given a cake of soap.

The peasant workers came forward to receive their prizes, their faces blushing and beaming. All the hardships, arduous labour, inclement weather, and miscellaneous weals and woes was encapsulated in the prizes. For them, such a reward was an honour and a recognition. To the Chinese peasants who had worked year in and year out on the farmlands and shared the difficulties of the young People's Republic, as long as the motherland acknowledged their participation as a "contribution" to socialist construction, they felt happy.

Landslide

When the diamond wall appeared, the excavation team appointed specialists to put up a temporary shelter.

The technicians assigned by the mat shed section of Dongdan District in Beijing came to the excavation site to design the plan for the shed. Shortly afterwards 11 trucks loaded with bamboo poles, bamboo mats, timber, asphalt felt, hemp rope and steel wire arrived, and 20 builders began work. Fir poles were used as supports, hemp rope and steel wire bound them together. The roof was covered with a layer of reed matting and two layers of bamboo mats, between which was placed the asphalt felt. Most of the workmen were skilled masters hired by privately-owned companies before 1949, who specialised in erecting temporary constructions for wedding ceremonies or funeral services; they had much experience and special skills. In a very short time a big shed 60 metres long and 26 metres wide was erected, with several roll-mat skylights for ventilation and lighting. The combination of the ancient tomb precinct and the temporary shelter looked like a long bridge across a deep river. The big, solid shed serving as a barrier was to be a perfect safeguard for protecting the stone tunnel, the diamond wall and the gate to the underground palace.

Unfortunately, as it turned out, events proved otherwise. In the dead of night on August 3, a strong gust of wind was immediately followed by a thunder shower, with rain beating down on the wooden shacks. All members of the excavation team woke up and peered outside through the small windows. Everything was enveloped in the dark curtain of night. Only when lightning struck, did they see sheets of rain blurring the sky and the earth into one, wreaking havoc.

"I'm afraid something might go wrong with the ditch," Bai Wanyu said in a low voice, watching the rain stream down.

"What's there to be afraid of? We have a solid

shed which can resist the strongest rainstorms," Liu Jingyi said nonchalantly, as he stretched out his hand to pat Bai Wanyu on his glistening forehead.

"You scamp..." Just as Bai Wanyu was about to hit back a sudden rumbling put everyone on the alert. Bai shouted: "Damn it, something's wrong at the worksite!" From his long experience in archaeological field work, he was the first to tell that the rumbling came from a landslide at the worksite.

Almost everyone rushed there without stopping to dress. Torch lights flashed through the torrents of rain. They searched from east to west on both sides of the shed. Zhao Qichang stopped at the end of the stone tunnel and called out: "It's here!" They all ran over. There they saw a large mass of loose earth which had slid down from the top of the tumulus above the diamond wall. Precisely at that moment, they heard a cry from inside the shed, muffled by the swirling wind and rain.

"Damn it all, there are people in the ditch!" sharp-eared Liu Jingyi reported.

They all fell silent and made their way down the steps of the ditch to the bottom of the stone tunnel. Then they heard piercing cries from under the diamond wall: "The earth is sliding...help!"

Rushing to the foot of the wall they saw two public security soldiers almost buried in the loose dirt. To ensure the safety of the underground palace and prevent mishandling of the buried relics, 15 soldiers from the public security forces had been dispatched to Ding Ling on May 30 to stand guard day and night.

Fortunately, the landslide had buried only the legs of the two soldiers. Their rescuers climbed up the landslide, moved the earth away and helped them out.

"How did you happen to come down to this place?" Zhao Qichang asked.

"We just came over here to look around and make sure everything was secure. We did not expect that as soon as we got here the land would give way..." one of them answered nervously, rubbing his hands up and down his legs.

"Well, your luck was with you, otherwise you'd have been finished!" As he spoke, Bai Wanyu flashed his torch over the collapsed land. They found that the wall had become buried in the landslide. The two soldiers had been standing above the wall; it would have been a different story if they had been half a metre further away.

Exploring the shed with their hand torches, they found rain water leaking in one corner. This was what had caused the slide. Zhao Qichang quickly organised a group to place blankets of asphalt felt and bamboo mats over the leaks in the roof. When they returned to their shacks, their faces were plastered with mud. They were forced to laugh when they looked at each other.

The rain stopped the next morning and the air in the precinct was pure and fresh. Zhao Qichang, together with some other members, went to the landslide in front of the shed to determine the cause of the leakage. It turned out that the asphalt felt used for the shed was of inferior quality. Some of it had cracks which split under the pounding of the rainstorm and erosion by the flow of water so that rain seeped through the crevices and caused the landslide. Only several days later did Zhao Qichang learn that one of the rear-service personnel had bought the substandard goods from a factory in Changping. This cost the peasants 12 days' labour to clear the ditch and placed two lives in mortal danger.

Hidden Mechanism

Rumours circulated widely about the underground palace of Ding Ling, much the same as those about the pyramids in the West. The tombs were enveloped in mystery and the rumours inspired terror. Long before the diamond wall was found, these rumours were already rife among the peasant workers and villagers around the Imperial Tombs area. Some whispered that behind the wall was a hidden mechanism which would shoot poisoned arrows once a certain stone slab was removed, and a person would surely die instantly if an arrow hit any part of his body. After the diamond wall was exposed, some people inspected the seal carefully. When they found nothing out of the ordinary, they began to suspect that there was no such hidden mechanism behind the wall after all, but there might in fact be hidden arrows and flying sabres waiting to be released in the underground palace. Once the gate of the palace was opened, they would have to look out! The arrows would be shot out in a steady stream and at the same time flying sabres would drop down so that no one could escape death. The rumours grew ever more fantastic and fearful.

They dared not disbelieve, but if anyone had doubts, more "proof" was forthcoming. Ten days after the wall was discovered, an old man in rags with a wide-brimmed reed hat and straggling white hair on his head came to the worksite quietly, and solemnly greeted every peasant worker he met. He confided to them with an air of mystery: "All these years, I've kept a tomb genealogy passed down to me by my ancestors. On it is clearly written that there's a stream running through the underground palace of Ding Ling. A small boat floats on it, and whoever wants to see Emperor Wanli's coffin must first cross the stream in the boat. On the other side of the stream is a chasm 100,000 feet deep. At the bottom of it are barbed wires with a stepping board on them. Only those born on an auspicious day will succeed in crossing the chasm. Otherwise, they will lose their lives..."

Judging by his appearance, the peasants wondered if the old man might not be an immortal; they went to see him one by one to have their fortune told. The old man readily complied, charging 20 cents a time. In all, he collected more than ten yuan, quite a handsome income at that time. On hearing of the old man, Zhao Qichang and Bai Wanyu also went to see him, but by then, the "immortal" was nowhere to be seen. He had quietly slipped away.

The rumours and the mysterious old man posed one riddle after another. The ensuing consternation finally came to the attention of the leaders of the nation's cultural circles and produced great repercussions. Guo Moruo, Wu Han, Deng Tuo and Zheng Zhenduo of the Chang Ling Excavation Committee personally came to the site one after another and left instructions: "Preferably believe it, rather than not believe it. Make necessary preparations to ensure the absolute safety of the workers' lives and the burial objects." Guo Moruo, who had studied medical science in his college days, issued further instructions: "There will be poison from the corpses in these ancient tombs. You must take precautions."

Members of the excavation team, who had originally regarded the rumours as a big joke, could no longer treat them lightly after receiving such instructions from the great cultural masters. Now they could take nothing for granted. Since the rumours had stirred the hearts of the people, they could not but adopt a solemn view of the situation.

With these questions in mind, Zhao Qichang consulted closely with Xia Nai. They agreed that excavations of the pyramids and other large tombs in the West revealed that corpses of tomb robbers were indeed buried in some tombs, but it had never been clear whether they were killed by some mechanism inside the tomb or by greedier accomplices. The same phenomena had also been observed in Chinese tombs. When some graves were opened, the corpses of three or four robbers might be found inside. However, on the basis of the positions and expressions of the corpses and the surroundings of the tombs, it could be concluded that most of these deaths were caused by the latter. When the robbers found the coffins, they would open them from one end, then tie one end of a rope around the neck of the corpse and the other end around the robber's neck. When the robber lifted himself up slightly, the corpse was also raised. In this way, the robber could freely search for valuables in the coffin and even remove the clothes from the corpse. After the valuables were thrust out through a hole, the robber waiting outside could stop up the hole with stones or lumps of soil without waiting for the man inside to come out, so that he had the valuables all to himself. The robber inside was left to wait for certain death by suffocation. Therefore, as a precaution whether in the West or in China, most tomb robbers would be a combination of father and son, or brothers, very seldom of friends.

A Chinese imperial tomb was being excavated scientifically for the first time, and the questions of what it would be like inside and whether there were hidden weapons installed there had to be treated with extreme caution. Special precautions had to be observed against gases inside. In order to prevent decomposition of the corpses, it might be necessary to use some protective drugs; but this raised the possibility that when these drugs mixed with the gases from the decomposed corpses, they may become toxic and harmful to human beings. Avoiding possible accidents required the study of more historical data as preparation prior to the opening of the underground palace. All agreed that they would fight no battle they were not sure of winning.

Therefore in preparation for the opening, Zhao Qichang and Liu Jingyi together studied all the historical data available. They were determined to be absolutely sure of success.

Of all the imperial tombs in Chinese history there is only one for which authentic records exist. This is the tomb of the first emperor of the Qin Dynasty (221-207 BC) in the Li Hills in Shaanxi Province. Emperor Qin Shihuang ascended the throne at the age of 13, and shortly afterwards work on his tomb was begun at Li Hills. After he unified the separate states, he enlisted more than 700,000 people from all over the land to continue the work. The tomb was not finished when he died at 50. Construction continued for another two years after his son, Qin Ershi, succeeded him. The gigantic project took 40 years to complete.

The book *Records of the Historian* by Sima Qian contains the following description: "The underground palace was deep and solidly built. It not only had 'veined stones' to block the underground streams and springs, but was also painted with cinnabar to keep out moisture. Halls were built with seats for high-ranking officials. There were pearls, jade and all kinds of treasures. Candles made of dugong (a large aquatic herbivorous mammal) grease were lit and kept burning. Hidden crossbows and arrows were installed inside with an automatic propulsion system to prevent robbery. The coffin, surrounded by mercury which was kept flowing mechanically, seemed to be encircled by rivers and seas. Above was a celestial body with the sun, the moon and stars, and below was a landscape with rivers and mountains..." The historian also informs his readers that when Emperor Qin Shihuang was buried, Qin Ershi ordered all palace maids without children to be buried alive with him. All builders of the tomb were buried alive in another place. Two thousand years after Emperor Qin Shihuang was buried, tomb excavators found a burial place for executed criminals near Yaochitou and Zhaobeihou villages, about 1,400 metres southwest of his tomb. At this burial place of 1,020 square metres, the pile of bones was more than one metre deep. This may have been the final resting place for the builders of the tomb which Sima Qian described in his book.

According to *Historical Records of the Han Dynasty*, Emperor Wu began to build an underground palace for himself in the second year of his reign. The tomb took 53 years to complete. When the emperor died, the trees planted in the area had grown so large that a man could barely encircle them with his arms. The tomb was more than 120 feet high and 130 feet deep; the coffin chambers were over 17 feet high. The doors were equipped with hidden swords and crossbows to prevent robbery. As soon as construction began, rich families, whose households totalled 270,000 people, were moved to the tomb area to live. It was at this time that the famous historian Sima Qian moved his family here from Xinyang. In the late years of the Western Han Dynasty, the Chimei (Red Eyebrow) Army occupied the capital city of Chang'an, destroyed the emperor's tomb and made off with the objects buried there. In fact, prior to this, the tomb had already been looted by local bandits.

In order to save manpower and materials, and at the same time to prevent robbery, the imperial tombs of the Tang Dynasty were built against hills, the hilltops being used as the tops of the tombs. Zhao Ling, the burial place for Emperor Li Shimin, was built by digging into the Jiujun Mountain 1,188 metres above sea level northwest of Chang'an. According to historical data, this burial method was introduced by Emperor Li Shimin's wife, Empress Changsun. She died before the emperor and before her death asked him to give her a simple burial to save expenses. "Bury me in the hill, please, without building a tomb." This was in fact Li Shimin's own idea which he expressed in the name of his empress. In the inscription on the tablet for Empress Changsun, he wrote: "The emperor regards the entire land as his home, why should so many objects be buried in the tomb as his own? Since the Jiujun Mountain is to be used for my tomb, no gold or jade should be buried there, and figures, horses and vases should all be made of wood, so that robbers will cease to covet them and there will be no need to worry."

Today we see that the Tang imperial tombs of Zhao Ling for Emperor Taizong (Li Shimin), and of Qian Ling for Emperor Gaozong and his wife Empress Wu Zetian, both built in the mountain, are even more majestic than the tomb of Emperor Qin Shihuang. Nevertheless Zhao Ling did not escape robbery. When the Tang Dynasty was overthrown, warlord Wen Tao led his troops in plundering the tomb and took away quantitis of gold, pearls and other valuables. This revealed that Li Shimin had not really meant what he had said about wanting a "simple burial". Only Qian Ling remained intact over the years. This may have something to do with the solid structure of the mountain rocks and the use of huge stones and molten lead to seal the gate.

Talk of hidden arrows, crossbows and poisonous gas persisted regarding most of the imperial tombs after the Tang Dynasty, but still a great number of them were looted. However, no records can be found in official historical data about what role these threats played in preventing robbery. Only unofficial history described in detail how the tombs were robbed and how dangerous the hidden weapons were. But this is not sufficient as evidence. There were various stories and detailed descriptions of how the warlord Sun Dianying looted the imperial tombs of Qing-dynasty Emperor Qianlong and Empress Dowager Cixi in the 20th century. But even if there had been hidden weapons in the tombs, they would have been destroyed in the explosions that Sun

Dianying set off.

But one aspect should not be overlooked. When Emperor Wanli began to build Ding Ling, he could not have been ignorant of the fact that most of the imperial tombs of previous dynasties had been robbed. The people in charge of the construction must also have read *Records of the Historian* by Sima Qian and *Historical Records of the Han Dynasty*; they should have had no doubts about the hidden mechanisms installed in the tombs. If so, it was impossible that they should neglect the installation of equipment to counteract robbery. By the Ming Dynasty, capitalist industrial civilisation had dawned in China. This was confirmed by the large fleet commanded by Zheng He on his voyages to the Indian Ocean in the early years of the Ming. If equipment to prevent robbery was to be set up in the underground palace, it should have been a matter of course that more scientific and advanced devices would be used in place of the out-moded crossbows, arrows and other sharp weapons of the Qin and Han dynasties. Then, what could the hidden weapons installed in Ding Ling's underground palace possibly be like? This riddle perplexed every member of the excavation team for a long time.

Chapter Seven
THE UNDERGROUND PALACE OPENS WITH A BANG

Rumours Under the Wall

It was a sultry summer night in August. The quiet of the Ding Ling tomb precinct was shattered by new terror and mystery because of fresh rumours and the recently discovered opening in the diamond wall.

Under candle light, members of the excavation team were still busy probing the obscure situation of the underground palace. With further analysis veil after veil was being removed...

The founding of the Ming Dynasty ended the rule of the Mongolian nobles of the Yuan Dynasty. The Mongolian burial system for the ruling family reverted back to the system of building tombs against mountains. According to the imperial funeral system of the Yuan, "there is no part of the tomb visible at the burial place; horses trample on the grave to level the ground. One thousand mounted troops are stationed there to guard it. When the grass grows in spring, the tents are moved away. The grassland looks just as before and nobody knows where the tombs lie underneath."

Zhu Yuanzhang, the founding emperor of the Ming Dynasty, was the son of a peasant; he and his descendants all hoped their family would continue as rulers of the empire from generation to generation. The theory and practice of geomancy, transmitted from remote antiquity, was revived and widely invoked again. The Imperial Ming Tombs were built on principles of *fengshui* largely as described in the *Book of Funerals* written by Guo Pu, a scholar of the Eastern Jin Dynasty. It says: "*Feng* refers to the shelter provided by mountains and the solidity of the earth, while *shui* refers to the height and moisture content of the terrain and its proximity to flowing water." The whole theory of the book, though immersed in superstition, is based on natural features of landscapes. Many of the special terms used, such as the "four terrains", the "lay of a mountain" and "cicada's wings", evoked an aura of mystery over natural landscapes, but were in essence nothing but synonyms for certain land formations and topography. In selecting the site for Ding Ling, Ke Ting, imperial censor, said in his memorial to the emperor: "Dayu Hill rises like ten thousand horses galloping ahead. Its four inclines are perfect, and the real dragon is hidden by Heaven for your majesty." Therefore, it is clear that Ding Ling was built at the foot of these mountains, with the mountains as a protective screen to the rear, in accordance with the theory of the relations of the four terrains described in the *Book of Funerals*. In his preface to and annotations for the book, Song Lian, a scholar in the Ming Dynasty, wrote: "Guo's *Book of Funerals* was truly and simply written. Nobody else could have done it better. It is indeed a suitable guide for selecting tomb sites. It is one matter if the world does not believe it. But if it does, there can be nothing else needed but this book."

Since the construction of the Imperial Ming Tombs conformed to the principle of "the shelter of the mountains and the solidity of the earth", the underground palace must have been built on a "high and dry" terrain, "far from" flowing water. Therefore, the last thing either the emperor or his ministers could have intended was that the underground palace should fill with accumulated water and place the coffins in danger of inundation. Quite the contrary, under the funeral customs from the first emperor of the Qin Dynasty (Qin Shihuang) down to the emperors of the Qing Dynasty, all-out efforts were made to avoid the intrusion of water into the coffin chambers. Numerous past excavations of ancient tombs showed that in almost all tomb chambers there were raised stone platforms on top of which the coffins were placed to avoid their being soaked in water. Thus water that seeped in, due to imperfections in design or construction which caused cracks in the soil layers, could only accumulate in the chambers.

This did indeed happen in the case of Tai Ling, the tomb of the Ming-dynasty Emperor Xiaozong. It was recorded in historical data that after Tai Ling was finished, water was suddenly found seeping out from a golden well* in the underground palace. The supervising eunuch and officials of the Ministry of Works were all stupefied, and decided to conceal it from the emperor. However the matter was reported secretly to the court, and the emperor hastily ordered the

---

*A golden well is a rectangular hole left in the stone platform, on which the coffin was to be placed, and in the stone floor right below. It was believed to connect the dead to the earth.

Ministry of Rites and the cabinet to inspect the tomb. When the officials went to the underground palace, they saw no water seeping from the well. It turned out later that a workman had proposed the idea of using wooden slips to fill the cracks, and a mixture of soil and lime for surfacing the area so that no water would seep into the chambers for some time at least.

From the Qin and Han dynasties to the end of the Qing Dynasty early this century, all emperors regarded it a matter of special importance to protect and oversee the tombs of their ancestors. This was because China's cultural heritage fostered the belief that the souls of one's ancestors would never die. It was only after the concept of souls first emerged that the construction of tombs originated. About 18,000 years ago the burials of the Upper Cave Man in the early period of the matrilineal commune at Zhoukoudian in Fangshan County reflected the concept of souls of a primitive religion or superstitious cultural ideology. The dead bodies were dusted with haematite powder; burial objects included firestone, stoneware, stone beads, perforated teeth of animals, simple hand tools, articles for daily use and crude ornaments. All these portrayed the daily activities of living people. Graveyards were found among unearthed ruins of the Yangshao culture of the late period of the matrilineal commune dating back 5,000 years. They were found scattered in several places: Shouling in Baoji (Shaanxi Province), Banpo Village of Xi'an, Yuanjunmiao in Hua County and Wangwan in Luoyang (Henan Province). Their layout was similar to that of the villages of primitive man. Most of the skulls of the dead faced one direction, fully reflecting the firm blood relations of the clan system. Many of the graveyards were public burial grounds for a second interment of the deceased. Among the excavations at Banpo Village were the tombs of four men, of two women, and of a mother and son. This provided evidence that in the matrilineal commune, the children "knew only their mothers, but not their fathers". It showed a new advance in the burial system. It also foretold the arrival of a new system under which a married couple could be buried together, a practice continued up to the present.

As the imperial tombs were huge in size, the burial objects both numerous and valuable, protection measures had to be taken to ensure safety, and prevent robbery and destruction. A large protection agency was established for the tomb of Emperor Qin Shihuang. In the early years of the Western Han, Emperor Hui moved the families of all meritorious generals, ministers, people of imperial lineage and wealthy families to Chang Ling, tomb of Liu Bang, founding emperor of the Han Dynasty. This led to the setting up of Chang Ling County to the north of his tomb. The practice was followed from reign to reign so that more counties were set up around imperial tombs. As a result, prosperous new towns emerged one after another around the capital city of Chang'an (today's Xi'an). The most famous among them were: Chang Ling County of Emperor Gaozu (Liu Bang), An Ling County of Emperor Hui, Yang Ling County of Emperor Jing, Ping Ling County of Emperor Zhao and Mao Ling County of Emperor Wu.

Therefore, the area of Xianyang where the five tombs were located was called "Wu Ling Yuan" (Five

Tombs Region). Wealthy families and their children in this region idled away their time at cockfighting and horse racing, when they were not engaged in perpetrating outrages against the common people. "The rich people take in profits from business while the gallants rove around and commit adultery." Du Fu, a poet of the Tang Dynasty, wrote in one of his poems: "None of my classmates in the prime of their youth are humble, they wear expensive clothes and ride fat horses in Wu Ling." This aptly described typical scenes in the Wu Ling region at that time. A new town was set up near the imperial tombs of the Qing Dynasty in Zunhua, Hebei Province, as an additional protection to the tomb supervisory station. When Zhu Di, Emperor Yongle of the Ming Dynasty, first chose the area for the Imperial Ming Tombs, it had military importance, apart from meeting the requirements of the four mountainous terrains described in the *Book of Funerals*, that is, "on the left is the green dragon, on the right is the white tiger, in front is the rosefinch, and behind is the tortoise." In fact, the Imperial Ming Tombs were guarded not only by a large tomb protection staff, but also by large numbers of troops. It was located opposite the Juyong Pass to protect Beijing against attacks from the northern tribes.

With such a numerous tomb protection staff and so many troops stationed there, the emperors, ministers, generals and advisers certainly could not conceive of anyone's opening the tombs to steal valuables and rob corpses. This being so, it would not be necessary to install poisoned arrows, flying sabres and other hidden weapons inside the underground palace. Even if there were hidden weapons, the mechanism would have long ceased to work in the passage of over 300 years. Now with the small stone tablet clearly pointing out how to find the road to the underground palace, it would likewise not be difficult to find the hidden mechanism if one existed. Once exposed to science, superstition inevitably succumbs to fact.

All rumours were ignored, but one possibility could not be dismissed. Because of the special position and status of the emperors and empresses, disinfectants might have been used in the coffins to prevent decomposition of the bodies and these could contain poisonous chemicals. Moreover, decomposition of the corpses could produce poisonous gases. Therefore, preparations had to be made beforehand to safeguard the health of the excavators against exposure to harmful gases.

The excavation team members paid no more attention to rumours and horror stories. They now had to go all out to prepare for the opening of the underground palace. Thirty years after the excavation, a yellowish-white slip of paper was found in the pile of data kept by team leader Zhao Qichang. Recorded in detail was a list of items bought before proceeding. From the list one can easily imagine under what material and technical conditions China's first imperial tomb was excavated.

Candles	10 boxes
Barn lanterns	10
Mine safety caps	60
Gas masks	10
Rubber gloves	5 pairs
Work clothes	5 suits
Darkroom	1

Enlarger	1
Formalin	2 pounds
Medical ethyl	10 catties
Absorbent cotton	5 catties
Gauze	20 feet
Camphor balls	5 catties
Talcum powder	2 bags
Water glass	1 pound
Wooden boxes	50
Iron scoops	10
Wood wool	100 catties
White silk thread	2 reels
Double-stranded hemp rope	2 catties
Iron wire	4 catties
2-inch wood screws	2 boxes
Oilcloth	10 feet
Tissue paper	500 sheets
Kraft paper	20 sheets
Pink paper	200 sheets
Big drawing board	1
Thick glass plates	3
Adhesive tape	15 rolls
Putty	5 catties

A Glimpse of the Underground Palace

After the tunnel had been cleared of earth, most of the peasant workers went back home. Only Wang Qifa and a few other stalwarts stayed on to continue working with the excavation team.

In the evening they sat around a barn lantern in the wooden shack discussing how to remove the wall bricks and what concrete measures should be adopted the next day. After analysing the internal structure of the underground palace together with all the information they had gleaned through scientific inference, the excavation team members had gained an accurate picture of what it would be like, and appeared calm and self-confident. But the peasant workers felt somewhat uneasy. They were still upset by the fearful rumours. Their trepidations were not lost on Bai Wanyu, who read their thoughts. With a bottle of liquor, he went to their quarters and stood them all a drink. He looked particularly animated that evening, his aged face beaming with good cheer. He sat in the centre of the group, and drained his glass with a flourish. Wang Qifa, beside himself with curiosity, could not help touching on the crucial yet sensitive question: "How are we going to open the gate of the underground palace?" He immediately felt abashed for having asked.

"You must climb the ladder to the top of the wall gate, remove the bricks which I point out to you, and write down the serial number of the bricks according to their location." Bai Wanyu had assumed the air of a general commanding a huge army.

The peasants bit their lips in silence, their faces revealing how ill at ease they felt over the prospect.

Finding them all very nervous, Bai Wanyu broke into laughter. "You're worried about the hidden weapons behind the wall, right?" He surveyed every face and said provocatively: "Then who will remove the first brick?"

This only made them more nervous. If there really was a shooting mechanism hidden behind the diamond wall as rumoured, the first one to remove the bricks would surely be the unlucky one. None of them could summon the courage to take such a risk. They could only gaze at their shoes in silence.

Bai Wanyu smiled. "Then, okay, how about deciding by lot! Here are some slips of paper. I'm going to write something on one of them. Whoever gets the slip with writing on it will have to be the first to climb up."

There was no other way to decide. Since nobody volunteered to run the risk, each had to rely on his own luck. Not one of them could believe that he himself would get the fatal slip. At the same time each was mortally afraid that he would be the one to pick it out.

Bai Wanyu got the slips ready, cupped them in his hands, shook them for a few seconds and dropped them on the table. The peasants stared wide-eyed at the folded slips as if one of them contained a time-bomb that would explode at any moment. Silence fell; every one could feel his pulse throbbing and his heart beating.

Wang Qifa glanced sideways at Bai Wanyu. The old man was fingering his short moustache, eyes half closed, and staring at him with a smile. Wang tossed his head, clenched his teeth, stepped forward and took the first lot. Everyone followed.

They opened their slips together. Someone shouted: "No words on my slip!"

"No words on mine!"

"None on mine!"

When the shouts died down all eyes fell on Wang Qifa. Liu Jingyi went over to him, looked at his slip, and read aloud: "Beware of the hidden arrows!"

The other peasants, greatly relieved, laughed with joy at their good luck. Wang Qifa, blushing, remained quiet.

Bai Wanyu rose and went to him. Patting him on the shoulder, he said jokingly: "Young fellow, get ready for tomorrow — you'll have to think of how to deflect the hidden weapons."

Wang Qifa was awake almost the whole night. The dangerous contingency looming ahead forced him to mull over effective countermeasures. He spent hours calling up an action plan for the next day.

The cameramen from the film studio suggested that the wall be opened after dark in order to avoid the uneven sunshine in the daytime. This proposal met with the work team's consent.

At twilight on September 19 the peasants came to the worksite. The excavation team members, all dressed up, went down into the ditch and placed the ladder against the wall. For them, a great moment in the history of archaeology was at hand. They were almost breathless with anticipation. A dozen gas lamps were suspended in the air illuminating the worksite with dazzling brilliance.

"Everything ready?" Zhao Qichang climbed up the ladder, then looked down at the gathering below. The people respectively in charge of photography, film shooting, drawing, recording, measuring and numbering, all with tools in hands, were in high spirits, awaiting orders. It was all silence at the worksite.

"Wait a minute!" A sudden cry was heard coming from inside the ditch further back. They turned around to see where the voice came from. There was Wang Qifa running toward them, his head damp with sweat, a rectangular basket in his hand.

He pushed through the crowd, put the basket down at the foot of the wall, removed a piece of red cloth covering the top, and took out two roosters. No one understood what this was all about, but without waiting to explain, he snatched a kitchen knife from the basket, pressed the necks of the poor fowl down on one side of the ladder, raised the knife. With a chop, the heads dropped down. As Wang Qifa waved his hand, the two headless chickens scampered helter-skelter around the ditch, blood spurting from their necks. Everyone had to jump aside to avoid getting blood splashed on their clothes. After a brief commotion, the chickens dropped dead at the bottom of the ditch. All this happened in less than a minute.

"What trick are you up to, Wang Qifa?" asked Bai Wanyu, who had kept his presence of mind throughout the brief scramble.

Wang Qifa, honest and straightforward as ever, rubbed his knife on the ladder and answered: "Mr Bai, didn't you tell me to beware of the hidden weapons? I spoke to some old men at home, and they all told me that chicken blood would protect me from harm. As long as two chickens are killed, all hidden weapons are powerless. I just want to avoid trouble!"

"So that was why..." They all looked stunned, as if awakening from a dream, not knowing whether to laugh or cry. Bai Wanyu shouted at him: "I was just joking yesterday evening! Why should you have taken it all so seriously! You're such a fool...When will you grow up?"

Science and superstition, culture and ignorance coexisted in the minds of the team members as well as the peasant diggers. The first excavation of an imperial tomb in New China proceeded exactly in this sort of climate.

The commotion over, Bai Wanyu turned to Zhao Qichang: "Shall we start?" "Wait," signalled Zhao Qichang.

Before long Xia Nai arrived from the city. He asked Zhao Qichang: "Have you drawn the map?" Xian Ziqiang handed him the map, and he nodded: "Very good, a large-scale map, OK. How about the restoring tools?" Bai Wanyu pointed to a big box nearby: "They've all been moved here; everything is ready." Xia Nai pondered a moment, then asked: "Don't you want to test the lighting?" Zhao Qichang promptly motioned cinematographer Shen Jie to switch on the lights. The assistant cameraman immediately dialled and the three powergenerating trucks outside the rampart went into operation, illuminating the diamond wall in a noonday light. Both the intensity and the angle were right. Xia Nai then signalled: "OK, start."

Nobody noticed that Zhao Qichang had already climbed to the top of the ladder. When Xia Nai nodded the signal, he raised his specially-made shovel, struck the seam of the first brick on the top of the inverted-V opening in the wall and pried it loose without much effort. Wang Qifa also climbed the ladder, seized hold of Zhao's shovel and said: "Let's pry it out together."

Zhao Qichang said, half jokingly: "There are hidden weapons inside. You'd better stay below to receive the bricks. I'm single, and if I'm killed, there's nothing to worry about!" Wang Qifa blushed, and squatted down next to Zhao Qichang to pass the bricks down.

Everything went smoothly according to plan; the

film crew began shooting those first unforgettable moments.

As mortar had not been used to fill in the seams, Zhao Qichang had easily loosened one corner of the brick, which weighed 24 kilogrammes. He hung his shovel by one side of the ladder, grabbed hold of the brick with both hands and began pulling it out slowly. Wang Qifa and the others in the ditch below held their breath and watched closely. All was silent except for the grinding sound of the loosened brick. Zhao Qichang then mustered all his strength and pulled with a sudden jerk. The heavy brick was gouged out of the wall with a crunch. Xia Nai standing at the foot of the ladder shouted in a loud voice: "Watch out for poisonous gas!"

Hardly had he finished before a muffled puffing noise was heard, as from a punctured rubber ball, and a heavy black mist poured out of the opening. It was followed by a hoarse growling, similar to the snarling of wild beasts in the dark night. All shuddered at the sound.

"Lie down quickly!" Bai Wanyu called out.

Zhao Qichang held on to the brick firmly and lay flat on the ladder, his head lowered.

The black mist kept streaming out with its strange rustling sound. It carried a mildewy, rotten, damp smell out with it. The mist turned from black to white, and emerged as thin wisps of smoke, floating up from the bottom of the ditch. Even with their hands cupped over their mouths, the people were suffocated by the smell and began to cough.

Zhao Qichang passed the brick to Wang Qifa and jumped down from the ladder coughing too and with tears in his eyes. Bai Wanyu asked: "Anything wrong?" Zhao Qichang rubbed his face with a sleeve, and shook his head. Xia Nai explained, pointing to the floating mist: "This is gas from the rotten substances which has accumulated underground for more than 300 years. Once it is released, you can enter the palace."

The mist grew thinner and thinner. Wang Qifa and Liu Jingyi climbed up the ladder to remove bricks. The workers below laid them to one side in order. Xia Nai numbered the bricks at the bottom. At the same time, the specialised personnel were drawing, taking pictures and recording. The cameramen from the Central Newsreels and Documentary Film Studio were shooting the scenes from the best locations possible.

The bricks were removed layer by layer, the opening becoming larger and larger. When the 15th layer of bricks was taken away, the aperture was already more than two metres high. Xia Nai ordered a halt. He climbed the wooden ladder and used his flashlight to see if he could distinguish anything inside the hole. All was pitch dark. His light circled like a firefly in the night. Nothing could be seen from the outside so he pushed his head into the hole and listened intently. The tomb passage was filled with a dead silence so overpowering that everyone felt tense. He asked for a small stone, threw it down and heard a sharp sound as it fell to the ground. Zhao Qichang said eagerly: "Mr Xia, let me go down there to have a look."

Xia Nai climbed down the ladder, raised his arm and measured the length of wall still untouched. He pondered for a while, then assented with a nod: "Be careful!" Bai Wanyu ran to them with a rope. "For your safety, we'd better tie a rope around your waist."

Zhao Qichang put on a gas mask, bound his sleeves tightly at the wrist, tied the rope around his waist, picked up a flashlight and climbed the ladder to the opening.

"If all goes well inside, flash a straight line of light upward. If something goes wrong, pull the rope and we'll help you out," Bai Wanyu advised.

Zhao Qichang nodded and turned around. Calmly and full of confidence, he placed his hands on the bricks at the opening and jumped down inside.

The people outside heard a loud sound and their hearts jumped. Bai Wanyu called into the hole: "What's happened?"

No response. Only rustling sounds were heard. "It's all over now," Bai Wanyu thought to himself. He turned to Xia Nai: "What shall we do?"

Xia Nai frowned, and said calmly: "Wait another minute."

The excavation team members climbed the ladder one after another, leaning over the wall to see if they could find out anything. Wang Qifa brought some ropes and appealed to Xia Nai urgently: "Let's go to the rescue at once! Zhao Qichang will be done for if we delay any longer." Xia Nai was just about to answer when an orange light flashed straight up from the darkness inside, and remained fixed on the upper side of the opening.

"Nothing's wrong!" Cheers broke out and those outside calmed down again.

"Keep going." As soon as Xia Nai spoke, Liu Jingyi, Xian Ziqiang, Cao Guojian and Wang Jie all tied ropes around their waists, and jumped down one after another.

"Place the ladder inside," Bai Wanyu ordered, directing the excavation people to stand the ladder on the other side of the hole. Xia Nai and Bai Wanyu, both with gas masks, climbed down the ladder from the opening.

"What was that all about just now?" Bai Wanyu took off his mask and asked Zhao Qichang, who flashed his torch around to reveal some rotten timber pillars scattered by the northern wall. According to an analysis afterwards, these must have been temporary gates used for the opening of the passage after the underground palace was completed, which were abandoned after the burials. After the palace was opened, the two gates were restored on the basis of the ruins; each was 2.1 metres high and 1.1 metres wide, and constructed of five banisters between the main pillars. At one end of the gate the door axles were above and below. Zhao Qichang had tripped over the timbers as he jumped down, thus producing the sound that gave everyone outside the jitters.

They flashed their torch lights in the dark, deathlike tunnel and inched their way forward. They were all concerned that something unexpected might happen. The space inside was enormous. Surrounded by darkness and putrid odours, they could not touch the sides, nor could they see the end. The red and yellow lights moved up and down through the darkness but the bright columns of light revealed only dust and mist suspended in the dank air. No one could keep track of the time. The whole concept of time became meaningless. Which century were they living in? They strode forward, nervous and excited.

Suddenly Liu Jingyi and Xian Ziqiang shouted almost in the same breath: "The gate! The gate of the underground palace!"

The deep, silent tomb passage reverberated with strange humming. They all shivered and, looking ahead by the beams of their torch lights, saw two huge white stone doors looming directly in front of them. In the thick mist their lights were reduced to small luminous dots, so that the lineaments of the doors were lost in a haze. They suppressed their excitement and moved forward step by step.

"Hidden arrows! Lie down quickly!" Xian Ziqiang, sharp-sighted and quick-witted, shouted loudly and threw himself on Zhao Qichang. The others also reacted instantly and lay down.

The humming echoes gradually abated and no hidden arrows appeared. They rose slowly. Now all was darkness and silence, and their breathing could be heard clearly. No one spoke. Their torch lights flashed here and there, soon focusing on the centre of the massive doors. Carved on each of the doors was the head of a mythical animal under which hung a circular ring. Each had two wide-open eyes staring ahead. Surrounding the animal heads were mysterious, circular devices which would ostensibly spring out and kill whoever approached, as soon as the beast gave the signal...

Advancing right up to the doors they could now clearly make out the features in detail. They were made of white marble, still crystal-clear and as white as snow after 300 years of burial. Each door had 81 (nine-by-nine) carved nipple-like knobs on it, as well as the carved animal head with a circular knocker in its mouth. The carvings were symmetrical, mirror reflections of each other, lending the marble doors an awesome dignity and an aura of power. The "hidden weapons" which Xian Ziqiang had suddenly caught sight of were none other than these animal heads and protuberances. Led on by his own imagination, he had been the first to utter cries of alarm.

Zhao Qichang pushed the doors lightly, but they did not budge. Xia Nai flashed his torch light through the two-centimetre-wide crack between them, and saw a stone slab securing the doors firmly from the inside. No matter how much force they used, the doors did not yield. Now at an impasse, they stood musing before them with one thought in common: "What a strange entrance!"

Key to the Doors

The 23 layers of bricks in the inverted-V opening were all removed in a single day. What lay behind the diamond wall was a rectangular tunnel with a floor space of more than 60 square metres. The walls on both sides were composed of nine layers of stone slabs. The arched top was all brick while the floor was paved with smooth stone slabs. The height between the floor and the arched ceiling was 7.3 metres. The rear part of the tunnel was connected with the gate to the underground chambers. The tunnel to the underground chambers behind the diamond wall was in fact the final part of the stone tunnel and the leading structure of the underground chambers. It is referred to as a "tunnel arch" by archaeologists.

The back wall of the tunnel arch was the outer part

of the gate of the underground chambers. It was an arched gate built entirely of flat stone slabs. The tiles, the ridge animals and the rafter heads were all carved of white marble. Under the arch was a stone carving of Buddhist architectural style with finely executed lotus flowers, emanating a strong religious power and mysterious aura. The whole arched gateway was designed according to the doctrines of Oriental architecture, but blended in with it were the style and flavour of ancient Greek architecture. It was a refined mixture of the simplicity, elegance, beauty and mystery achieved by the ancients. Under the arch were the two magnificent marble doors.

Another sleepless night followed the discovery of the marble doors.

In the morning the team members gathered in the wooden shack for a discussion. They were still excited about the mystery of the doors to the underground chambers. It was certain that a stone buttress had been used inside to secure the doors so that no outside impact could force them open. Then, who set this block in place? How did the people come out after the burials were complete? Did the buried concubines and palace maids move the buttress to secure the doors after the funeral staff withdrew from the underground chambers? This would have been impossible. According to historical records, all the concubines and palace maids were first put to death and then buried together with the imperial coffins. This had been confirmed by subsequent excavations except in the case of slave society. Moreover, under the funeral system of the Ming Dynasty, only emperors and empresses were entitled to burial in the imperial tombs, while concubines and even high-ranking imperial concubines had to abide by a strict system in which it was absolutely forbidden for them to be buried inside. Although there are Ming Dynasty records of burying concubines and palace maids alive with emperors and empresses, they were in fact hanged and then buried in another place. Was there then another secret passage to the underground chambers from which the workmen exited after they had buried the emperor and empresses, and secured the doors with the stone buttress? Two other passages to the underground chambers were indeed discovered in the course of later excavations, but the theory of using workmen to seal the doors was excluded. Since it was necessary to prevent people from entering the chambers, who would seal the secret passage by which the workmen left after securing the doors? If this secret passage was discovered later, would that not mean all previous efforts made by the workmen were wasted?

Since the idea of using concubines and palace maids to seal the doors was proved wrong, there was only one other possibility. That was, after the emperor and empresses were buried, after all living people had exited and the doors were closed, the stone block inside secured the doors automatically. Then, how could the stone move itself to seal the doors?

The discussions went on in the smoke-filled shack. One theory followed another, none of which stood up to scientific analysis. The countless riddles plagueing their minds wasted both their physical and mental powers.

The following afternoon Zhao Qichang and his group went again to the marble doors to investigate how to open them. Before returning to Beijing, Xia Nai enjoined them to hurry: "Time is pressing. We must not allow anything to delay the work. We must find out how to get them open so we can proceed."

Zhao Qichang tried in vain to find a secret code around the marble doors, like the "road-indicating stone" they had come upon earlier. Although some of the 81 knobs on each door had been inserted in chiselled holes, the whole stone wall was a tight construction with no traces or clues of an opening. They had to go back to reading historical records and data.

Long before the underground palace was opened, Zhao Qichang had already dug tombs of the nobles of the Ming and Qing dynasties in the western and eastern suburbs of Beijing. The stone doors of some internal tomb passages were locked by rolling stone balls. That is, a sloping surface was constructed on the inner side of the stone door, a groove was made inside the threshold, and the stone ball was placed at the top of the groove and held by the opened door. After the burial was finished and all the people had left the tomb, the doors closed slowly, and the stone ball rolled down along the sloping surface until the stone doors were tightly closed and the stone ball stopped at the deepest part of the groove thus securing the doors.

The use of a stone ball as a lock gave them some inspiration. Looking through the crack between the marble doors, they surmised a similar function for the stone slab they had glimpsed. A ball differs from a slab, but the principle is similar: When the doors were half closed, the slab was put in a groove on the inside of the door; when the people left, the slab tilted slowly as the door closed. When the doors were completely shut, the upper part of the slab slid into the central position against the doors and locked them. This conjecture carried conviction; it seemed the only method for securing the doors from within.

Once the principle was understood, the next step was to remove the slab. Members of the excavation team, after searching through oceans of historical data, finally came upon the "key" in records relating to the burial of Emperor Chongzhen at the end of the Ming Dynasty.

On the 17th of the 3rd lunar month of 1644, Li Zicheng led his army up to the city wall of Beijing after capturing Juyong Pass in the Great Wall.

The same evening Zhu Youjian, Emperor Chongzhen, realised his days were over as he watched the flames spreading outside the city and heard the roar of cannons. Looking up with a sigh of anguish, he cried: "What a painful misfortune this is for my people!" and drained a cup of wine. When Empress Zhou saw the emperor completely demoralised and the Ming Dynasty doomed to perish, she spoke to him in tears: "I've served Your Majesty for 18 years, but you've never once listened to me. This is the result today." Without another word, she took a sword, cut her throat, collapsed to the floor and died.

The 16-year-old Princess Changping seized her father's robe, tears streaming down her face. The emperor clenched his teeth and said with a sigh: "What a pity that you should have been born in my family!" He unsheathed his sword and, hiding his face in his robe, chopped down with his right hand only to cut off the left arm of the princess. She fell to the ground with a terrified cry. The emperor tried to strike again, but his arm was too weak. Taking a blunderbuss with him,

Emperor Chongzhen led dozens of eunuchs out of the Hall of Heavenly Purity. Mounting their horses, they rode straight towards the Gate of Stability in an attempt to flee. They found the gate had been sealed. The outer city wall had been forced open, through which the peasant troops were running towards them. The emperor had to dismount. All the eunuchs ran away. Only Wang Cheng'en remained. The two of them abandoned the emperor's horse and clambered up Coal Hill (called Jing Hill today).

Chongzhen removed his outer robe, and took a brush and ink from Wang Cheng'en to write his last edict on the white satin garment, under the light of the moon and the raging flames:

> In the 17 years since I ascended the throne, people from the east have invaded the hinterland three times, and rebel bandits now overrun the capital city. Although I have not ruled by virtue or brought greater good to the dynasty, and am therefore severely punished by Heaven, my ministers led me astray. I am ashamed to face my ancestors in the nether world. I now take off my crown and clothes, cover my face with my loosened hair, and leave my body to be dismembered by the rebels. Keep the common people unharmed.

Emperor Chongzhen hung his clothes on a tree, took off his crown, dishevelled his hair to cover his face, and hanged himself from a pine tree on the side of the hill.

On the 30th of the 4th lunar month Li Zicheng,

defeated by troops of the Qing Dynasty, was forced to flee with the remnants of his army and Beijing submitted to occupation. Some wealthy personages in Changping County, out of loyalty to the Ming emperor, organised themselves to contribute money for his funeral. The last Ming emperor had not had time to build a tomb for himself, but had built a luxurious tomb for Concubine Tian, his favourite, at the foot of Jinping Hill in the tomb area. The country gentlemen therefore moved the coffins of the emperor and his wife to the tomb of Concubine Tian for burial. According to historical records, the workmen spent four days digging at the tomb before they found the gate to the underground chamber. After opening the doors with an L-shaped key, they moved Concubine Tian's coffin to the right side of the dais, placed Empress Zhou's coffin on the left side and set Emperor Chongzhen's in the middle. After the burial was finished, the stone doors were closed again and the pit was filled with earth. The mention of an "L-shaped key" so inspired Zhao Qichang that he slapped his thigh and shouted: "I have the answer!"

He found a steel rod the thickness of his little finger and bent one end of it into the shape of a squared hook. He showed it to the other members of the team, saying: "Take a look — isn't this an 'L-shaped key'?" Everyone suddenly understood. What had seemed at first so puzzling was in fact very straightforward.

On the morning of October 5 members of the excavation team went to the underground palace prepared to open the marble doors with their own "key", the steel rod with one end shaped like a hook. They proceeded under the direction of Zhao Qichang and Bai Wanyu.

The marble doors were buried deep down underground, but their magnificent construction and perfect craftsmanship were by no means inferior to the huge gates of the Forbidden City.

It was still dark and damp in the vaulted tunnel, and the smell was nauseating. Although this was no longer their first experience at the site, their hearts beat fast as they gathered at the huge marble doors.

Torch lights flashed through the heavy mist and darkness to focus on the crack between the massive doors. Zhao Qichang took the "key" in his hand, held up the hook-shaped steel rod and inserted it slowly through the crack. When the rod touched the upper part of the slab, he twisted the rod vertical and scooped the top of the slab. He got everything ready, held his breath and pushed the rod slightly. The rod stretched inside bit by bit and the slab was also moved bit by bit until it stood erect.

"I'm holding up the slab tightly. Now you open the doors," Zhao Qichang said to Bai Wanyu as he grasped the "key" firmly with all his strength.

They had thought that the huge marble doors couldn't possibly be opened without Herculean effort. Therefore, Bai Wanyu divided the team members into two groups and lined them before the doors. When he shouted "open", they pushed the doors with concerted effort. The doors opened with a loud crash. The large door axles produced friction, so that the stone doors gave off sounds like metal against stone, clear and appealing to the ears in the deep and dark tomb passage. This was accompanied by rising mist from inside the gate. Echoes from the walls resounded through the mist and dust, and reverberated in the darkness as if the whole underground palace was trembling with shock.

Bai Wanyu had moved the slab to one side before entering the gate to look inside. Liu Jingyi was already flashing his torch here and there. When the light reached the upper side of the doorframe above them, they saw many shining tapered objects hanging down, which looked like unsheathed sabres pointing at the ground. Liu Jingyi shouted: "Flying knives on the doors!"

Bai Wanyu demanded quickly: "Where! Where?"

Liu Jingyi pushing the others aside, led Bai Wanyu to the doorframe. Pointing his torch up, he said in a frightened voice: "Look up!"

"Ah!" Bai Wanyu was also alarmed. Indeed, there hung a row of sabre-like weapons above the doorframe indistinct in the mist and dim light, but perceptible nevertheless. To ensure safety, they decided to withdraw from the chamber until they could light a gas lamp.

The gas lamp lit up the whole tomb chamber. It was a huge rectangular structure built entirely of stone blocks, including a vaulted stonework ceiling without supporting beams or pillars — a fine example of Chinese architecture. Archaeologists call this spacious chamber the front hall.

Under the light of the gas lamp the dozen or so sabre-like objects turned out to be peculiar rock-like formations. As the underground chambers had been closed for more than 300 years, moisture had accumulated. This caused erosion of the stones above the doors. Calcium carbonate was produced and dropped down with the water, gradually forming into sharp "stalactites", which looked exactly like suspended flying sabres in dim light.

Another false alarm was put to rest.

Above the doors was a rectangular bronze lintel, at either end of which as a round mortise into which the upper axles of the doors were inserted. The bronze lintel was 3.6 metres long, 84 centimetres wide and 30 centimetres thick. One year earlier Zhao Qichang had come across a reference to the use of bronze in a history book. When Qing Ling was built, Wan Jing, an official of the Ministry of Works searched for scrap bronze inside and outside the palace to make "tube fans" (mortises). He collected a great deal, such that a eunuch accused him of amassing it as a personal fortune. The emperor immediately summoned him to the court for trial. After a merciless beating, Wan Jing, defending himself tearfully, was exempted from further punishment. Only when the bronze lintels were made and put to use in the tomb did the emperor and court officials understand his original idea.

For more than a year Zhao Qichang had thought over and over again about the "tube fans" mentioned in the history book, but found no answer. He suddenly saw the light when he noticed the bronze above the arched gate. If bronze had not been used for the lintel at the upper side of the arched gate, it would have been difficult to find any material which could bear the force of friction of the heavy marble doors. It was now clear to him how earnestly that official had racked his brains to solve the problem.

The marble doors showed not only careful and detailed workmanship, but also exquisite finish. The side of the door with the axle was 40 centimetres thick while the other side with the animal head was 20 centimetres thick. The axle side was thicker because it had to bear more weight and avoid damage caused by the opening and closing of the doors. The other side was thinner to reduce the weight of the door and the load of the axle so that the huge marble doors, 3.3 metres high and 1.7 metres wide, could be opened and closed with relative ease.

On the inner side of each marble door immediately behind the animal head on the outer side, a raised section was used to bear the pressure of the stone buttress. When the marble doors were being eased shut, the upper end of the buttress, which had been propped upon the protruding section of one of the doors, gradually slipped under it. With the lower end inserted into a groove on the ground inside the gate at the centre of the marble doors, the stone buttress held the doors firmly locked. On examining the magnificent marble doors, the excavators were filled with admiration for the extraordinary creativity and artistic talent of the ancient craftsmen.

Between the beginning of the excavation and the opening of the underground palace to tourists, the marble doors were opened twice. They were closed and re-opened for the shooting of the documentary film *Underground Palace*. The cinematographers were not asked to enter with the excavation team when the doors were first opened in order to avoid any contingency. Thus the lively feelings of mystery, tension, alarm and excitement were absent at the time of filming.

All measuring, drawing and picture taking proceeded in an orderly way. When they surveyed the stone buttress carefully, they discovered some indistinct small characters written in regular script in black: "All the *zilai* stones for the seven gates of the underground chambers have not been examined." This not only told the excavators that the stone buttress was originally called a *zilai*, or self-locking, stone, it also told them that there were six more stone gates in the underground palace for them to open.

Chapter Eight
THE PERPLEXING DAIS

Hope and Despair

As indicated on the stone buttress, at the end of the 20-metre long front hall they found another gate with tightly closed stone doors. The 81 nipple-like knobs on each door twinkled in the dim light. Since nine is the highest single digit numeral, the knobs on the stone door were arranged in nine rows and nine columns to symbolise the highest luck and authority of the emperor. When they flashed the torch light through the crack between the doors, they found them locked by another self-locking stone buttress on the inside. After taking strict protective measures, they used the hook-shaped steel rod to open the second pair of stone doors. With experience, they opened them without much effort to the accompaniment of clear and harmonious sounds produced by the friction of the huge stone against the bronze of the lintel, mixed with heavy "humming" echoes.

They were all stupefied when they entered the main hall, which appeared endless, dark, ghastly and terrifying in the gas light as dim and poor as an oil lamp. Heavy mist, wafting a rotten, mildewy odour, blocked their vision. They had to feel their way carefully, hands linked.

Through the haze, as if by a miracle, three white marble thrones gradually floated into view. The middle one, much larger and facing east, was obviously meant for the emperor, with the other two on either side and facing each other, for the empresses. Carved on the back of the middle throne were two dragon heads, one on each side. In the centre of the back was a dragon playing in the clouds, chasing a pearl. Phoenixes were carved on the other two. Before the thrones were altars, each with five sacrificial objects. In the centre was a yellow glazed incense burner, in which a round sandalwood joss stick was placed. On each side of the burner were yellow glazed candle holders each with a candle. On both sides of the candle holders were yellow glazed vases. In front of the altar was a large blue and white dragon vase filled with oil, and on the surface of the oil was a round bronze ladle with a wick, the end of which looked burned. This was the "everlasting light" described in history books. Judging from the burned wick, the lamp had been burning at the time of burial and had gradually gone out for lack of oxygen after the doors were closed. The oil had long solidified on the surface by the time the chambers were opened. Tests revealed it to be sesame oil. The blue and white dragon vase was not only a treasure amongst the unearthed objects in Ding Ling, but also a rare work of art in the field of Chinese blue and white porcelainware. The height and diameter of the vase were both 70 centimetres. Its outer side was inscribed with the words "Made in the Jiajing Reign of the Great Ming Dynasty". Both the neck and the base were painted with lotus flower petals, and the middle part with dragons flying among clouds. The clouds seemed to be floating, the two dragons chasing one another, mounting the clouds and riding the mist. With a lively sense of motion, the whole vase is full of imagination and charm.

The porcelainware of the Ming Dynasty boasts the highest repute in the long history of Chinese ceramics; the pieces with blue designs on a white base in particular are of the best quality, known as "blue and white porcelainware". Jingdezhen, a town in Jiangxi Province, was a centre of porcelain production during the Ming Dynasty. An imperial factory was set up there to produce special ware for the imperial family. Production was supervised by officials assigned by the court and guarded by troops. Connected to it was a prison with instruments of torture for punishing workmen who violated any rules or regulations.

According to historical data, the making of huge dragon vessels required complicated skills and a difficult firing process. Each kiln could make only one or two a year, with a very low percentage of success. To meet the needs of the court, the imperial factory set up 32 kilns specialising in dragon vessels. Craftsmen with special skills in firing dragon vessels were called "dragon vessel men". There were also clay mixers, painters and labourers. If the firing temperature was not properly controlled, the vessels would crack; if the blue clay was insufficient, they would be flawed. A passage in a history book describes the life of a worker named Lu Dingxin. He became an apprentice at the pottery kilns after his parents died, leaving him in poverty. He was upright, brave, and benevolent toward others. Emperor Jiajing wanted a dragon vessel; he sent the eunuch Pan Xiang to supervise its production at the imperial factory. Firing was a demanding job, and none of the craftsmen had the courage to take it on. Lu Dingxin accepted the responsibility, but after several attempts he failed to produce the vessel as specified. The eunuch became enraged and ordered the workmen severely punished, but still not one dragon vessel came out right. Pan Xiang ordered the food supply cut off and had the workmen and craftsmen beaten again. Five of them died. Unable to stand by and see his fellow workers go on suffering, Lu Dingxin jumped into the burning flames in the kiln at night. The following day when the kiln was opened, it contained a dragon vessel that matched every standard. All his fellow workers shed tears. They buried his remains at the foot of Phoenix Hill. Later they built a temple by the kiln in memory of his sacrifice.

This passage, with its legendary overtones, clearly falls outside the scope of historical evidence as such, but it is a fact that women were indeed killed as sacrifices in the firing of dragon vessels in the Ming Dynasty. Very often workmen could not escape being killed following the firing procedure.

The production of blue and white porcelain reached its peak in the reign of Jiajing. The material used as glaze was called *sunipo* blue, imported from Southeast Asia. It was very valuable and when fired produced a beautiful hue of unique charm. The resulting product was unmatched by any other porcelainware. In the 41st year of the Jiajing Reign, a supervising minister was scheduled to return to the capital to claim an award after he oversaw the successful firing of 12 blue and white porcelain vats. Before leaving he hosted a dinner for the craftsman in charge of the firing. During the meal, he praised the firing master: "You have superb skills in firing blue and white porcelainware. You have worked hard and done an excellent job!" Then he asked: "After I leave, if the court sends another supervisor here, could you fire even better ware?" The master, not really knowing what the official was getting at, replied: "There is no end to artistic improvement!" On hearing this, the supervising minister ordered one of his followers to secretly put some poison in the master's cup, and poisoned him to death. Afterwards, exquisite blue glazed porcelainware could no longer be fired in Jingdezhen. The dragon vessels used for Emperor Wanli's burial were chosen from among those made in the reign of his grandfather, Emperor Jiajing. This record is also of a legendary character. But historians have drawn the conclusion, based on research, that after the Jiajing Reign, the supply of *sunipo* glaze from Southeast Asia gradually became exhausted, and the porcelainware fired afterwards no longer matched its predecessors in quality.

At the time they discovered the thrones and everlasting lamps, they also found two arched gates, one on the northern, and the other on the southern wall of the hall. The gates had no protruding eaves or decorations, and each had a stone door without a carved animal head or nipple-like knobs. Above the arched gate was a bronze lintel through which the door axle passed. The stone door was the same as the marble doors of the central hall in form, but was much smaller in size. It was only 2.2 metres high and 90 centimetres wide, also locked by a stone buttress from inside. The team members used their hook-shaped key to open the left door. Walking through the misty arched passage, they came upon a huge dais. There was nothing on it at all except an empty cavity in the centre which had been filled with loess. Bai Wanyu cried out: "It's over! Finished!"

The others, astonished, rushed over to him and asked: "What do you mean — over?"

"The coffins have been stolen!" he gasped. "There must be a secret passage leading to the outside."

Everyone became jittery. Lifting up the gas lamp and flashing their torches, they searched for the passage.

Bai was right. There on the west of the left hall they found a small stone-arched opening and stone door. The door opened on the inside and was sealed by a stone slab. If the tomb had been looted, the robbers must have come into it through this secret passage. "Come on, hurry up! Move the slab away," Bai Wanyu ordered. The younger men removed the slab and opened the stone door.

This time they were not assailed by misty gases. Through the door a dark wall could be seen under the gas light. It was built of square bricks, the seams filled with mortar. There were no traces of robbery, not even the slightest. Now they realised that the possibility of robbery was out of the question, because the 20-metre long dais showed no traces of any coffins ever having been placed there, and no traces whatever of decay. Moreover, no signs of abrasion or damage could be seen on the smoothly-paved bricks on the dais, pointing to the same conclusion.

When the gas lamp was put on the dais, it lit up the golden well in the middle. They wiped the sweat off their faces and gazed silently into the well seeking an explanation of the newest riddle — a dais with no coffins.

The golden well was located inside the dais. It was bottomless and uncovered, designed to facilitate the flow of the positive and negative forces of Nature. When the coffin was consigned to the vault, it had to be placed above the golden well so that the dead, or his soul, could receive energy from the earth. Human beings originate from Nature, and must return to it after death. Heaven and the earth are the realm in which mankind lives and only in coalescence with Nature can the souls of the dead live on forever...It was owing to these particular paradoxical religious ideas that, when building began on an imperial tomb, the first shovel of earth had to be carefully kept, and then filled back into the golden well when the tomb was finished. Some researchers said that this practice was based on inspiration from Buddhism, while others argued that it was influenced by ancient burial traditions. The conclusion awaits further confirmation, but it shows how profoundly human beings love the earth and how much they are dependent upon it. The common people as well as the emperors and their ministers unquestioningly believed that the earth was the eternal mother of all human beings.

When Empress Dowager Cixi of the Qing Dynasty went to the Eastern Imperial Qing Tombs to inspect the underground palace built for her at Putuo Hill, she threw a priceless pearl bracelet into the golden well. After she returned to the palace, she sent a minister back to the tomb area with a sizeable trove of jewels and jade ornaments to be put into the golden well. Gold, silver and other jewels were also found in the golden well under the coffin of Emperor Guangxu in the underground palace of Chong Ling in the Western

Imperial Qing Tombs. Together with them were half a catty of loess wrapped in yellow satin and one of the emperor's molars which had loosened and come out before his death. Therefore, it can be seen to what extremes superstition and idolatry had evolved in regard to the golden well among the emperors and empresses of the Qing Dynasty. They believed that once they received the energy from the earth, the imperial power would never die and the regime would last forever.

Judging from the dais of the left chamber and the laying of the golden well in the Ding Ling underground palace, the coffin of an empress or a concubine should be laid in this chamber. Why was it not there? Were the coffins all laid in the right chamber? The team members discussed this while they approached the door of the right chamber, which they opened without difficulty. Their steps quickened as they entered in hopes of finding the coffins. As the right chamber was lit up under the gas lamp, their hopes were dashed. Their feelings gradually turned to despair. The dais, which was of the same size as that in the left chamber, had nothing on it but a solitary golden well in the centre. After a careful survey, they found no traces of robbery. There was another stone door at the western end of the chamber. When they moved the stone seal away, they found only a solid wall of square bricks inside as intact as when it was first laid.

"Could it be that this underground palace is a 'fake' one, and that the emperor and empresses are buried somewhere else?" Liu Jingyi's question was put in a very low voice and produced consternation among the others. Yes, could this underground palace be a ruse? Cases of false imperial tombs in the past were far from rare. Were the tombs of Fuxi in Gansu and that of the Yellow Emperor in Huang Ling County (Shaanxi Province) real or not? It is difficult even today to know which of the 72 tombs of Cao Cao is the real one. Also, according to a folktale, coffins were taken out through the 13 city wall gates simultaneously after the founding emperor of the Ming Dynasty Zhu Yuanzhang died. Moreover, according to the villagers living in the Imperial Ming Tombs area, when Emperor Wanli was buried, 18 coffins were buried separately in the tomb area...All this reminded them of the "road-guiding stones" found during the excavation. It was unlikely that these "road-guiding stones" were buried in this huge tomb to make it easier for people to open later on. By this time, they were no longer worried about poison gas or hidden arrows. They were more anxious to find the imperial coffins, and the sooner the better. If this turned out to be an empty tomb, their hard work of two years would be a waste. Fortunately, there was yet another gate to be opened, as indicated on the first self-locking stone slab. This gave them one last gleam of hope. Success or failure of the whole excavation now depended on what lay behind this last gate, if they could only find it.

The team members left through the narrow arched doorway of the right chamber and searched along the central hall as they proceeded inward. Their pace quickened perceptibly. The decayed wooden planks lying scattered on the floor rumbled under their feet. The dim gas lamp shone like a beacon in the dark, guiding nocturnal navigators forward through a vast rolling sea of fog.

The last pair of stone doors emerged.

It was as if they saw the first light of dawn through clouds of despair. A newly-awakened exuberance now spread throughout the length and breadth of the hall. Thirty years later, Zhao Qichang, leader of the excavation team, described the scene in his recollections: "We practically raced to the doors, but when we got there, no one was willing to open them. The stone doors were the same as the first two pairs. Once the self-locking stone slab inside was moved away, we could see everything. My heart was beating like mad and I was very nervous. We had been nervous before because we were afraid in the dark and worried about possible exposure to toxic gases. We were nervous this time because we feared that the last gleam of hope would vanish like a soap bubble. I took the hook-shaped key and tried to insert it through the crack, but failed three times as my hand trembled too much. Finally, Bai Wanyu took over the key from me and moved the slab away. The doors swung open to both sides with a clatter of stone against metal, sending echoes through the depths of the dark hall just as if a hurricane had suddenly struck in the quiet night, whipping up sea waves and sending cold shivers down my spine. At that time, no one gave a thought to hidden arrows or poison gas, everyone simply looked ahead, wide-eyed and breathless. In fact, the clouds of mist pouring through the doors were the heaviest of all, as if someone intended to scatter dust in our eyes so that we could not open them, and tears came running down our cheeks. The gas light grew dim and flickered. A strong draught of air and humming echoes indicated that the space inside must be enormous.

"Hope rose up and prevailed over disappointment.

When we entered the gate in the teeth of the mist and mildew, we saw a marvellous vision that stunned us all: Three giant red-coloured coffins lay silently in order on the dais. We embraced each other, deeply moved. No one uttered a word; all was quiet in the chamber. In the dim light, we could only see tears streaming down our colleagues' faces... It was a glorious, unique embrace of a rare occurrence any time, any where."

A Black Love Tragedy

The underground chambers of Ding Ling, built with painstaking efforts under the rule of Emperor Wanli, its huge expenditures paid for by the Great Ming Empire, were opened to the public after 300 years. Its excavation has provided posterity with the opportunity for objective study and assessment.

In 1578 acting upon the order of Empress Dowager Cisheng, the Ministry of Rites chose the eldest daughter of Wang Wei, commander of the imperial guards, as the empress for Emperor Wanli. The 19th of the 2nd lunar month was selected as the auspicious day for their wedding ceremony held under the auspices of Zhang Juzheng and other important ministers. The lady later became known as Empress Xiaoduan.

To the 14-year-old Emperor Wanli, the grand wedding was far from exciting or emotional. His marriage with the 13-year-old girl was a mere matter of obedience to his mother, Empress Dowager Cisheng who, in her old age, was anxious to have grandsons. To her, the earlier grandsons were born, the better; and the more, the better. Once the empress was officially established, it was customary that the emperor should have concubines, who would all give birth to children for him.

Emperor Wanli had no interest to speak of in either the empress or his concubines. The woman who would occupy an important place in his life would come to him years later. He found his life dreary and devoid of interest. The red halls and chambers were magnificent, but they were reduced to nothing by a lack of the beauty and charm of nature.

The palace maids in the Ming Dynasty mostly came from ordinary families in Beijing and the surrounding provinces. Like the empress and concubines, beauty was not the only criterion for selection. All those at the age of 13 or 14 or even younger could be listed as candidates, but their parents must be benevolent and virtuous people of good breeding. The criteria for the empress and concubines were: dignified deportment, delicate features, well-proportioned ears and nose, good teeth, bright hair, scarless body, a genial disposition and good manners. The criteria for palace maids were different and slightly lower. After repeated selection, the chosen were carried into the palace in a special palatial sedan by female bearers. Once they entered the palace, they found it difficult to leave. These poor maids had beautiful looks and led a romantic life only in descriptions written by men of letters. In fact, the thousands of palace maids were all privately owned by the emperor. Most of them led a life no different from that of slaves. Only a few "lucky" ones wasted their time in endless anticipation. Chen Chen, a poet of the late years of the Ming Dynasty, wrote these lines about the palace maids in his poem "To the Hall of Heavenly Enlightenment":

> Thousands of beauties locked in the palace,
> Waste most of their youth in bitterness.
> As lions and dragons whirl in shadowy light,
> The emperor dallies with maidens the whole night.

Since reality could not be changed, the girls in the palace could only do their best to win the favour of the emperor. Only in this way was it possible for them to change their bitter fate, and achieve an honoured position for life. This was vividly shown in the life of Emperor Wanli's mother, Empress Dowager Cisheng. She had been a palace maid who accidentally found favour with Emperor Longqing. After a private affair with him, she gave birth to a boy named Zhu Yijun, gradually became his favourite and finally the empress.

In the 10th lunar month of 1581 a rare opportunity arose. Emperor Wanli, now 19 years old, was on his way to see his mother in the Hall of Benevolence and Tranquility when he came across a slender, graceful maid named Wang, who came to greet him and serve tea. Miss Wang was a 17-year-old beauty with dignified, elegant deportment. It happened that the Empress Dowager was not in her hall. It is not hard to imagine what might take place when a full-figured girl of her age at the first dawning of love and a young emperor with absolute power find themselves in the same place. Emperor Wanli, moved by a sudden and strong desire, embraced the girl passionately, and thus began their relationship. The young emperor at that time had no idea that his sudden unpremeditated act would influence his whole reign and lead to a long-lasting tragedy.

According to the demands of imperial etiquette, after a private affair of this nature, Emperor Wanli should have given some token to Miss Wang as evidence of his regard for her, especially when his act was already recorded in the Imperial Diary by a eunuch of the Imperial Document Office. This was to guard against any misrepresentation in the posterity of the emperor. However, as Miss Wang was a maid in the chamber of his mother, the young emperor himself did not regard his behaviour as entirely respectable, although nobody else would condemn the encounter as illicit. He simply dressed himself again and left without paying any attention to her woebegone expression, thinking that everything would be over as time went by. Little did he suspect that Miss Wang had conceived as a result of that one episode.

Miss Wang was pregnant and the changing contours of her body after several months were recognised by the empress dowager, who questioned her in detail and was reminded of her own miserable days as a palace maid. She expressed sympathetic understanding for the young lady's predicament and was at the same time very happy at the lucky prospect of having a grandson. She had established the empress for her son and also arranged nine concubines for him, but these women had shown no sign of giving birth. Wang's pregnancy was as welcome as long-awaited spring rain, and the old lady could not but be overjoyed. One day as the emperor waited upon his mother at a banquet, she questioned him about the situation. He flatly denied being involved. The empress dowager, who had always subjected her son to strict discipline, ordered the eunuchs to show him the record in the Imperial Diary. He had no way out but to admit the truth. Seeing her son driven to distraction, the mother sought to comfort him; "I'm getting on in years, but I still have no grandson. If it turns out to be a boy, what a blessing it will be for the Imperial Ancestral Temple and the realm!"

At the insistence of the empress dowager, Miss Wang's status as a respectable concubine was established in the 6th lunar month of 1582. In the 8th month the same year Respectable Concubine Wang fulfilled the dowager's hopes by giving birth to a boy. The prince, Zhu Changluo, the short-lived Emperor Guangzong of the Ming Dynasty, was to be discriminated against and cold-shouldered by his father all his life.

The birth of the emperor's first son was naturally a happy event in a land permeated with feudal ideas, and especially so in the imperial family. Accordingly, the emperor issued an order to reduce taxes and exempt criminals from punishment or reduce their sentences. Also he sent an envoy to convey the joyful news to the king of Korea, who had friendly relations with the Ming Dynasty. What had dawned brightly became shrouded in clouds of tragedy. The cause, at least in its surface manifestations, was related to the emperor's subsequent meeting with another woman, Miss Zheng, who had been established as a concubine in the 3rd month of 1582. A charming beauty born to a well-off family, Miss Zheng came to the imperial family at the age of 14. Two years later she became the emperor's favourite. Once she became an important part of the young emperor's life, Miss Wang was all but forgotten. The emperor and the younger girl remained passionately in love for life, and consequently brought about an extremely grave political crisis.

Indeed the beauty of Imperial Concubine Zheng was such as could cause the fall of a city or a state. However, she won the favour of the emperor, not simply because of her outstanding looks, but because she was also intelligent, sharp-witted, highly cultivated in the literary arts and of a determined cast of character. These talents were rarely found in imperial ladies. If based simply upon her looks, their love could not have lasted so long.

In the course of fathering and nurturing his children, Emperor Wanli, like most young men, developed and matured. Now he no longer had time for revelry with the young eunuchs or any interest in their merry-making. Harsh political reality forced him to make vigorous efforts to bring prosperity to his domain and to ward off disaster. He ordered the grand academicians to have copies of the "True Narrations" of his ancestors made for his reference. He also ordered his eunuchs to buy newly-published books in Beijing, including poems, ballads, essays, medical treatises, dramas and scripts for story-telling, which he read to increase his understanding of Chinese culture. Sometimes, after reading a legendary novel or tragic play, he could not but feel sad. His was the respect due to him as the Son of Heaven, but sometimes, he did not even have as much happiness or freedom as ordinary people. While he worshiped heroes, he even more yearned for the kind of love Zhang Sheng and Cui Yingying had for each other, in the hope of finding a paradise of freedom.

One night when Emperor Wanli was staying in Concubine Zheng's chamber, he happened to start singing a passage from *Romance of the Western Bower*:*

> Green hills and forests stand between him and me,
> Thin mist and evening vapours screen him from my view.
> No human voice is heard on the sunlit ancient way
> But rustling of the crops in autumn wind and horse's neigh.
> I am reluctant to enter the cart,
> So eager to have come with you;
> So slow to go back afar!

As soon as the emperor finished, Concubine Zheng followed with the connecting passage:

> Surrounded by mountains east and west,
> He flips his whip on the sunlit road.
> All the world's grief seems to fill my breast.
> How can such a small carriage bear such a heavy load!

As concubine Zheng finished, colour rose to her face, tears filled her eyes. She looked indeed like Cui Yingying when parting from Zhang Sheng at the roadside pavilion. Emperor Wanli was surprised. He did not expect any woman among his acquaintances to be so cultivated in poetry and so emotional. He drew near her, taking her delicate hand in his, and said: "My dear, how do you know this passage?"

"Who does not know the story of Cui Yingying

---

*The following lines are taken from an English version of the drama translated by Professor Xu Yuanzhong of Peking University and Published by Foreign Languages Press, Beijing, 1992.

and Zhang Sheng?"

The young emperor's surprise turned to happiness. For years he had been searching and now he had found the woman of his dreams. After that he went to Zheng's chamber more and more often. He confided in her, telling her of his melancholy feelings and political ambitions. With her intelligence and sharp wit she quickly understood the role fate had in store for her. It can be said that she came into the life of Emperor Wanli at the most opportune time. Since a chance had presented itself, she was determined to grasp it and take every possible initiative to achieve her goal. She clearly understood that Emperor Wanli was respected as the Son of Heaven and his wealth extended over the whole land, but he was weak and soft-hearted. Nobody had sympathised with or understood the vacancy of his spiritual world and his utter loneliness. His own mother often regarded him as an automaton for carrying out his life's mission, ignoring him as a human being made of flesh and blood, one who was both impulsive and sentimental.

These factors enabled Concubine Zheng to form a coherent conception of what role a partner of the opposite sex could play and of how she could use her youthful enthusiasm to compensate for the emperor's spiritual alienation. All other concubines were obedient and submissive to the emperor, but inwardly kept their distance and maintained their guard against him. Concubine Zheng alone was simple and unaffected and had no reservations in his presence. She had the courage to tease him and ridicule him while at the same time she could listen sympathetically to revelations of his innermost feelings. She helped free him of his worries and anxieties. In status she was a concubine, but in her own mind, she no longer regarded herself in that light. And in fact the emperor himself appreciated the vitality of their intellectual rapport. When talking to the emperor, she did not lower her head or bend her back like a serving maid, as the other concubines did. On the contrary, she embraced him and stroked his head with her hand. None but she had the temerity to hazard such a "disrespectful" approach to the emperor. This was a dangerous course of action. If there was the slightest carelessness, disaster could strike. However, Lady Zheng was fully aware of this and had made up her mind to proceed along this path. It was precisely because she acted differently that the emperor came to love her even more fervently. In less than three years, she was promoted from a concubine of the third rank to one of the second rank and then to the status of imperial concubine.

In the Chinese empire one who was destined to become the emperor was brought up not as a human being but as a deity from the day he was born. Once he ascended the throne, he was the incarnation of the deity and the symbol of its power. He owned everything and decided everything. And for this very reason, he became the most restricted and most unfortunate man in the whole empire. All his acts were strictly controlled and kept within the set norms of conduct to serve as examples in the eyes of the people.

Accordingly, Emperor Wanli's mother often urged him to attend the morning court sessions while his eyes were still heavy with sleep. Zhang Juzheng pressed him to read certain books, however dull, and his ministers tried to persuade him to emulate the behaviour of his ancestors. In spite of all, he was still an "ordinary human being", prone to "bad habits", in the grip of the seven emotions and six desires just like everybody else. Therefore, when he attended the court, he watched the officials going through the same boring motions day after day, kneeling and bowing to pay him homage; when he left the court he coolly mingled with the beautiful ladies in the imperial chambers and saw their expectant looks, all alike, the same as ever. He could only sense how intolerably restricted he was in life and how painfully vacant his thoughts were. Especially, as the descendant of a dynasty with remittent crises erupting in the frontier areas and a decaying court administration which he was incapable of dealing with, where could he turn for emotional sustenance?

It was undeniable that Concubine Zheng was intelligent and perceptive of the feelings of others. She was bound to use her vital instincts and abilities to do all she could to win the favour of the emperor, as she had already been placed on the bleak but majestic altar of the imperial court. In 1586 Concubine Zheng gave birth to a son, who was named Changxun. As the emperor treated Concubine Wang and Concubine Zheng differently, the birth of Changxun raised the curtain on the "dispute over the rightful imperial successor" that was to last for 15 years.

Concubine Zheng was not at all surprised to find herself established as an imperial concubine by Emperor Wanli after giving birth to a son, and felt she fully deserved the honour because of her close relationship with him. The emperor announced the rite in advance so that necessary preparations could be made by the administrative department concerned. When the news spread, an old minister raised an objection, saying that according to imperial ethics and customs, this honour should be granted first to Concubine Wang, mother of his first son. Since Concubine Zheng was the mother of his third son (the mother of his second son being unknown in official historical data), the emperor's decision constituted a "reversal of the fundamental and the incidental". Although this made Emperor Wanli unhappy for a moment, the ceremony was held according to plan.

Beyond a doubt Concubine Zheng wanted her son to be the crown prince. Since there was hope, most likely the clever Concubine Zheng would spare no effort, and would ensure that all her actions were above criticism. However, to those determined and unyielding ministers, frustrating Concubine Zheng's "conspiracy" was equivalent to stopping "the devil" from undermining the court system and subverting the cause of the empire.

Under this dilemma, Emperor Wanli, with characteristic weakness, adopted tactics of "delay": Since opinions were divided, establishment of the crown prince would have to be postponed. The reason given was that as the empress was still young, she might yet give birth to a boy, and it would not then be too late to appoint the crown prince at that time. In fact, however, Emperor Wanli had ceased his intimate relationship with the empress after he fell in love with Concubine Zheng. So where could this boy come from? The emperor was obviously not quick-witted enough to use this excuse to stall the court officials.

Emperor Wanli was fully occupied with deflecting the repeated questions and objections of the ministers.

Throughout his treatment of Concubine Wang and her son was cruel and unusual. He himself had begun learning to read and write at the age of five, but he had still not arranged a teacher for his first son who had now reached the age of 14, consigning the future emperor to a state of virtual illiteracy. Concubine Wang herself was banished to an isolated chamber, and nobody dared to show concern for her.

Zhu Changluo had turned 19, yet the emperor had arranged neither his marriage, nor for him to be established as the crown prince. His neglect was finally probed by the ministers and it was discovered that Empress Wang often fell ill. Apparently the emperor planned that if and when Empress Wang died, Concubine Zheng would succeed her. In that case, Zhu Changxun would logically become the crown prince. After Imperial Instructor Huang Hui arrived at this conjecture, he promptly reported it to Wang Dewan, saying: "This is a state affair, one which may give rise to contingency at any time. If Emperor Wanli and Concubine Zheng's wishes are fulfilled and the events recorded in the historical archives, future generations will laugh at the absence of officials loyal to the dynasty." On hearing this, Wang Dewan asked Huang Hui to draft a memorandum, which he himself would approve before copying and submitting to the emperor. As a result, Wang Dewan was flogged 100 times and expelled from the court. A number of other officials who appealed on his behalf were reprimanded for disobeying an imperial edict.

After punishing Wang Dewan, Emperor Wanli angrily declared: "I will establish the crown prince after one year!" without stating who the prince would be. It seemed as if the emperor had a plan, but what was it?

At this critical moment it was Wanli's own mother, Empress Dowager Cisheng, who made the choice.

Although the old and ailing empress dowager passed her late years secluded in her chambers and no longer attended court sessions, she closely followed developments concerning the crown prince. In this, she once again sided with Concubine Wang and the ministers, and decided it was time she personally took a hand in the affair. When Wanli came to her hall to pay his respects, the old empress questioned him in all seriousness: "Why haven't you established Changluo as crown prince?"

Wanli, perhaps caught unprepared and overwrought, unwittingly blurted out: "He's the son of a palace maid."

The emperor had unaccountably forgotten that his own mother had been a palace maid. When Empress Dowager Cisheng, pointing at him, exclaimed in a towering rage: "You are also the son of a palace maid!" Emperor Wanli woke up to his *faux pas*, fell to his knees and bent his head.

The emperor's mistake redoubled the empress dowager's determination. Emperor Wanli had no choice but to accede under her pressure. He made Changluo crown prince in the 10th lunar month of 1601.

When Concubine Zheng first heard that Wanli intended to establish Changluo as the crown prince, she made one last effort for her son. Some years earlier, when Emperor Wanli had promised to make Zhu Changxun crown prince Concubine Zheng had been clever enough to ask the emperor to write a personal edict. This she placed in a brocade container, which she then hid in the roof beam in her own chamber to preserve as evidence. Now the time had come to wield this "magic weapon" against her enemies. When she opened the box in great anticipation, she was shocked to find the emperor's personal edict chewed to pieces by worms, and the two characters "Changxun" completely obliterated. The superstitious emperor observed with a long sigh: "This is the will of Heaven." Zhu Changluo was established as crown prince in spite of Concubine Zheng's tears, and Zhu Changxun granted the title of Prince Fu with a fief in Luoyang.

This put an end to the 15-year dispute over the establishment of the crown prince which had led to the flogging and exile of many high-ranking officials, exhausted Emperor Wanli physically and mentally, and destabilised the empire.

Failure to raise Zhu Changxun to the rank of crown prince enraged Concubine Zheng. It also gave the emperor an uneasy conscience. He had no alternative but to grant a rich reward from the national treasury to compensate her for her loss. Concubine Wang however, was looking forward to better days, expecting to lead a life like Empress Dowager Cisheng. Unfortunately her days were numbered. The unlucky woman was granted no favours at all, but was instead confined to her solitary chamber. Even after her son Changluo was elevated to the status of crown prince, the dire circumstances of her life did not change. She grieved over her unjust fate and the emperor's unfaithful love while the absence of her son, whom she missed beyond measure, added to her sorrow. She spent her days in tearful despair. Flowers blossomed and withered, winter followed autumn, but the day when she could appear in public never came. As described in a poem:

> "Tears wet her silk kerchief, dreams unfulfilled,
> The voice in the front hall is subdued, singing at midnight;
> Still young and beautiful, she is no longer loved,
> But sits reclining by the fire till dawn."

Concubine Wang's eyesight began to fail. Then she gradually became bed-ridden and helpless, unable even to turn over. When Zhu Changluo was permitted by Emperor Wanli to visit his mother, he found the door of her chamber locked. Breaking the lock to get the door open, he entered and saw her lying in bed utterly miserable. Her face was ashen, but she was still breathing. Overcome with grief, he knelt down to hold her in his arms and burst into loud sobbing. The eunuchs and maids accompanying him all shed tears. Although the son was crown prince, the mother had to die grief-stricken and outraged. Adding to her distress was the fact that she could no longer see her son. Slightly comatose, Concubine Wang heard her son crying, stretched out her thin arms and felt his head with trembling hands. She said in a choked voice: "That my son has grown to this age, I die without regret." With these last words, she stopped breathing. She was only 47.

When Concubine Wang passed away, the whole court was shocked. By this time Shen Yiguan had succeeded as chief cabinet minister. He and Grand Academician Ye Xianggao submitted a joint report to Emperor Wanli: "The mother of the crown prince has died; she should be buried with a grand ceremony according to the rites." Emperor Wanli viewed it coldly without replying. Later he granted Concubine Wang the title of "Mild, Serious, Dignified, Quiet, Pure and Exemplary Imperial Concubine" at the request of the ministers. She was permitted to be buried on the flat ground of Eastern Well at the Heavenly Longevity Hills. Ten years after her death, in the 10th lunar month of 1620, when Emperor Wanli and his son Changluo had both passed away, her grandson, Zhu Youxiao, who had succeeded the throne, put her and Emperor Wanli together by ordering her coffin moved to the underground palace of Ding Ling. In spite of all this, Concubine Wang remained nothing but an offering to embellish the austere sacrificial altar.

In the 2nd lunar month of 1614 Empress Dowager Cisheng breathed her last. Just before her death however, she accomplished one more great exploit which gratified the ministers, confounded Emperor Wanli and set Concubine Zheng's teeth on edge.

Under the ancestral system of the Ming Dynasty, all princes who had been granted fiefs were obliged to live in their vassal states. They were forbidden to go to the capital city without permission. However, Changxun, son of Concubine Zheng, had remained in the imperial palace for more than ten years after his grant, without leaving for his vassal state Luoyang. In this, he had the backing of his parents. The ministers, in order to consolidate their achievements and also to show their loyalty to the dynasty, more than once pleaded with the emperor to arrange for Changxun, Prince Fu, to leave. On this matter, Wanli once again became enmeshed in clumsy quibbling.

He first pressured the ministers with the excuse that the mansion for Prince Fu had not yet been completed, forcing the Ministry of Works to accelerate the construction. After the mansion was ready, Emperor Wanli said that travel in winter was too inconvenient and that he could go in the spring. However, when spring came, Wanli demanded "Prince Fu be granted 40,000 *qing* (one *qing* equals 6.67 hectares) of land" if he should be required to go to his vassal state. This time ministers and other court officials rallied together to challenge him. Grand Academician Ye Xianggao was the first to speak, saying that it was stipulated in the *Official Book of Political Affairs* that a prince was entitled to a salary of 10,000 *dan* (one *dan* is equivalent to one hectolitre) of rice and it must not be increased at will. Farmland of the empire was limited and the imperial family would have more and more children and grandchildren. If this went on, not only would the common people have no land, but even the royal court would have no land. Prince Jing and Prince Lu had both demanded 40,000 *qing* each, which was now regarded as undermining the ancestral system. The overturned cart ahead served as warning to the carts behind. "It is hoped that Your Majesty will not follow their example."

Just when the emperor and his ministers were locked in disagreement, a ghost-like vision appeared — the dying empress dowager. She first summoned Concubine Zheng and asked her: "Why has Prince Fu not yet gone to his fief?"

The clever, sharp-witted Concubine Zheng was not as flustered or bungling as Emperor Wanli had been at his last meeting with the dowager. She replied calmly:

"Next year will be the 70th birthday of Your Majesty. Prince Fu has stayed on to celebrate your birthday." Empress Dowager Cisheng had after all experienced many vicissitudes in her life. She retorted coldly: "My second son Prince Lu lives in Weihui. Will he be permitted to return for my birthday?" Concubine Zheng, finding no reply, had to promise to urge Prince Fu to leave for his vassal state.

Emperor Wanli, unable to withstand the successive attacks by the empress dowager and his ministers, asked Prince Fu to go to Luoyang to take up his post one month after the death of Empress Dowager Cisheng. It was overcast the morning he left, with brief flurries of snow and a cold shivering wind from the north. Concubine Zheng and her son faced each other in front of the door, tears streaming down their cheeks. Emperor Wanli bade farewell to his son in front of the Meridian Gate and repeatedly exhorted him: "It's a long way, and you should take care..." When Prince Fu was in his carriage ready to start his long journey, Emperor Wanli could no long suppress his feelings. He raised his long sleeves to hide his wet eyes, but the tears ran down all the same.

In the underground palace built for the use of Emperor Wanli, he knew for whom the "beds" in the chambers were intended: the rear chamber was for himself, the left chamber for Empress Wang, whom he did not like but could do nothing about. Who would occupy the right chamber? His son Changxun, if he had been established as the crown prince, could beyond doubt arrange this position for his mother, Concubine Zheng. But now the course of events had completely eliminated this possibility. Who would take into account his life-long love for Concubine Zheng and his utmost efforts to defend it? Obviously he could not have his wish fulfilled while he was still alive, but as emperor, he should in all justice be granted the right to be buried together with the woman he loved, a right which even ordinary people took for granted. A man may be motivated and manipulated by various factors: money, honour, power, woman... These factors, complicated as they are in themselves, operate in alternating ways, with differing force. But to Emperor Wanli, whose riches extended throughout the empire, who held the most exalted position in the land, who in spite of all he possessed felt isolated and lonely, Concubine Zheng was his only source of comfort and spiritual sustenance.

With these ideas uppermost in his mind, Emperor Wanli issued one last order before he died: Lady Zheng was to be established as an empress and buried in the underground palace of Ding Ling. However, when Ding Ling was opened 300 years later, no sign of Concubine Zheng was to be found. In the rear chamber, among the three red lacquered coffins, Emperor Wanli was in the middle, while on the left was Empress Wang, whose temple title was Xiaoduan, and on the right was Empress Xiaojing, mother of Zhu Changluo, the crown prince and later emperor. This arrangement in violation of Wanli's intent and expectation was, in that sense, tragic. However, since he had already lost all power over his court before he died, it could hardly exist after his death. His last order was not carried out, because the ministers believed it went "against the rites".

However, this tragedy was not perpetrated by Zhu

Changluo. He was on the throne for only 29 days before he died. It was the son of Zhu Changluo, the 16-year-old Zhu Youxiao, who established his grandmother, Concubine Wang, posthumously as Empress Dowager Xiaojing, after he became the emperor. He had her coffin moved from the flat ground of Eastern Well to Ding Ling for burial together with Emperor Wanli and Empress Xiaoduan.

As for Concubine Zheng, whom Emperor Wanli loved most, she lived ten years longer than he did. Because she was regarded as an evil-doer who brought calamity to the country and people, she rated no sympathy from the court officials. During these ten years she lived a solitary life in her chamber in the Forbidden City, distantly separated from her beloved son Prince Fu. In the 5th lunar month of 1630 she died, miserable and depressed, having lived to the last in despair and resentment. She was buried in a lonely tomb at the foot of Silver Spring Hill. Her son, Zhu Changxun, Prince Fu, brought on one disaster after another while he governed. His actions in Luoyang were marked by stupidity and disorder. Eleven years after Concubine Zheng died he was killed by the peasant army led by Li Zicheng.

Empty Chambers Still Unexplained

The ancient buildings in China were elegant and awe-inspiring in their magnificence. This is most vividly demonstrated by the Imperial Palace, or Forbidden City, in Beijing. Once within its gates, the precinct evokes a forceful, quiet awe, as human beings suddenly appear small. The deeper one goes, the stronger the force. Overpowered in this sea of brilliant and splendid art, one can not but feel impelled to kneel, or prostrate oneself in worship. Herein lies the intended architectural artistic effect of the Imperial Palace. The underground chambers in the Imperial Ming Tombs, apart from their solidity, spaciousness and resistance to pressure, exude a feeling of freedom from mundane cares and vulgarity. The northern and southern walls of the underground palace of Ding Ling were built of nine layers of stone slabs to symbolise good omens, supremacy over and ownership of all under Heaven.

The application of mechanics in the construction of the underground chambers for Ding Ling was extremely ingenious. From the diamond wall to the rear chamber, it is 70 metres in length, the maximum width is 9.16 metres and the minimum 6.03 metres. Moreover, the design for an underground space required the excavating of earth from below and, when the palace was completed, concealing it under loess laid over above. This involved a large amount of work and built up a heavy load on the roof of the palace. To build up adequate resistance to the stress, the workmen, relying on their experience and extraordinary creativity, used principles of mechanics and aesthetics to engineer a vaulted structure. This kept the underground chambers of Ding Ling intact for 400 years.

Placed in the rear hall were three red lacquered coffins and 26 wooden boxes; conspicuous in the central hall were three white marble thrones and three blue and white dragon vats. Other odd decorations were found here and there. These seemed dwarfed by the immense void of the lonely underground palace. It invoked a dreary and desolate world, and pleaded for a fresh inquiry into the enigmatic question of life's ultimate meaning.

Few inscriptions were found in the underground palace. Only on the back of the marble door on the left side of the central hall were there some Chinese characters written in black ink at eight places. They were recognised as:

> Wang Zhong, below
> Chen Hong
> Liu Zuo, below
> Zeng Wanpan
> Liang Ye, below
> Wang Tang
> Wang Bin, below
> Zheng Xue

These characters were written with a small pointed bamboo stick. It was a tradition among Chinese masons and carpenters to use a bamboo stick and black ink to make marks on the prepared stone or pieces of wood. Analysis showed that the ink marks were probably the names of the masons who made the marble doors. According to an inference drawn from the fact that the names are arranged in order and every other name is marked with "below", the workmen might have been divided into groups of two with clear responsibility for the division of work so that it could be checked later.

The wooden planks laid over the ground floor of the underground palace were rarely seen in other previously excavated tombs. From the front and the central hall to the rear chamber, the whole ground floor was covered with wooden planks. Although they were eroded by moisture and most had decayed, traces of cart wheels which had rolled over them were still visible in places. The traces were without doubt left by the carts that carried the coffins, the wooden planks being laid to protect the floor bricks from damage. No wooden planks were found in the side chambers, because no coffins had ever been placed there.

Here arose the riddle that has yet to be solved: since there was both a dais and a golden well in each of the side chambers why had no one been buried in them? Whose coffins should have been placed on these daises? The empresses' or concubines'? These questions have been asked not only by archaeologists and historians, but also by many tourists who have visited the tomb.

After the founding emperor of the Ming Dynasty, Zhu Yuanzhang, established the system of burying the emperor and empress in the same tomb, all the succeeding emperors of the dynasty followed the practice. Emperor Yingzong, Zhu Qizhen, of the sixth reign, wanting to avoid any dispute after his death as his wife Empress Qian had no son, issued as his last edict: "Empress Qian has been officially appointed. She should be well looked after until her death." He decreed that the empress should be buried together with him after her death. After Emperor Xianzong ascended the throne, he appointed his own mother Concubine Zhou as the empress dowager.

Trouble arose when Empress Qian was buried. Empress Zhou thought that from the emperors Hongwu to Renzong, each imperial tomb contained one emperor and one empress. If Empress Qian was to be buried with Emperor Yingzong in Yu Ling, she herself could not be buried together with Yingzong after her death. Therefore, she insisted that Empress Qian be buried elsewhere.

When the word spread, the ministers resisted her proposal on the strength of the last decree of Emperor Yingzong, but Empress Zhou refused to give up her demand. The ministers, finding their memorandum useless, all knelt in front of the Hall of Literary Excellence in tears as a last resort, to demonstrate their opposition to her proposal. Seeing this Emperor Xianzong, Zhu Jianshen, decided to divide the underground palace into three chambers so that both Empress Qian and his own mother could be buried together with his father. When things had developed to this stage, Empress Zhou could not but agree, but she produced another demand: The tunnel gate for the left chamber where Empress Qian would be buried should be blocked; only the right chamber where her own coffin would be placed should be linked with the central chamber. When Empress Qian was buried, Zhu Jianshen did as his mother insisted. Therefore, one of the side chambers of the Yu Ling underground palace was blocked and the other linked with the central hall. The burial system established by Zhu Yuanzhang was abolished henceforth but this passage of historical data reveals that the side chambers were built for the empresses.

This being the case, why were the side chambers of Ding Ling unoccupied and the coffins of the two empresses placed in the rear chamber?

Some researchers argue that the side chambers in Ding Ling were built for concubines. The question remains why then, were they not occupied by Concubine Zheng or any of the others? Could it have been that since Emperor Yingzong had already abolished the system of burying concubines and palace maids alive, Emperor Wanli lacked the courage to go against the ancestral system by using concubines and palace maids as burial sacrifices?"

Over 400 years have elapsed since Ding Ling was constructed, making it extremely difficult to interpret all its mysteries. Further research and evidence are needed. However, one fact should not be ignored: Since the coffins of the emperor and empresses had all been buried, why was it that the wooden planks covering the floor had not been moved away? Why were the strings tying the boxes undone and the boxes left scattered in disorder? All signs indicate the coffins were buried in great confusion. Then, what happened after the burial? People still keep guessing and investigating.

The day when the underground palace was opened, Wu Han, Deng Tuo, Guo Moruo, Shen Yanbing, Zheng Zhenduo and Xia Nai of the Chang Ling Excavation Committee came to Ding Ling. After inspecting the deep, dark, splendid underground palace, these men of learning, with their wide knowledge of Chinese and Western cultures, all expressed unbounded admiration for this massive space constructed without a single column or beam to prop it up.

Chapter Nine
TWO FEMALE CORPSES

A Rich Tapestry of History

To the excavation team members, this was the most exciting, the most memorable day! They had for the first time opened one of China's imperial tombs in keeping with archaeological principles and scientific methods. This was a significant event for all archaeologists as well as for the individuals who took part. How many excavations of as great an historical significance as this could an archaeologist participate in? The team members did not know whether this was their first excavation of an imperial tomb as well as perhaps their last, but they knew its status and importance. Their achievement would certainly constitute an important page in the history of Chinese archaeology.

In dealing with the three ponderous coffins and the 26 boxes of funerary objects lying in disorder and decay, the first thing they had to do was to sort out the funerary objects quickly and study the three corpses.

The "sumptuous burial" system that had prevailed in China for over 1,000 years meant that the rulers of all dynasties went to their last resting places accompanied by quantities of wealth. Apart from gold, silver and other valuables, there were innumerable objects for daily use, miscellaneous works of art, the four treasures of the study (paper, ink, writing brush and inkstand), various books and paintings, tools and the latest scientific inventions. These burial objects, apart from having their own intrinsic value, represented the most highly treasured and exemplary goods of the times. Much of the head gear, costumes, textiles, bronzeware, jade objects, pottery, lacquerware, and ornaments of gold and silver were crafted specially for the burial, reflecting fairly accurately the level of production and scientific and technological achievement, and at the same time illustrating the prevailing habits, customs and artistic styles of the times.

As material witnesses to history, the unearthed objects were more reliable than the antiques circulating among the people. Apart from being absolutely authentic, these objects, hidden from air and sunshine, and kept in constant temperature and humidity, appeared almost "as good as new" even after hundreds or even thousands of years. They were far better both in quality and colour than the antiques that had been preserved by the people. Among the piles of funerary objects, those found in the imperial tombs were the most precious and of the greatest value to archaeological study, because these objects were produced by concentrating the wealth of the entire dynasty, and by enlisting the ingenuity of the skilled craftsmen of the whole country or even of several countries and various dynasties.

The team members had put forth various conjectures and made preliminary preparations regarding the underground findings at Ding Ling. What form of burial had been used? Were the three corpses well preserved or had they already decomposed? How were they clothed? The Peking opera stage costumes in current use are supposedly based on styles of the Ming Dynasty. Did Emperor Wanli and his two empresses dress the same way as the emperors and empresses in Peking opera?

Of the three coffins, the one on the right was the most seriously damaged. The outer coffin had decayed and caved in, and examination of the inner one also revealed crevices. This was the coffin of Empress Xiaojing. The pitiable woman had died ten years prior to Emperor Wanli and had been buried in the flat ground to the left of Eastern Well. This was why her coffin had rotted faster. The damage was even more serious after it was moved to Ding Ling by her grandson Zhu Youxiao.

Xia Nai made the decision to open this coffin first. Once the underground palace was opened, the temperature inside was no longer constant, and the current from outside, when mixed with the air inside, would seriously damage the corpses and burial objects. So Xia Nai assigned some of the team members to examine Empress Xiaojing's coffin, while the others took measures to protect and preserve the decaying funerary objects in the wooden boxes.

In order to ensure smooth progress in the work, Xia Nai stayed with the excavation team. He lived in a wooden shack and gave on-the-spot guidance. Before his death, Emperor Wanli, who had spared no cost to build his magnificent tomb, must have done his utmost to find a method for preserving his body; therefore it was possible that the corpses had not yet entirely decomposed. Xia Nai asked the team to make a wooden box big enough to contain the three corpses and make preparations for preserving them.

In the gloomy, humid underground halls, there was only one small generator to supply electricity for lighting. Members of the excavation team took photos, drew sketches, took measurements and noted down numbers all under a dim light in front of Empress Xiaojing's coffin. When everything was ready, they began to dismantle the outer coffin.

It did not take much time or effort to take the planks of pine and China fir apart and expose the decaying inner coffin.

In the history books of the Ming Dynasty, not all records correspond to historical facts. In one description, Empress Xiaojing was said to be an older woman who had already lost her youthfulness by the time she met Emperor Wanli; she later lost the sight of one eye, this being the reason why she fell out of favour with the emperor. In another account, it is related that Emperor Wanli fell seriously ill and realised he would not recover. One day he woke up to find Concubine Wang sleeping with him, her arm under his head, her face wet with tears, whereas Concubine Zheng was nowhere to be seen.

These stories were not only the subject of gossip among the people, but were immortalised as woodblock prints in books. The question of Lady Wang's age when she first met the emperor was cleared up in the excavation of Ding Ling. According to inscriptions on a stone tablet, which had been moved from her original burial place and now stood on the western side of her outer coffin, she was only 16 when she first met the emperor who was 18.

There are discrepancies between entries in some

history books of the Ming Dynasty and the tomb inscription concerning specific dates in Concubine Wang's life. For example, in the tomb inscription, Lady Wang was established as Respectable Concubine in the 6th month of the 10th year of the Wanli Reign, while the books record it as the 4th month of the same year. In the tomb inscription, Concubine Wang died in the 39th year while the books record her death as having occurred in the 40th year.

When Empress Xiaojing's coffin was opened, the first thing seen was a light-yellow brocade quilt and some Buddhist scriptures. The brocade was woven in a floral pattern and the scriptures were bright red. Long years had rendered the scriptures almost unrecognisable, with only a few characters in the centre faintly visible.

The corpse was not under the quilt, which instead, covered a trove of brocades and objects of gold, silver and jade, making the coffin look more like a cache for jewellery.

The internment of funerary objects, like the imperial tombs themselves, underwent a process of evolution. Excavations have shown that in the early stages of primitive society people were not overly attentive to burying the dead, less of burying valuable objects with them. Archaeological excavations have confirmed that the custom of burying funerary objects with the dead emerged only after burying the dead became a conscious act. When people buried the corpses of their forbears or companions, they often thought of burying the personal belongings the deceased had used or loved. They served approximately two purposes: The first, relating to remembering the dead, was not necessarily inspired by religious or superstitious ideas; the second was connected with the notion of the soul — a person travelled to another world after death, lived there as in this world, and therefore needed production tools, daily necessities, and things enjoyed during earthly existence.

Under the brocade quilt were two sets of exquisite, bright coloured costumes. The upper garment was a lined satin jacket in yellow, stitched with gold threads, with the front opening in the centre and the sleeves long and wide. At the waist was a red satin skirt; the lined trousers were made of yellow satin, with an opening at the left. The waist was tightened by a yellow satin ribbon. The lined jacket was one of the few best preserved and most precious treasures among the nearly 200 bolts of finished textile materials and costumes unearthed from Ding Ling.

The jacket was embroidered with 100 boys to show that the imperial family would thrive from generation to generation. The front and the sleeves of the garment had nine dragons embroidered with gold thread in different postures against the background of hills, rocks, trees and flowers. They formed a painting in which human beings, animals and Nature share a common fate. The 100 boys were each portrayed in a different stance, wearing different clothes and playing different games, all lively and in high spirits, making up 40 individual patterns to form a colourful children's playground. In the "Cat's Game", for example, a cat plays with a butterfly amidst grass and flowers while the boys chase the cat. In "The Examination," one boy pretends to be the teacher, one writes in earnest, and another, with a book in his hands, gazes out the window. "The Bath" is the most lively and provocative: Four children are acting out a farce in which a naked boy is bathing in a wooden tub, while another sprinkles water on him. Just at this moment two other boys come running. They poke a stick under the tub, tip it up, and spill the water. The bather, about to fall over with the tub, waves his hand wildly to beg for mercy.

In other patterns, boys play various roles dressed as grown-ups. In "Officials on Duty," boys wear long robes, black gauze caps and jade belts, and ride bamboo horses. Some hold banners, some umbrellas, while some play music and others beat gongs to clear the way. The scene is lifelike and funny, but also serious. It portrays different activities and attitudes of real court officials. While it elicits joy and delight, it provides leeway for thought.

Other motifs include "Skipping Rope", "Catching Birds", "Shooting Firecrackers", "Hide-and-Seek", and "Picking Peaches", each depicting the most vivid scene of the story in a true-to-life style. The drollery, liveliness, simplicity and innocence of the boys are all clearly described.

The lined jacket was not only beautiful in design but rich in skilfully embroidered detail.

Embroidery dates back to remote antiquity in China. According to the *Book of Documents*, under the official garment system of more than 4,000 years ago, there was a rule that "the upper piece be painted and the lower piece embroidered". It is also stated that in the Zhou Dynasty "both embroidery and painting were used together". During the period of the Western and Eastern Han dynasties, embroidery was common in

Changsha of Hunan, Huai'an of Hebei, Minfeng of Xinjiang, and Wuwei of Gansu. It was dominated by a braid stitch, while allowing for a small amount of plain and herring-bone stitch.

Impressive progress was made in embroidery techniques during the Tang and Song dynasties. The use of knot stitch, couching and other plain stitches in particular greatly helped bring out the expressiveness of the craft. Its patterns and designs gradually formed a consummate artistic style.

Although embroidery in the Ming Dynasty was based on the fine traditions of the Tang and Song, it experienced a new creative development. The jacket decorated with 100 boys was a palace embroidery, which may have been an official garment worn by the empress at her wedding ceremony or at rites. According to an official Ming record, in the 26th year of the Hongwu Reign, craftsmen in the palace worked in rotation or on a fixed basis. The one-year group consisted of 150 embroiderers and the three-year group had 1,043 weavers. Perhaps some of them were skilled craftsmen and women from other parts of the country. After coming to Beijing, they also learned the characteristics and style of Beijing embroidery. Therefore, the materials, stitches and techniques of the palace embroideries are characterized by the particular features of Beijing embroidery.

The embroidered children's games and the designs of the props they used had a strong northern folk flavour, while the banana trees and the boy's bath were based on the landscape and customs of the south. The use of plain stitch over a large area, and the use of gold threads and wrapped threads for outlining reflect the characteristics of Guangdong embroidery; the use of multi-coloured threads characterizes that of Suzhou.

Apart from landscapes, trees, grassland, woods, dragons and beasts, the jacket was also decorated with the symbol of the swastika. It invoked a strong religious sense together with enjoyment of the poetic and picturesque charm of Nature.

The swastika " 卍 " was probably introduced to China from India and Persia around the time of the Tang Dynasty. Whether it was introduced by Monk Xuan Zang (famous monk of the Tang) and his disciples is not known. But the character, or word, was created in the second year of the Changshou Reign of Empress Wu Zetian and was pronounced *wan*. It is clearly recorded that the swastika " 卍 " was called the "*wan* character design".

According to the Chinese *Dictionary of Religion*, the meaning of the swastika, which is given a peculiar Sanskrit pronunciation is "an auspicious symbol on the chest". In ancient times, it was translated as "auspicious sea and cloud expression", one of the 32 expressions of Sakyamuni.

The swastika was originally an incantation, an amulet or a religious symbol and was believed to be the symbol of the sun or fire. It was used in Brahmanism, Buddhism and Jainism in ancient India, Persia and Greece. In the writings of Tibetan scholars, the swastika was introduced into Tibet by Buddhists after the 7th century.

One researcher found some significant rock paintings in Rutog west of Nagqu in Tibet. Devoid of any religious flavour, they simply represented the whole process of evolution from the sun to the swastika:

$$\odot \rightarrow \text{☼} \rightarrow \text{⊗} \rightarrow 卐 \rightarrow 卍$$

The rock paintings indicate that this symbol may even have originated in the sacred place of Buddhism in Tibet. In the progress of world civilisation, there have been many coincidences. For example, the pictographic character "$\odot$" was commonly used in Chinese, Tibetan and ancient Egyptian scripts. The early history of Tibet shows that the swastika was not a result of the introduction of Buddhism into Tibet. The swastika had been a sacred symbol of the Bon religion (the pre-Buddhist animistic religion of Tibet) long before Buddhism came into Tibet, where it was worshiped by the Tibetan people.

The swastika attracted the attention of the excavation team and tourists because the same symbol was used by Hitler's army during World War II. Why did Hitler choose the swastika as the symbol of fascism? There are many stories but no clear answer. A woman who was once Hitler's maid recalled that Hitler discovered this ancient auspicious symbol of India in the early years of his life and interpreted the image and its implication in the light of his own ambition. The pity was that he remembered the symbol as in the opposite direction, and thus used the form reversed.

The many brocades unearthed from Ding Ling bear this symbol rotated in both directions, indicating that people at that time did not pay much attention to its direction.

When the two sets of costumes and the two brocade

quilts were taken away, the corpse of the pitiful empress was revealed. She lay peacefully, with pins of gold, jade and precious stones in her hair. Her face turned slightly to the south. Her left arm at her side, with her hand at her waist; her right arm was bent upward, her hand near her head. The upper part of her spine was slightly bent; the lower limbs were straight. Only the skeleton was left as the flesh had already decomposed.

When the excavators started to remove the skeleton, in order to put it into the prepared wooden box, it came apart. Only the joints of the lower limbs were still tenuously held together. It took a great deal of time and effort to move the skeleton piece by piece.

When the task was completed, a layer of ritual paper money and copper coins was revealed underneath. These had been put there supposedly for the use of the empress' soul in the next world. It may have been hoped that this symbolic money would console her sad, lonely soul.

Waxed Wooden Statuettes and the Burial System

The eight wooden chests placed at both ends of the stone dais were filled with carved wooden statuettes and horses. Seven of them contained human figures, and the eighth, horses. The wooden boxes had been eroded by moisture and had disintegrated. Many of the figurines were also in a state of decay and broke into pieces upon the slightest touch, making them difficult to handle. Traces on the floor indicated that the underground chambers had been flooded several times.

The slow evaporation of the moisture had accelerated the wood rot.

The excavation team assigned Bai Wanyu to sort them out and take what protective measures he could to preserve them while the others opened the coffins.

It was impossible to tell exactly how many statuettes there were, but they must have numbered over 1,000. Only 300 or so were relatively intact. Careful observation revealed that they had been carved out of pine, poplar and willow wood. Most of the human figures were male, a small number of which were old men with long beards. The minority were females, short in stature and likely depictions of palace maids. Whether male or female, young or old, they were all neatly dressed and full of vigour. Each horse was fitted with a saddle carved in a different posture. Together all these figures formed a vivid picture of life inside the palace.

By the Ming Dynasty, the emperors and their ministers had begun to feel somewhat uneasy about the practice of living people being buried with the emperor. Few records were ever entered in the imperial documents with regard to this practice. Only the bare minimum of information was included in historical data to provide later generations with some insight into the entire scope of burial customs.

The Ming Dynasty differed from the slave societies that preceded it in that concubines and palace maids were used as sacrifices buried with the dead, instead of such being war captives or slaves. The practice was no longer to bury them alive, or to decapitate them first; instead most of the victims were hanged before being buried in the imperial tombs area or in some other place of burial. An example was provided in a gruesome record entered during the reign of Emperor Jingtai of the Ming Dynasty: "Lady Tang and other concubines were all given red ribbons with which to hang themselves." If a large number of concubines were to be buried with the dead (46 being buried with Zhu Yuanzhang), they were ordered to hang themselves collectively. Before they died, they were invited to a banquet and were obliged to dress up in their finest garments. One can hardly imagine how these beautiful women, about to end their young lives, could partake of a banquet, however sumptuous. Wailing and weeping resounded in the hall until after the banquet, when they were led to the designated hall, made to stand on wooden platforms and put their heads into the nooses. After that, the eunuchs moved the platforms away and the young ladies departed from this world forever.

Emperor Yongle of the Ming Dynasty had a Korean concubine named Han. She was ordered to be buried with him after his death. She knew that she was going to die and could do nothing about it. When she stood on the wooden platform, and was about to put her head into the noose, she turned back abruptly to call out to her wet nurse Jin Hei: "Mother, I'm going! Mother, I'm going!..." The sight was so sad, the cries so plaintive, that even the execution supervisors were moved to tears. A eunuch forced her head into the noose and moved the platform away. Jin Hei, wet nurse to Lady Han from Korea, made these details public after she was permitted to return to her native land. The story was entered into the Korean collection *True Narrations of the Lee Dynasty*.

To deceive the public and to make a show of

kindness, the emperors often granted posthumous titles to console the close relatives of the deceased. The ten palace maids buried with Zhu Zhanji, Emperor Xuanzong, were all made concubines and granted titles posthumously. Their fathers and elder brothers were given generous pensions and official posts. Their children and grandchildren also benefitted from the hereditary system. They were called "women's family members entitled to imperial pensions".

In general the names of the palace maids who failed to receive official status were not recorded in the court annals so their true histories remain unknown. However, there was one exception. As recorded in a passage in the *History of the Ming Dynasty*, a girl named Guo Ai in Fengyang, who, born in a scholar's family, was innocent, beautiful and intelligent, and had literary talent, was chosen to become Emperor Xuanzong's concubine at the age of 14. When she left Fengyang for Beijing to see the emperor, with high hopes of finding happiness, she did not expect that death was fast approaching. In just 20 days after she arrived in the palace, while everything was still quite unfamiliar to her, the emperor died, and she was chosen to be buried with him.

When the imperial decree was issued, the lovely girl was utterly shocked and grief-stricken. At the last moments of her life, she wrote a poem to express her sorrow and resentment, which she asked a friendly eunuch to send out of the palace. It became an immortal poetic masterpiece written by a wretched young woman in the Forbidden City:

Life is short,
This is fate that can not be challenged.
Life is a dream,
You know only when you die.
I'm parting, ashamed to lose my parents,
This is filial impiety.
Though sad, I am helpless.
If true, mourn over it.

The poem is a tearful complaint about the shortness of her life. Hers is regret over her outstanding debt of gratitude to her parents, and grief over her fate and brief youth.

With the advancement of feudalism in China, the use of statuettes to replace the living for burial began to prevail. However, even as late as in the Qing Dynasty, there were still cases of burying the living with the dead.

Unlike gold and silver objects, wooden statuettes are vulnerable to decay. Special care and treatment are required to preserve them. In some countries a method of freeze-drying was used in the 1950s.

Since this technique did not exist in China at the time of the excavation, Bai Wanyu had to treat the figures with the method he had learnt from Sven Hedin and Andersson in the Western Regions in the 1920s.

Inside the underground palace he melted wax in a flat-bottomed bronze pot, then dipped the figures into the pot one by one to seal them. They whirled about in the boiling wax as if they were dancing at an imperial celebration.

However, the excavator's joy soon turned to sadness; the wax-covered figurines were all shrunken and deformed as a result of vaporisation when they were taken out of the pot. In an instant youth stiffened as if paralysed and turned into ugly old age. All Bai's sincerest efforts were to no avail. But the curtain had just opened on the tragedy of the excavation of the imperial tomb. The transformation of the expressions of these "boys and girls" was merely a brief, ironic overture to a larger, more sweeping tragedy.

Empress Xiaoduan

To the left of Emperor Wanli's coffin was that of his wife, Empress Xiaoduan. In size and shape, it was the same as that of Empress Xiaojing, but it was better preserved. Although there were cracks on the outer side of the outer coffin, no part of it had caved in. The part from which the paint had flaked off revealed that the coffin was also made of pine and fir wood.

On the lid of the outer coffin were two blue and white plum vases with dragon designs. Their colour and workmanship were equal to the quality of those in the imperial chambers. One vase was inscribed on the bottom: "Made in the Wanli Reign of the Great Ming Dynasty", and the other: "Made in the Jiajing Reign of the Great Ming Dynasty". Thus one might conclude that these had been on display in the quarters occupied by Empress Xiaoduan.

Plum vases of this kind were also unearthed in the tombs of Ming-dynasty concubines in Dongsi Tomb Village in the western outskirts of Beijing. The concubines of the Ming emperors were mostly buried in these tombs except a few favoured ladies who were buried in the Imperial Ming Tombs area. The use of plum vases as burial objects was probably a burial custom of the imperial court.

The opening of the outer coffin revealed a wooden inner coffin used to protect and preserve the corpse more efficiently. In the excavation of the tomb of Pharaoh Tutankhamen of Egypt, the outer coffin was found to be made of stone while the inner coffin was a double casing made of gold. In China in later dynasties, both the inner and outer coffins were made of wood. This has been confirmed by the excavations of Ding Ling and the Eastern Imperial Tombs of the Qing Dynasty.

Four pieces of jade were placed in Empress Xiaoduan's coffin on both sides of the corpse. In all, 27 pieces of jade had been found outside the three coffins. The jades differed in size and shape, and most were inscribed with Chinese characters; some had characters written in black ink, some had paper slips stuck on them on which characters were written, while others had both. Most of the characters written on paper were done neatly and clearly, a contrast to the bold, rough and indistinct strokes of the characters incised on the jades. Some of the jades were numbered which greatly aided the keeping of records of all the pieces as to type and weight. For example:

Jade piece, 13 catties
Cabbage jade, one piece, 13 catties
No. 68, jade piece, 15 catties
Cabbage jade, one piece, 15 catties and 12 taels
No. 72
Milky jade, one piece, weighing ten catties
Milky jade, one piece, 11 catties

Two catties and eight taels
Milky jade, one piece, two catties and eight taels.
...

According to written records, the smallest piece weighed one catty and ten taels whilst the biggest totalled 48 catties. One, recorded as weighing 13 catties, actually weighed 16 and a half catties. It is now difficult to tell whether this was a mistake or if some changes had taken place in the jade. Another piece of jade bore marks of sawing which may have been caused by the binding string. Yet another was marked by three characters identifying the recipient.

Jades were among the emperor's funerary objects in all Chinese dynasties. While the golden well was intended to receive vital energy from the earth to ensure the soul would live forever, jade was believed to prevent the corpse from decomposing. A passage in the "Biography of Yang Yusun" in *Chronicles of the Han Dynasty* says: "With a jade in the mouth, the body will not decompose but gradually become mummified."

A change began to take place in burying jades with the dead in the Warring States Period (475-221 BC). In archaeological excavations in Luoyang of Henan Province, a number of flat stones shaped like human faces were discovered on the faces of some corpses, flat stones were also found on their bodies, and two flat stones shaped like animals under their feet. All flat stones had perforated holes which might be used for stringing them together to cover the faces and bodies of the dead. This was the prototype of the jade suit that appeared in later dynasties.

By the time of the Western Han Dynasty (206 BC—AD 24), the emperors were firmly convinced of the efficacy of jade to protect their bodies. No longer satisfied with simply burying jade with their bodies, they had suits made of jade pieces to wear when they were buried to ensure that their bodies would be preserved forever. This notion reached its peak in the period of the Eastern Han Dynasty (AD 25-220). The jade suits sewn with gold thread, worn by Liu Sheng and his wife Dou Wan, unearthed from the Han tomb in Mancheng of Hebei Province shattered the myth recorded in the *Chronicles of the Han Dynasty* that "with jade in the mouth, the body will not decompose but gradually become mummified". Although the couple wore jade suits and had many flat pieces of jade on their backs and chests, jade in their mouths, jade plugs in their noses, jade drops in their ears and jade lids over their eyes, only the jade suits and coverings were found by the excavators, when the tomb was opened up in 1968, the bodies had already decomposed completely with only a few decayed teeth and bits of broken bones left.

Use of jade suits as burial clothes lasted from the Western Han Dynasty to the late years of the Eastern Han. In the later period of the Three Kingdoms (AD 220-280), Cao Pei, Emperor Wen of the Wei, banned it as "a silly practice". In fact archaeologists have never found jade suits of the Wei, Jin and later dynasties.

Jade objects and uncarved jades were also unearthed from the imperial tombs after the Jin Dynasty, but they were buried only as tokens. The 31 jade pieces unearthed from Ding Ling belonged to two categories: milky jade and cabbage jade. Milky jade is slightly greenish, with a glossy surface. Cabbage jade looks like a dried cabbage leaf, light yellowish mixed with light green in colour. According to *Inquiries into Antiques*, these two types are of inferior quality, perhaps mined in Xinjiang and Gansu.

However, the jade vessels found in the boxes were altogether different. The bowls, basins, pots, cups and wine vessels were all of the finest jade and exquisite craftsmanship. Many of them were fitted with gold attachments, and inlaid with precious stones and pearls. One jade bowl found at Ding Ling is so fine that if stood before a window, the other side of the jade bowl can be seen through the side nearest the viewer. It would have been impossible to achieve such splendour if there had not been special designs and highly-developed skills at that time.

Comparing the raw jades with the jade vessels, it is not difficult to see that the burying of jade in the tombs was no longer intended to protect the bodies; in the Ming Dynasty it was no more than a formal custom.

The *nanmu* coffin for Empress Xiaoduan was next opened. Inside were a brocade quilt embroidered with lotus flowers and nine dragons, clothes, gold objects, and a lacquer basin. After carefully taking these out one by one the excavators found the empress' body.

She lay in a jacket embroidered with dragons, a skirt embroidered with dragons and a pair of yellow satin trousers. The dragon jacket had wide sleeves made of yellow damask, embroidered with bats, the ancient Chinese character for long life and the swastika. As the fabric was not wide enough, the upper ends of the sleeves had obviously been sewn together with another piece of fabric. The Chinese characters for longevity and the bats were inverted. This was clearly not a mistake, but an indication of the "arrival of blessings and long life". (In the Chinese language, the character for arrival and that for inversion are pronounced the same.)

The flesh of Empress Xiaoduan had decomposed, but her skeleton was intact. Her head was placed toward the west, her feet toward the east, her left arm was at her side, with her hand at her waist and her right arm straight. Her legs were crossed, the left foot over the right. The lower ends of her trousers were inserted into her stockings bound with cord at the ankles. She wore a pair of yellow satin shoes with soft soles. She lay on her right side, facing south, looking as dignified and refined as when alive in the palace.

In the more than 30 years during the reign of Emperor Wanli after Zhang Juzheng had died, the imperial court gradually lapsed into confusion and further decline. With the emperor increasingly inept, court officials became increasingly corrupt and embroiled in intrigues against each other. During this period, it seemed only two people remained sober-minded: One was Chief Cabinet Minister Shen Shixing and the other Empress Xiaoduan.

As early as 1587 Shen Shixing stood head and shoulders above all the others like a crane among barnyard fowl, concerned only with the interests of the empire. It was he who came to the conclusion: "Since ancient times, no country in a situation like this has been able to rule in peace for long." At the critical time when the Great Ming Empire was on the decline, he did all he could to heal the rift between the emperor and the court officials, and settle the dissension among the officials themselves. However, all his painstaking efforts to effect a reconciliation among them ended in failure owing to the deep-seated inertia of the imperial system.

Empress Xiaoduan had reason to feel bitter, but she was able to make a sober appraisal of her status and situation, and to perform whatever came within the range of her duties with a submissiveness and tolerance characteristic of Chinese women. She found her own *modus vivendi* in the narrow cranny between moral integrity and human feeling. Her eager attentiveness and her strict observance of the rites made a good impression on Emperor Wanli's mother and the court officials. Her sober manner was well exemplified in her attitude during the dispute over Emperor Wanli's heir apparent. In the whirlpool of ethics and politics that lasted 15 years, she neither inclined towards the officials, nor blamed the emperor, but with her intelligence and resourcefulness, stood on neutral ground between them, and saw the question so clearly that neither side could do her any harm. Even when Emperor Wanli wanted to depose her as the empress after he had lost in the struggle, he had to give up the idea just because she had handled so many problems with outstanding skill.

She had no son, nor any love from the emperor; this was surely a tragedy for the empress who had the greatest power to enjoy it all. However, she recognised the situation, buried the pain in her heart, soberly prepared herself for the role she wished to adopt in this tragedy, playing it out like a professional. In this way she managed to avoid the extremely miserable lot which the Respectable Concubine Wang, the Imperial Concubine Zheng, the other concubines and the palace maids had to endure all their lives. At best, this may perhaps be counted as luck among the luckless.

She lay in serenity by the side of Emperor Wanli, her head on a rectangular brocade pillow, with many gold hairpins inlaid with precious stones in her wispy hair. She seemed to be gazing coldly at the world.

Her head ornaments were obviously more expensive and striking than those of Empress Xiaojing. Almost every gold or jade hairpin was inlaid with emeralds and "cat's eyes". The "cat's eye" gem was the most precious of all precious stones in the Wanli Reign. It was said to originate in Southeast Asia. As precious as it is rare, the cat's eye gem may be considered a priceless treasure.

Under Empress Xiaoduan's body was a cotton-padded mattress with 100 gold coins, cast with four Chinese characters meaning "dispel calamities, prolong life". On both sides of the mattress were large numbers of gold and silver ingots inscribed with words filled in red, and reading as follows:

Top: 90 percent gold, ten taels
Bottom: All bought by Xu Guanglu, owner of the jewellery shop in Wanping County, and presented to the Ministry of Revenue in the 46th year of the Wanli Reign.
Top: 90 percent gold, ten taels
Bottom: All bought by Yan Hong, owner of the jewellery shop in Daxing County, and presented to the Ministry of Revenue in the 46th year of the Wanli Reign.

The inscriptions further confirmed statements in historical records that jewellery shops in the region administered by the capital area had to buy gold for the imperial court at whatever cost, in addition to the gold levies provided by Yunnan.

Gold and silver ingots were not found in Empress Xiaojing's coffin. Some historians argue that this was because the emperor ordered an economical burial for her. This argument is somewhat biased. Since Xiaojing was only an imperial concubine when she was buried, while Xiaoduan died as empress, under the hierarchical system of that time their treatment was naturally different.

Chapter Ten
AUDIENCE WITH THE EMPEROR

Flowers Will Fade, Do What One May

At the critical moment when the excavation team was busy dealing with the skeletons of the empresses and their burial objects, the anti-rightist political storm* was gathering momentum along the tortuous mountain roads to Ding Ling after sweeping over cities and villages throughout the country.

By this time the excavation team was no longer led directly by the Chang Ling Excavation Committee, but had been formed into a new collective unit with the group preparing to establish the Ding Ling Museum. Actually, the team had been "taken over" by the museum's preparatory group. Acting on the instructions of the group leader, the excavation team members stopped their cataloguing work in the underground chambers to take part in the political movement.

Although Xia Nai explained to the Chang Ling Excavation Committee several times what harm and what losses would result if the excavation work was interrupted, the committee members, themselves in a

---

*The Anti-Rightist Campaign in which many intellectuals were persecuted.

precarious position and on the defensive, could only sigh and remain silent.

The storm had long been anticipated by Xia Nai, but he had not expected it to come just at that moment. It was now that Zhao Qichang understood the true implication of Xia Nai's plea after they had discovered the diamond wall several months earlier: "Do your best to open the gate of the underground palace as soon as possible, *or it will be too late*!"

It was now too late.

Members of the excavation team worked day and night to open the palace gate and the coffins, and catalogue the burial objects. Xia Nai joined them, despite a painful stomach ulcer. But all their efforts were in vain. As they reluctantly laid down their tools, put aside the bones and burial objects and walked out of the underground chambers aggrieved by this painful reverse, the excavation of Ding Ling was doomed to become a tragedy unprecedented in the history of New China's archaeology.

Xia Nai was requested to return to the Institute of Archaeology to take part in the anti-rightist movement. When he was about to leave, Zhao Qichang grasped his teacher's hands tightly in his, and asked: "Professor Xia, is there anything else you want us to do?"

In a choked voice Xia Nai said: "Take care of the relics as best you can when you've time out from your political study. Let me know as soon as you have even a hint of a problem." Zhao Qichang nodded.

"Take good care of yourself!" Xia Nai wore a forced smile, his face as pale as a withered autumn leaf. After waving his skinny hand in the air, he turned and walked towards the car parked in the square in front of the gate. He had become very thin, yet still, his bearing was one of determination and self-confidence. As the car moved off, Zhao Qichang's heart tightened, the blood pounding in his veins. He turned and strode into the tomb precinct. Climbing the tomb mound, he looked up at the green Dayu Hill and slowly exhaled, as if divesting himself of all that was foul and wearisome.

The excavation team members now sat all day long in the wooden shacks listening to reports on the anti-rightist movement by a newly-appointed leader. Faced with what already seemed a critical situation, it was beyond their expectation that history could retaliate against them too.

The brocades, which had undergone simple technical treatment and were stuck on plexiglass, gradually hardened and turned brittle, while the colours faded. The beautiful, dazzling embroideries developed large black spots and then began to rot. What would happen to the corpse of the emperor still hidden deep in the vault, his coffin still unopened?

One day, Bai Wanyu met Zhao Qichang by appointment in a secluded corner and told him in a low voice: "I heard the warehouseman whisper that the things inside are beginning to rot."

Zhao Qichang was terribly upset, his head hummed. He seized Bai by the hand: "Is this true?"

"I happened to overhear the man report this to the leader of the preparatory group confidentially," Bai explained.

Zhao Qichang hammered his head in despair: "Everything's finished!"

The news hit him like a bolt from the blue. Bai Wanyu asked anxiously: "What is to be done? Speak up. Say something!" This reminded him of what Xia Nai's parting words: "If you run into any trouble, let me know right away! Report it, if it's only a hint of a problem!"

The current situation was no longer a "hint of trouble", but an irreversible disaster. "Tell Director Xia at once! Let him try to find a solution!" Zhao Qichang told Bai Wanyu hastily.

Bai Wanyu hurried to the city that very day. On learning what had happened, Xia Nai went out to Ding Ling at once.

The warehouse was opened. Xia Nai, Zhao Qichang and some others went in. The dim interior was filled with a smell of decay and mildew. The panes of plexiglass had been stood up against the wall. The brocades stuck on them had already faded and lost their former gloss. The original light yellows, light greens and bright reds had all turned into dark clouds. At first Xia Nai had thought it was the dust and dim light that had produced such a dull effect. When he held the glass in a good light, the truth was clear for all to see.

The warm sun shone over the brocades, already shrunk and puckered into a formless mass. He stretched his shaking hand out to touch them; the satin-silk felt like a hard iron sheet. On contact, the warped parts all fell to the ground. Xia Nai put down the "woven fabrics" with his trembling hands without a word. He paced up and down the warehouse. The others grieved as they watched him.

Xia Nai had been the most sober-minded participant

of the excavation not only because he had a profound knowledge of archaeology, but also because of his deep understanding of Chinese politics, culture and the general situation. At the beginning of the excavation, he had already anticipated what the future held in store. What was happening now represented just an inkling of his forebodings.

On seeing the reams of ruined brocades, Xia Nai deplored his inability to change the situation. He returned to the city the same day.

Before long, the decision that was made in Beijing reached Ding Ling. It relieved, temporarily, the plight of the team members and their project, thus dropping the curtain on the first episode, before the tragedy reached its climax. The excavation was resumed.

Lights Switched on Again

The dim lights shone once more in the damp, ghastly underground chambers. Work resumed after a six-month stoppage, the most pressing task being to open Emperor Wanli's coffin.

The huge coffin, which was 1.8 metres high, 1.8 metres wide and 3.9 metres long, lay undisturbed in the centre of the rear chamber.

The red planks of the outer coffin were made of delicately-worked pine wood, and the four sides, mortised together, were fastened with iron nails. The thick bottom was extremely heavy, and four big bronze rings were fixed on either side, apparently for convenience in moving and burying the coffin. Above the planks were wooden processional banners and other burial objects, arranged in good order, as if two opposing armies were pitted against each other in the heat of battle.

Xia Nai was present at the worksite to give personal guidance. The team members used sharp iron tools to slowly pry loose the planks, and remove them. The inner coffin made of *nanmu* wood was exposed. The coffin was covered with an inscribed yellow silk banner, both ends of which were fixed with wooden plates with dragon designs. In the centre of the banner were six bold, golden characters: "Coffin for the Deceased Emperor".

The exterior of the coffin was painted red. The lack of cracks on the painted side showed that the painting was done after the deceased was put in the coffin. The inner coffin and the outer coffin were exactly the same shape: higher and wider in front, lower and narrower in the rear. Both were slightly narrower at the top, wider at the bottom and widened in the middle. The two sides were bowed outward to maximise space inside the coffin. The lid was fixed on with four big iron nails.

The last coffin was about to be opened. All was quiet in the hall. The excavation team members pried at the seams of the coffin lid, the rusty nails gave way slowly, and a crack between the lid and the coffin began to widen. Iron levers inserted into the crack emitted creaking sounds as if the spirit of the emperor was complaining at the intrusion.

The team took hold of the ponderous lid with all their might and at an order from Xia Nai lifted it up and shakily placed it down on the dais.

Then needing no signal, they returned to examine the emperor's inner coffin. Inside were all kinds of dazzling treasures and valuables. A red brocade satin quilt embroidered with gold threads and floral patterns served to protect the gold, silver and jade objects and a brocade dragon robe beneath.

Zhao Qichang, his camera ready, took the first batch of pictures after the coffin was opened. Xian Ziqiang busied himself at his drawing board sketching the coffin and buried objects. The other members measured, numbered, recorded and registered, everything done in accordance with proper archaeological procedures.

Xia Nai and Zhao Qichang carefully examined the coffin in silence. Both were considering how to sort out the hundreds of burial objects inside. The emperor's inner coffin was different from those of the empresses. It was in a perfect state of preservation. It was 1.5 metres high, which made their work difficult even if they stood on benches. They needed to find a way to work conveniently without damaging the burial objects.

Later that evening Xia Nai discussed his idea with Zhao Qichang: "I thought we might put up wooden stands around the coffin. We can lie prone to sort out the objects." Zhao Qichang hesitated: "It's a good idea, but working in that position is too hard. Young people may be able to stand it, but you are not really well, how can you work like that?" The two of them thought of one method after another, but unable to come up with a better idea, they decided to give it a try.

Up went the stands around Wanli's coffin. Lying flat on these planks, they began to work.

When they put the brocade quilt aside, they found Taoist robes of various kinds and colours, inner garments and imperial robes. The uppermost garment was a Taoist robe made of plain yellow damask lined with gauze, with an opening on the right side and a ribbon under the armpits to hold the robe together. It looked similar to those worn by Taoist priests today. The only difference was that there was an alternate opening at the back, and the openings on both sides reached to the armpits. This design perhaps made it easier to put on. Visible on the inner side of the lower front were the characters embroidered with silk thread:

> Made on the 18th of the 1st month in the 43rd
>   year of the Wanli Reign,
> Three *chi* nine *cun* and six *fen* long,*
> Silk floss, nine taels.

There was a paper slip inside the robe, and the words on it were almost the same as those embroidered except for the following:

> Plain colour damask Taoist robe with big
>   sleeves and lining,
> The robe is two *chi* one *cun* wide.

The robe was padded with silk floss, which was unevenly distributed. The date it was made and its colour showed that the robe had not been worn by the emperor before he died. In fact, all rulers of the Ming Dynasty advocated Buddhism and adopted a cold attitude toward Taoism. During their reigns, both Zhu Yuanzhang and Zhu Di had high-ranking Buddhist monks help them with political affairs. When Zhu Di

---

*One *chi* is approximately 1.1 feet, and is equal to ten *cun*. One *cun* can be divided into ten *fen*.

was still prince of the Yan State, it was none other than Monk Dao Yan of Qingshou Temple on whom he relied for help in seizing the throne. Empress Dowager Cisheng, mother of Emperor Wanli, made several contributions to help build Buddhist temples. The pagoda in Cishou Temple in the western outskirts of Beijing was built with contributions from the empress dowager. After Emperor Wanli met Concubine Zheng, the two of them often paid homage to the Western Buddhist Temple to pray for lasting love.

Though indifferent towards Taoism, the rulers of the Ming Dynasty did not exclude it. They permitted it to exist as part of the cultural heritage. The Taoist robe found in Wanli's coffin seemed to be confirmation of this policy.

Under the robes and garments was a priceless treasure — the emperor's ceremonial dragon robe with 12 coiled dragons and 12 patterns. This robe was used only on ceremonial occasions such as sacrificial rites for Heaven and Earth, for ancestors at the ancestral temple, for the god of the land and the god of the grains, for the ancestor who introduced farming and for the memorials conducted for sages. It was the most precious among his dragon robes.

The background patterns of the ceremonial robe included swastikas, characters for longevity, bats and *ruyi* (s-shaped) clouds to symbolise "long life and good luck". The 12 coiled dragons were woven separately on the front, back and sleeves, and each coiled dragon formed a separate circular pattern, in the centre of which was the dragon, flanked by the "eight auspices", namely: wheel, sieve, umbrella, canopy, flower, vase, fish and plate. Above the dragon were floating clouds, and below, rolling waves and rising cliffs. In addition, there were 12 patterns representing the sun, the moon, stars, mountains, dragons, *huachong*, *zongyi*, algae, fire, rice, *fu* and *fo*. The patterns each had its own implication: The sun, the moon and stars radiate light, day and night, shining over the whole land. The mountain is used to "keep watch over" the earth, the dragon is used to symbolise "power". *Huachong* is a pheasant with beautiful plumes to show "bright literary colours". *Zongyi* is an ancient wine vessel with a long-tailed monkey pattern, used in the imperial ancestral temple. According to legend, the long-tailed monkey was the most filial creature. These monkeys lived in trees, the eldest at the top and the young ones in the lowest branches to protect the safety of the elders. Thus, *zongyi* symbolised "filial piety". Algae is a water grass with figures, representing "its literary content". Fire means flame, representing "brightness". Rice means food. *Fu* is a pattern half black and half white, like an axe, to indicate "resoluteness" and "authority". *Fo* is a combination of two bows back to back, a pattern half black and half green, which stands for "good against evil". In short, all these patterns implied that the emperor was well versed, cultivated in both literary arts and martial arts, handled state affairs brilliantly and resolutely, and his holy light shone over the land while his kindness and grace were shown to all. Emperor Wanli possessed none of these qualities except one — the autocratic handling of political affairs. It is hard to imagine how he felt about the care and thought his forebears had given to the preparation of all these patterns when he wore this "ceremonial robe".

As it required complicated skills to make the fabric for the ceremonial dragon robe, even the most skilled weaver could produce little more than an inch each day. It took approximately ten years to make one ceremonial dress. That made for Emperor Wanli is probably the only imperial ceremonial dress, woven by the tapestry method, still extant in China. In 1983 Ding Ling Museum entrusted the Nanjing Brocade Research Institute to make a reproduction of it. The new garment, which took five years to complete, bridged a gap of more than 300 years in the making of Ming Dynasty imperial dragon robes.

In order to revive the original weaving of the imperial dragon robes, it was necessary to make "colour analysis" and "warp and weft analysis" of the original material. A craftswoman named Wang Daohui, with 30 years of experience, worked day and night to trace the designs of the dragon robe and completed them, with accurate details, in 48 days. The replica weighed 900 grammes; 121, 370 warps and wefts were used, each over 500 feet long from head to tail. The peacock plumes were carefully chosen, split and twisted into threads. They were woven with coloured silk into clouds and dragon patterns and then fixed with genuine gold threads to produce a refined and brilliant decorative effect. Many specialists agreed that the new ceremonial dress equaled the Ming Dynasty original in materials weave, colour, design and craftsmanship. This "rare treasure" won the "Gold Cup" award at the Fourth National Arts and Crafts Hundred Flowers Award Selection.

When the team members began to sort out the 11th

layer of objects, they came upon a brocade quilt folded in half. When the quilt was opened, Emperor Wanli's corpse was revealed.

He was no longer a well-preserved mummy, but a ghastly skeleton, his head toward the west, feet toward the east, his face turned toward the south. The upper part of the spine was slightly bent; his left arm was down, his hand on his abdomen with a string of beads entwined around the thin, long fingers as if he was praying for the blessing of the gods. The right arm was bent upward, the hand near the chin. A yellowish-brown beard hung by his lips, as if he was leisurely stroking his beard whilst pondering issues of state. Obviously the posture was arranged artificially when he was buried. Much of the robe in which he was dressed had completely decayed, while a jade belt at the waist remained intact. On his head was a crown made entirely of fine gold thread woven into gauze-like material and shaped like a bonnet with two wings. The hair knot was neatly done. He wore a pair of long boots, with the trouser-legs tucked into them. His upper part was dressed as a scholar, whereas the lower part was in the manner of a warrior. Such a combination of scholarly and military clothes have been rarely found in other tombs.

The three skeletons demonstrated no particular characteristics of the burial system for emperors and empresses in the Ming Dynasty.

Emperor Wanli's skeleton was carefully taken out of the coffin. Professor Zhou Dacheng of the Stomatological College of Beijing Medical University made the following conclusion after examining the oral cavities and teeth of the emperor and empresses:

The oral diseases of Emperor Wanli were complicated. Apart from serious dental cavities and periodontosis*, he also suffered from gum decay and fluorosis**. Empress Xiaojing had many decayed teeth and suffered from periodontosis of a middling degree. Only Empress Xiaoduan had good teeth.

A common feature of the three skulls was that the wear of the teeth was very slight, and some teeth appearing almost "brand new". Unearthed skulls in China confirmed that the Peking apeman, the Upper Cave Man, the man in the Neolithic Age or in the Warring States Period all had seriously-worn occlusal surfaces, which was closely related to the coarse food they ate. The wear of the occlusal surface of the teeth of these three skulls was so slight as to show that the food eaten had been finely prepared. But it was precisely the finely-prepared food that caused their dental cavities and periodontosis.

The gum decay suffered by Emperor Wanli and Empress Xiaojing was caused by an improper method of brushing. It shows that the use of tooth brushes was already popular in the palace at that time.

The earliest fossils of fluorosis in China were unearthed in Xujiayao Village on the border between Shanxi and Hebei provinces in May 1978. These were the fossils of three human

---

*Weakening of the tissues surrounding and supporting the teeth.
**The mottling of teeth enamel due to fluorine poisoning.

teeth of the middle period of the Old Stone Age. The teeth showed well-defined yellow-brownish spots and small cavities. It has been reported that people living there today all suffer from fluorosis, and of a similar type to that of Emperor Wanli. This was an important discovery in the ancient history of China's oral diseases. Its origin is still to be verified.

The conclusion drawn by the Beijing Institute of Criminal Science and Technology after checking remnants of hair from Emperor Wanli and Empress Xiaojing was:

> One strand from Wanli, and one strand from Xiaojing.
> The blood type of Emperor Wanli was AB.
> The blood type of Empress Xiaojing was B.
> Note: Empress Xiaoduan's hair was entirely destroyed with her bones during the "cultural revolution".

The conclusion made by the Institute of Vertebrate Palaeontology and Palaeoanthropology under the Chinese Academy of Sciences after restoring Wanli's bones was:

> The upper part of Emperor Wanli's body was hunchbacked before he died. The measured height of the skeleton between the crown of the head and the left foot is 1.64 metres.

A Crowning Oversight

After taking away the tattered silk mattress under Emperor Wanli's bones, the team members found 69 bolts of neatly stacked brocade. Such bright colours and outstanding workmanship had never been found before in China and were also rarely seen among the objects unearthed in tombs in other countries.

The bolts were tied with silk thread at both ends and in the middle. The middle thread was split into the shape of an inverted V. Pasted under the inverted V was a square paper marked with the name of the product, its place of origin, the name of weaver and the date of manufacture. Some of them bore red seals on the date of manufacture. As they had been buried underground for hundreds of years, most of the words on the paper squares were almost invisible. The team members tried their best, but could recognise only few of them.

Brocade weaving in the Ming Dynasty blossomed and wrote a brilliant chapter in the history of Chinese textiles, and arts and crafts. The brocades became known throughout the world for their fine craftsmanship, bright colours and great variety. The first hint of capitalism in the Ming Dynasty manifested itself in the textile industry. Ancient textile techniques were raised to a new height at the time. However, with the rampaging of Qing troops as the new dynasty rose, the textiles produced in the Ming were almost all destroyed. Little was left for today, though some examples might be found in museums, research institutes and private collections, which are mostly remnants left after making robes and dresses. Those who take up the study of such brocades have to search out faded fragments from the covers of Buddhist scriptures for verification.

The brocades found in Emperor Wanli's coffin undoubtedly provided an abundance of valuable material data for studying the history of the Ming Dynasty's textile industry and its technical achievements. Moreover, they also provided inspiration to study the growing of mulberry trees, raising of silk worms, silk reeling, twisting and weaving, varieties of weave and dyeing.

These silk fabrics were a concentrated expression of the weaves and designs of all dynasties since the Han, including plain weave, twill, satin, double weave and complex gauze weave. The combination of varied construction of fabrics and changes in designs made the silk fabrics of the Ming more gorgeous and elegant than those of the Han and Tang dynasties.

When Emperor Yongle moved the Ming capital to Beijing, the imperial court often depended on areas south of the Yangtze River for the supply of large quantities of materials because northern China was less populated and most of the farmland lay waste. The silk fabrics unearthed from Ding Ling show that the bolts of woven fabrics for imperial robes and dresses, or the objects collected in the palace for other purposes, mostly came from southern China. The warm, humid areas south of the Yangtze River were good for growing mulberry trees and bast crops. In the early years of the Ming Dynasty, special weaving and dyeing offices were set up in Nanjing, Suzhou and Hangzhou to supply silk fabrics to the imperial court, which sent special officials to supervise their production. There was a strict quota and checking system. The sealed marks were made strictly in accordance with the official checks. Ironically enough, as the Great Ming Empire continued to decline, the number of bolts produced by the weaving and dyeing offices rose year by year, reaching its peak in the reign of Wanli. It was recorded that the annual quota set for these offices was 20,000 bolts, but the actual supply was more than 100,000 bolts in the early period of Wanli's rule.

Large numbers of weaving and dyeing craftsmen and women were employed in Suzhou, which during the Ming Dynasty was the brocade-making centre. The daily production of each weaver was only two or three *cun* (one *cun* being about an inch). To meet the amazing quota, the weavers had to work long hours every day. They were ill-fed and poorly clothed, leading a life of bare subsistence and untold misery. According to historical data, the weavers and dyers began to vent their anger in the 6th month of the 29th year of Wanli's reign when Ge Xian led more than 20,000 workers in a large-scale rebellion against the imperial court and its officials.

After carefully removing the brocades bolt by bolt, the team members found 79 shining gold ingots in the coffin. Most of them weighed ten taels each, some five taels or less. Marked on the back of most of the ingots were inscriptions giving the date of collection, the names of the officially assigned collector, the supplier and the craftsman. They showed that most of the ingots were cast in Yunnan. Although historical data indicated that Yunnan did not produce large amount of gold in the Wanli Reign, the province annually paid the court 5,000 taels of gold. This became an intolerable burden. Some righteous court officials realised the danger of levying gold and exhorted the emperor: "No calamity in Yunnan is more serious than the levying of tribute gold and taxes." In his memorandum to Emperor Wanli, Hong Qichu, a high official of the Ministry of Revenue, openly declared: "No calamity is as serious as the levy of tribute gold for Yunnan." However, Wanli did not pay attention to their memorandums, and the gold tribute quota kept rising year by year. As the local government in Yunnan could not meet the demands of the court, it had to buy gold from the neighbouring provinces of Sichuan and Guizhou, and was sometimes even obliged to purchase high-priced gold from merchants in the capital city.

Although tribute gold was raised by the local officials, it was finally shifted to the common people who not only had to pay taxes for it, but also had to transport it to Beijing. One can easily imagine how difficult it was for the local people to transport it on foot from Yunnan to Beijing, 5,000 kilometres away. One record recounts that when a group of courtiers and guards escorting the carriers was crossing the Pan River in Yunnan, a sudden mountain torrent rushed down sweeping all 50 people into the river.

After enduring oppression and hardship for a long period, the enslaved people of Yunnan finally rose in rebellion. In the 34th year of the Wanli Reign, more than 10,000 people surrounded the official residence of the mine supervisor, killed the eunuch Yang Rong and the more than 200 officials despatched to Yunnan by the emperor. Yang Rong's residence was burned to ashes, together with his body.

Among the many burial objects in Wanli's coffin were two inconspicuous pots for decocting herbal medicine. They were made of gold, with long handles, but were not as bright as the other gold, silver and jade objects. The abrasions on the surface of the pots indicated that they had been used for a long time, perhaps specifically for decocting herbal medicine for the emperor.

The Ming had a complete system of rules for treating emperors when they fell ill. The imperial hospital usually was ordered to send four to six physicians to see the patient in the palace. They first knelt by the side of the bed for diagnosis and drew up the prescription after joint consultation. Two doses for each medicine were put together in the pot, which was then sealed. It was decocted under the joint supervision of the imperial physicians and imperial eunuchs. When the medicine was ready, it was divided into two parts. After a physician or eunuch took one dose and it proved to have no negative effects, the other dose was sent to the emperor. This strict system was followed mainly to ensure the safety of the emperor.

Historical data reveal that Wanli was in poor health almost all his life and often took medicines. When his skeleton was restored, the right leg was found to be notably shorter than the left, which could explain why the emperor suffered from serious foot diseases among other illnesses before he died.

To the right of his skull lay a medium-sized round box. Regarded as an insignificant burial object at first, it was not opened until classification of the other objects was almost finished. When it was opened, everyone was stunned. Before them was a shining, magnificent headdress! A crown!

Made entirely of fine gold threads woven into a gauze-like fabric, the crown weighed only 826 grammes. It had two wings made of gold netting and a sun-shaped pearl between them. Two golden dragons facing each other climb to the top of the bonnet, as if pursuing the flaming sun. When worn, the effect is arresting. Heaven, earth and man blend into one, as if holding sway over the common people and dominating the universe. This was the first crown of such exquisite design ever unearthed in China, and is a prime national treasure. It is precious not only because it is made entirely of gold, but because of the finely-honed skills used in drawing the threads, weaving and welding. It represents the highest level of craftsmanship in the weaving of very fine gold threads in ancient China.

When the objects inside the coffins had all been documented, the wooden boxes on the dais were opened one by one. By the side of Wanli's coffin was a box of books, which were made of sandalwood slips in their original colour, neither painted nor dyed. Each book had ten slips, stitched together with a silk cord. It was covered with brocade and the inside was inscribed with words cut in intaglio, in the style of regular script, with vertical lines read from right to left. The slips at both ends of the book were painted with golden clouds and dragons. The text was full of undeserved praise for the merits and achievements of Emperor Wanli in his lifetime. These writings represent a picture of vigorous growth, peace and prosperity, concealing the sad reality of the Wanli Reign. On this point, Emperor Wanli and his officials were by no means as frank as Zhu Yuanzhang, the founding Ming emperor. In erecting the tablet for his own tomb, Zhu Yuanzhang personally wrote his autobiography. He described with true feelings and in a cold objective style how difficult it had been to found the Ming Empire, his purpose being to prevent any cover-up by the scholars, concerning him and the empire. What would be the good of Wanli's autobiography to the common people except as an expression of regret over his failure in life and the perishing of an empire?

Chapter Eleven
A TRAGIC LEGACY

Turn in Destiny

Eventually, as they neared the relics in the lower part of the coffin, the team members could no longer reach in far enough from their position up on the stands, not even by bending down. The main job now was for Xian Ziqiang to draw sketches of all the objects in their original state. He first made the drafts based on the original objects, after which they were labelled, and then catalogued. But he ran into a problem: "Director Xia, even with half of my body already in the coffin, I still can't touch these things. I doubt that I can work squatting inside the coffin!" With so many burial objects still untouched, there was no empty spot for him to stand in.

In other countries, established archaeological practice was to use plaster to cast small burial objects at the original site. When the casts were complete, they were taken to the laboratory for studying. In this way the researchers could measure the objects and conduct necessary tests. It was impossible to carry out these procedures in the underground palace because the imperial coffin was too massive.

As Xia Nai walked around the coffin Zhao Qichang followed behind. Xian Ziqiang's words weighed on his mind: "I doubt if I can work squatting inside the coffin!" An idea occurred to him: He looked at Xian's slight build, and then described his idea to Xia Nai, who nodded: "Good! That seems to be the only way. Only I'm sorry to put him to such inconvenience."

Walking over to Xian Ziqiang, Zhao Qichang asked him: "How about if we suspend you in the coffin, just above the articles?"

Xian Ziqiang was quite bewildered. Zhao explained: "We'll put a square bench upside down, with the four legs up, like this, and suspend it on a cross-beam. If you squat in it, can you draw?" After a long pause, he added: "I'm afraid it will be too much trouble for you." To their surprise, Xian Ziqiang replied: "I can work in whatever way is necessary, as long as I can get the drawings done!"

They made a square wooden box, with a wooden leg nailed at each corner. Two long beams were nailed on the tops of the legs. To move the box easily without damaging the coffin, they removed the original stands around the coffin, replaced them with higher ones. The box, now suspended with its two beams on the stands on either side of the coffin, could be moved back and forth freely. Xian Ziqiang crouched in the box and went on with his drawing.

A misty gloom filled the palace depths. In the heat of summer, the excavation team members had to wear thick cotton sweaters or even cotton-padded clothes to withstand the biting cold. The fusion of the acrid, mildewy odour and the fumes of formalin caused the workers to choke and cough.

When they were sorting out the imperial head-dresses and fur hats, they found the silk threads stringing the beads together had decayed, leaving the jade beads scattered in one corner. Some of the objects and materials had disintegrated or corroded, so that their original shapes were difficult to discern. Of the crowns and hats, which were so closely related to the hierarchical system of rites and ceremonies, no originals have been preserved. In view of this, Xia Nai personally sorted them out piece by piece. Climbing on to the stands, and lying on the plank with a pillow under his chest, for four days and nights he recorded the forms, shapes, structures, measurements, colours, strings of beads, and made sketches, thus providing an important basis for future reproductions.

The cataloguing demanded great attention to detail. The slightest carelessness might cause difficulties in future research. Zhao Qichang took notes amounting to 1,000 words a day and gave them all to Xia Nai to check over. When the team had finished work late at night, Xia Nai examined the notes carefully, marked them with small circles and dots and raised many questions. He often worked throughout the night and although his ulcer became worse, he put off going to a nearby sanatorium to recuperate until the work was finished.

It took two years and two months to excavate Ding Ling from the time work began in May 1956 to the time the cataloguing work was finished at the end of July 1958. More than 20,000 workdays and 400,000 *yuan* RMB had been spent to open the 368-year-old underground palace.

On September 6, 1958, the Xinhua News Agency released the story of New China's first excavation of an imperial tomb. The news, withheld for almost three years, stunned archaeological circles throughout the world.

Also in September the burial objects for the emperor and his two empresses were displayed at an exhibition on the rostrum of the back gate of the Forbidden City. A refreshing breeze blew that autumn morning when members of the Chang Ling Excavation Committee — Guo Moruo, Shen Yanbing, Zheng Zhenduo, Wu Han, Deng Tuo and Xia Nai — presided at a ribbon-cutting ceremony to open the exhibition. Wu Han was particularly happy and excited when he appeared before the exquisite head-dresses for the emperor and empresses and the various brocades, ornaments and jewellery of wonderful patterns, designs and elaborate craftsmanship. The excavation of Ding Ling was finally completed according to his ideas in spite of the many upsets. Zhao Qichang, who supervised the arrangement of the exhibition, returned to the Ding Ling worksite one day before the opening. He had a faint premonition that something might happen to him after the brilliant celebration.

Three days after the exhibition opened, events confirmed his fears. When he was sorting out his data, Zhu Xintao, leader of the Preparatory Group for the Ding Ling Museum, came to his wooden shack and sat down quietly by his side. Zhao Qichang found the affable old man, who ordinarily engaged in lively chatter, now wearing a serious look on his face.

With a forced smile he said: "Qichang, I want to tell you something. Prepare yourself and don't get upset when I tell you."

"If the sky falls, the mountains will prop it up," Zhao Qichang said as if he were not worried at all, though his heart was beating fast.

Zhu Xintao continued: "We have received instructions from the Cultural Bureau. Members of the excavation team must go to the countryside to do farm work. You are among the first group and will go to Doudian Farm in Liangxiang County."

Zhao Qichang was surprised. He stared speechless at Zhu Xintao. He had long expected a tragic turn in his fate, but once it came he was at a loss what to do. He stood up and asked: "Why?"

Zhu Xintao extended his hand, signalling him to sit down. "Originally you were to go next spring, but..." He stopped, swallowed the words already on his lips, and changed his mind. "I can't do anything to change it." He opened his hands in a gesture indicating there was no way to help him.

Zhao Qichang asked angrily: "Only me?" "Bai Wanyu has returned to the Institute of Archaeology. You alone have to go first." As if he was talking to himself, or seeking an explanation, Zhao Qichang murmured, "I don't remember having made any mistakes in my work..." Zhu Xintao, looking at his simple and naive face, felt impelled to explain just a little more: "Someone said that you were releasing toxic gas and enjoyed privileges." Then he added in an emphatic tone: "Plus the problems in your personal history."

Zhao Qichang had participated in the Youth League of the Three Principles under the Kuomintang and had been president of the student union in his school. These were problems in his history he could not evade, but what about the toxic gas? He calmed himself and sat on his bed. He recalled that when he was checking the objects in the emperor's coffin, he sprayed a mixture of formalin and alcohol in the chambers from time to time for purposes of sterilisation, to prevent mildew and putrefaction. A government leader and his family came to visit the underground chambers when he was spraying the liquid and the stinging odour spread. The leader withstood it, but his wife kept coughing and used a handkerchief to wipe away the tears. Their two children complained loudly. At this, the leader could only gather his family together and leave immediately. Zhao had never expected at that time that the incident would lead to his present predicament.

But if it had been toxic gas, how could he and his teammates have worked in it, on and on for months? Anger flared up in his heart; he felt wronged and indignant.

There was no need to ask for an explanation. As the situation had reached this stage, he could only face reality. "When do I leave?" he asked.

"The leadership said you should leave today, but I think the time is too short. You pack and leave tomorrow, or even the day after."

"Well, should I write the report on the excavation or not?" Zhao Qichang asked. He had in mind the accumulated records on the excavation running to millions of words collected in the past three years. They needed to be collated, summarised, analysed...

Zhu Xintao did not reply for the moment. As the leader of the Preparatory Group for the Ding Ling Museum, he was keenly aware of the importance of such a report. The archaeological excavation had been made strictly according to international set procedures. In digging up ruins or a tomb, a field survey was first needed to obtain a large quantity of clues and evidence for the excavation. This process should be coordinated with photographing, measuring, drawing and recording with no negligence or omission. After the excavation was complete, a report on it should be prepared immediately to summarise the results, and should be announced to the public in various forms to provide firsthand data for further study. The exhibition of the objects unearthed in Ding Ling was only part of the excavation work. The work as a whole should be considered complete only after the issue of the excavation report. This was common knowledge. Zhu Xintao had no answer.

Zhao Qichang decided to leave Ding Ling for Doudian Farm the next day. He was single and therefore had no family worries and it was not necessary to tell his old father. But he wanted to say goodbye to his teammates.

In the evening when he was busy packing, Liu Jingyi walked into the wooden shack quietly, with a cloth bag under his arm.

"Leaving tomorrow?" he asked in a low, strained voice.

"Yes." Zhao Qichang raised his head.

Their eyes met, but no words were exchanged. They stood silently in the dim light. Past events, joys, hardships and true friendship flooded their minds.

Liu Jingyi first studied in the department of history of Nankai University, but abandoned his schooling because of serious neurosis. After he recovered, he and his widowed mother left Baotou for Beijing to seek work. They met Zhao Qichang at the office of the Beijing Cultural Relics Investigation and Research

Group. As the excavation of Ding Ling was in need of people, Liu Jingyi joined the Ding Ling excavation team upon Zhao Qichang's recommendation. This was the beginning of a fast friendship.

Liu Jingyi was earnest and conscientious in work. When attempts to open the giant marble doors of the underground palace reached an impasse and there seemed no way to proceed, it was him who came up with the answer. After combing through many ancient books, he at last found the record of the hook-shaped key.

Later on, in sorting out the burial objects, Zhao Qichang developed lumbago for working nearly 20 hours in a row in the cold, with his back bent. He had no time to see the doctor. He would heat bricks and wrap them in towels to use as hot compresses in the evening. Liu Jingyi happened to see an advertisement about a special Chinese traditional medicine for lumbago in front of a drug store while waiting for the bus to the Ming Tombs. He bought several packs and every evening before bed-time, he mixed the medicine with vinegar to apply to Zhao's back. The magic "iron sand" mixed with vinegar released a penetrating therapeutic heat which helped cure Zhao Qichang's backache.

It seemed as if everything happened just today, or else sometime in the remote past. At this moment of parting, it was hard to know what to say.

Finally, Liu Jingyi opened his cloth bag, and took out a knitted woollen sweater and a pair of knitted woollen underwear: "I bought them for you in Chang Ling Commune this afternoon."

Zhao Qichang looked at him, tears trickling down

his face. He took his fountain pen from his pocket and stretching out both hands, gave it to Liu. In the cold night they clasped hands in farewell.

It was late autumn. The morning sun shone over the tomb precinct and lit up his face. Gusts of cold wind blew across the land, whipping up clouds of dust. He walked along the rugged mountain path to the grain supply centre of Chang Ling Commune to take the bus. He carried a stack of excavation records in his hand. The bundle was heavy, which annoyed him, but also gratified him. Ding Ling, a sort of companion with whom he had lived in close proximity for three years, was soon out of sight. The magnificent halls, the old pines and cypresses, the homey wooden shacks, the underground chambers in which he had worked so hard...All this would become a dream of the past. In material form, only the pack of excavation records was still with him, a heavy reminder. It was the most precious thing he brought with him from Ding Ling. He could not over-estimate its value.

Majestic Dayu Hill gradually turned blurry before his wet eyes. History had dispensed with the excavation team leader who had pioneered in opening up an imperial tomb. Beyond doubt, his fate had taken a deplorable turn. But the consequences of this turn would eventually prove more serious than his own personal predicament. A matter of years later an even sadder story would unfold, which would not be the tragedy of one person alone, but a disaster for the whole nation.

The First Imperial Tomb Museum

When the exhibition of Ding Ling relics in the Forbidden City was over, the personnel of the Preparatory Group for the Ding Ling Museum speeded up the repair, protection and reproduction of the burial objects.

These measures were first applied to the three skeletons. The three skulls were sent to the Institute of Vertebrate Palaeontology and Palaeoanthropology under the Chinese Academy of Sciences for repairs. Meanwhile, the people in the tomb precinct were busy applying technical and protective treatment to the unearthed brocades and fabrics. Someone suggested that the silk fabrics be mounted on tough paper lined like ancient paintings. Another suggested that the paste should be mixed with antiseptic so that they could be permanently preserved. Unfortunately, the mounting work was done without onthespot guidance from specialists. After it was finished, the noted writer Shen Congwen, who became an expert in the study of ancient garments and dresses in his late years, came to see the mounted fabrics. Carefully inspecting the pieces with the aid of a magnifying glass, he grew more and more puzzled and finally asked: "Why is the exposed side the wrong side of the fabric?"

"Doesn't research into the texture of fabrics also require study of the wrong side?" one staff member answered promptly.

The reply enraged Shen Congwen, but he explained with a smile: "In the study of fabric texture, we want to observe the wrong side, but more importantly the right side. If it is to show the texture of the wrong side, it is quite enough to set aside just one, two or five centimetres at most. Here the whole bolt has been mounted on the wrong side. In my opinion, it's a mistake in the work." His frank remarks, especially the word mistake, put the chief cadre at his side in an awkward position.

Shen Congwen walked out of the reception room and told his assistant: "The brocades of the Ming Dynasty, the cream of the textile techniques and skills of the Chinese nation, have been handled in such an offhand manner, and to think they should have given such an irresponsible explanation! If it was not pure ignorance, it was outright dishonesty!"

The treatment of some robes and gowns was also highly unsatisfactory. For example, they used a mixture of polymethacrylic methyl and a softener to coat the decaying garments. As time went by the colours darkened, and the fabrics hardened as the softening agent vaporised. The work had been started hastily without experiment, resulting in irreparable damage. It had to be stopped half way.

When news of the damaged silk fabrics reached Beijing, Zheng Zhenduo and Xia Nai were appalled. In the midst of their worry and frustration, they received news that in some provinces, people were being organised to dig up imperial tombs. Some provinces, reluctant to be left behind, had even gone ahead and followed the Ding Ling example. Trumpets blared, quickening the march into the imperial tombs of the Han, the Tang and the Qing dynasties.. In view of the situation, Zheng Zhenduo and Xia Nai, who were in charge of protection of relics and archaeological excavations countrywide, burned with indignation. They promptly submitted a report to the State Council requesting a check to this irregular onset of excavations. The report, approved by Premier Zhou Enlai without delay and circulated to the whole country, finally stopped the mad rush to open tombs.

In a year's time the unearthed objects from Ding Ling were almost all repaired and reproduced, with the exception of those destroyed through mishandling. The best preserved specimens were naturally chosen for public display.

On September 30, 1959 the Ding Ling Museum was formally set up, ready to open to the public.

In March 1963 the Ming Tombs, including the Ding Ling underground palace, were listed among the country's major relics under state-level protection.

Destroyed Coffins and Seven Lives

Since the Ding Ling Museum was opened to the public, tourists have been arriving in droves to visit the magnificent buildings which had slumbered underground for nearly 400 years. They all wanted to see with their own eyes what the emperor and empresses looked like and personally experience the exotic atmosphere of the imperial underground chambers.

It is a pity that in this 27-metre deep palace, there was only an empty cave to be seen. Although three huge coffins were placed on the dais in the rear chamber, what people saw was not the original coffins made of *nanmu* wood, but reproductions made of plaster and cement. During the first few weeks these painted replicas, looking like ordinary chests, still smelt strongly of paint. There was no aura of remote antiquity; the whole rear chamber contained a somewhat modern atmosphere. Many disappointed tourists asked: "Where are the original imperial coffins? Were they here when the underground palace was first opened?"

Well...ah...they have disappeared.

It was a dramatic coincidence that they disappeared on the same day that the Ding Ling Museum was inaugurated.

On the morning of September 30, 1959 Wang Qifa, who dug the first shovel of earth in the excavation of Ding Ling, received an instruction from the director of the general affairs office of the museum: "The museum will soon be opened. Now that the reproductions of the coffins are complete, the originals are useless. Bring some people to the underground chambers to remove them before the leaders come to check our work."

After the underground palace was opened, most of the peasant workers returned to their villages. Only Wang Qifa and a few who had distinguished themselves during the excavation stayed to work in the museum. On receiving this instruction, Wang Qifa called some workers together and had the coffins removed from the underground chambers.

"Where shall we put them?" he asked the director.

"There's no space for them in the warehouse. Throw them away!"

Wang Qifa hesitated. He recalled Bai Wanyu's words: "The unearthed objects, even a needle or a tile, are all priceless treasures. They should not be damaged."

"This isn't right..." Wang Qifa did not move.

"Why not? Do as you are told! Save the bronze

rings. Listen to me and there will be no problem. We can't delay the leaders who are coming to check our work."

Staff members stood around the coffins with iron implements in their hands. The heavy picks struck the coffins with resounding thuds. When the bronze rings were removed, they were all quite tired. Wang Qifa watched the four big bronze rings fall to the ground with a sharp clang which filled his heart with grief. In the three years of wind and rain, joy and sadness, fear and cheer, coming and going — how many people had toiled and struggled to excavate this imperial tomb? What had it all been for? What, if not to uncover the coffins and corpses of the emperor and empresses? Today, here they were; the coffins before their eyes, and they were destroying them. Why? Wang Qifa had only two years of schooling, not knowing much about the significance of the excavation, but he intuitively sensed the value of the unearthed relics.

"Director, we can't destroy the coffins! Store them anywhere, but don't destroy them..." he entreated.

The director was busy preparing for the museum's opening reception. Glaring at Wang Qifa, he snapped: "Are you thinking of keeping them for yourself?!"

This attack stunned Wang Qifa. His face flushed as his indignation rose. He was about to retort but suppressed his anger. At this adverse turn in his life, he had to consider what best to do. He withdrew from the office and retired to his wooden shack to calm his frayed nerves.

Dozens of armed guards followed the director over to the coffins.

"Please be so good as to throw these wooden

planks away for me!"

The guards struck up a work song and hoisted the heavy coffins up the rampart. Each time the director shouted: "Throw!" the guards flung the coffins one after the other over the rampart wall where they tumbled down the gully in pieces.

A week later, when Xia Nai heard how the coffins had been disposed of, he was shocked. The great master could only pace up and down in dismay. He hastily ordered the museum to retrieve the coffins and place them under protection. However, they had disappeared into the empty valley.

Thirty-one years later, at the Summer Palace we came across Li Shuxing, a former member of the excavation team, who told us in detail about this period. In the midst of our discourse, we encountered the former director of the museum's general affairs office. The meeting, as dramatic as it was unexpected, was at the same time most opportune.

His hair had turned white at the temples, and he had long been retired although he still worked for the cause of the Party in the spirit of "an old steed in the stable". We knew that he had been given a disciplinary warning for having the coffins thrown away and that this was a particularly sensitive political pain in his heart. Nevertheless since we'd been offered the chance, we still ventured to ask him about the matter.

"We heard that it was you who decided that the coffins be thrown away, is that right?"

His face puckered, his eyes narrowed in anguish. He answered in a heavy voice: "You are right in considering that was the case."

"Why do you say 'considering'?"

"As a matter of fact, before the coffins were disposed of, I asked for instructions from the leaders above, including those of the Cultural Bureau. Think about it, how could I, as director of a local-level office, dare to take such a decision on my own?" His voice grew louder, as he grew more excited. "But when the time came for the investigation, those leaders denied it. I had no choice but to recognise it as my tough luck."

We believed him.

In the autumn of 1990 when we came to Ding Ling in search of more fragments of the history, we heard a story both dreadful and inexplicable.

In 1959 after the *nanmu* coffins of the emperor and empresses were tossed over the rampart wall, they were taken away by peasants from nearby villages. When these peasants discovered these almost complete coffins, they felt they'd found the treasures of a lifetime. One old couple hired some carpenters to make two coffins for themselves out of the valuable *nanmu* planks. It so happened that after the first coffin was finished, the wife died. The second was barely completed when the husband also stopped breathing. The two deaths took place within the space of two weeks.

The sudden deaths of the old couple shocked all those who heard tell of it. As the story spread more widely, it inspired increasing awe. Within five months, further dreadful happenings occurred which were even more mysterious.

Among the peasants who took pieces of the imperial coffins, a peasant named X in Yu Ling Village benefited most. When the coffins were thrown down from the rampart, he and his wife were working on the slope just below the wall. X recognised the wood as rare and of excellent quality, and lost no time in picking up the big, thick *nanmu* planks and dragging them home with the help of his wife. Other peasants were quick to follow suit.

After dragging the planks into the house, X hired some carpenters to make two long, low chests. These he placed in the central room of his house. Some of his fellow villagers envied him his new fortune while some jealously warned: "That's imperial property! You can't just do whatever you like with it. You shouldn't take it, it might bring you ill fortune."

X did not take their words seriously until the ill wind blew.

It was noon on Sunday. When X and his wife returned home from the fields, they found their four children (three boys and a girl) missing. The mother had a fearful premonition that something was amiss which galvanised her into frantic action. She rushed about inside and outside the courtyard looking for the children. They were nowhere to be seen. At last when the couple returned to the house, they suddenly noticed four pairs of small shoes by the new chests. Struck with alarm, they flung open the lids of the chests. Inside one of them, the children lay pressed closely together. None were breathing. There was blood around their finger nails and scratches on the sides of the chest.

A police car, siren wailing, came to Yu Ling Village. Cameras flashed over the chests. After a detailed inspection, the police announced the cause of death of the four children: "suffocation due to lack of oxygen".

When we went to X's home we saw him standing in

the courtyard, a tall, grey-haired man with a dark face.

After the death of their four children, the couple had four more (three girls and a boy). It was both tragic and perplexing that his son, who had just completed his senior middle school education, also died mysteriously on the chest late one night. It was said that he suffocated after lighting the *kang** fire.

In X's home, a dreadful mood settled like a thick fog in our hearts. In the central room, the two red-painted chests stood quietly against the wall just like two coffins. Cold shivers ran down our spines. X's younger sister volunteered to tell us about the tragic scene of 30 years before by showing us the chests. She said: "There is an iron hook between the lid and the sides, which locks the chest when the lid is tightly closed. It must have happened that when the children were playing inside, the lid fell and locked automatically. If that was the case, there was no way for them to get out no matter how desperately they struggled."

As we looked at the two coffin-like chests an idea occurred to us: Would there be similar tragedies related to the chests in the future? When we asked X why he did not dispose of them to exorcise the painful memories, he looked at us blankly without replying. His sister spoke: "Many people have urged him to throw the two chests away, insisting that they are haunted by evil spirits. I for one, disagree. This is just a superstitious way of talking. I believe that everything is predestined. Even if the chests had not been here, who can say for sure that the five children would not have met with some other accident?"

---

*A *kang* is a heatable brick bed.

Chapter Twelve
SKELETONS IN FLAMES

Storm

In 1966 the "cultural revolution" was initiated across China.

Almost overnight the staff members of the Ding Ling Museum split into different factions, such as the "Fight-for-Truth" group, the "Red Banner Fighting" group and the "Rifle Fighting" group and so on. Before they began to fight each other, the common targets of their "revolution" were the unearthed relics of Ding Ling and the museum leaders. The fighting groups took a unanimous decision: Zhu Xintao and the other "capitalist roaders" should be kept in custody in the warehouse and guarded 24 hours a day to prevent them from "undermining revolutionary actions". Then they organised all forces to destroy the tomb buildings and all other symbols of feudalism in the Ding Ling tomb precinct.

Dozens of people swarmed to the stone bridge in front of the precinct to start the revolution. After destroying the small bridge, they climbed to the stele pavilion and used red paint to blank out the two characters "Ding Ling".

At 2:15 in the afternoon, the square in front of Ding Ling was filled to capacity with peasants from nearby villages, red guards and students who had come especially to watch the spectacle.

The three royal skeletons were placed together, with the emperor in the middle, surrounded by their portraits, photos and other "proofs of their crimes". When everything was ready, a young female member of the revolutionary committee named W led in shouting revolutionary slogans:

"Down with the royalists!"

"Sweep away all devils and demons!"

"Down with Wanli, chieftain of the landlord class!"

"Firmly carry the Great Proletarian Cultural Revolution through to the end!"

As the shouting of slogans finished, W shouted to the crowds: "The revolution starts right now!"

Hardly had she finished, when a dozen burly young men came forward carrying stones which they threw at the royal remains with all their might. A downpour of stones followed and the three skeletons were smashed to pieces.

The crowd began to move away, astonished, admiring, confused, benumbed, admiring or overjoyed ...All eyes were on W. Heartened, she ordered her followers: "Set them alight!"

Within seconds of the order being issued, flames rose and spread, turning the square into a sea of orange. The skeletons, mixed with firewood, crackled in the fire. Dark smoke rose in columns and the ashes flying about filled the air with a sickening stench.

Perhaps this mad onslaught on earth moved the gods above or the spirits of the emperor and empresses, for suddenly a clap of thunder burst out of the blue, followed by a heavy downpour. The crowd quickly dispersed and the flames were soon quenched. The burning skeletons were carried by the running water and churned together with the mud, where they dissolved into the bosom of mother Nature.

Afterthoughts

Twenty-three years after the skeletons were burnt, our research took us to the Ming Tombs Special District in search of any remaining traces of those turbulent years.

We came upon an interesting source in the generator room of the tomb precinct, where we met a man whom for convenience we will refer to as S. It was he who had climbed up the stele pavilion to paint out the two characters for "Ding Ling", and who set fire to the skeletons. No longer young, no longer the immature "revolutionary rebel" of the past, S showed no sign of his former fanaticism.

When our conversation turned to the burning of the skeletons, we wondered whether he would try to evade the matter. However, he was surprisingly frank. He made no effort to conceal his role and talked openly about what he had done, adding some details which we were not familiar with, and providing some explanations of his own:

"The 'cultural revolution' harmed a whole generation of people. It also caused damage to a large number of cultural relics. The two incidents you just asked about actually did happen. It was like this: The wind was very strong when I climbed up the stele pavilion to paint over the characters. The ladder was just like a scaling-ladder. On reaching the top, I fell. I could feel the damp clouds wafting by my ears. At that time, I was prepared to risk my life. If it were today, I wouldn't do it at any price. Just imagine, if I had fallen to my death, I would have lost my life for nothing. No one's interested in the scars on my legs and head. I myself am reluctant to seek treatment, just like a thief who has been injured during a robbery. I was really stupid at that time. The characters, Ding Ling, were inscribed high up on a horizontal board — what did that have to do with me? I took them to be a sort of reactionary slogan and insisted on climbing up there to cover them with paint. Why go to the trouble? I did it in all earnestness.

"When the Cultural Bureau sent people to investigate the burning of the skeletons and asked all who participated to sign their names, I signed mine. Since I did it, why not admit it? I'm not one of those who wanted to appear like a hero when smashing relics, but who sticks their heads in the sand when questions are asked. A real man should have the courage to accept the consequences of his actions. It was done in the overwhelming atmosphere of the 'cultural revolution'. Calamities like that took place at almost every site of ancient culture, at museums and parks throughout the country. Although after the 'cultural revolution' the public security department listed the burning of the skeletons at Ding Ling as one of three major cases in Changping County to be prosecuted, but up to today nobody has been dealt with. The law is never directed against people in great numbers; this is an old saying. If we are all thrown into prison, it would not be too severe a penalty. It was a great pity to destroy the skeletons. They're not like the bowls and chopsticks we eat with. If they are broken, we can buy new ones. But where can we find such skeletons? You should write about this whole tragedy and tell future generations never to permit such actions as this to occur again, otherwise our ancient Chinese culture will be utterly destroyed."

S provided a sharp contrast to another person we spoke with. When we met W, the then member of the revolutionary committee, she was a picture of dejection. Her hair had prematurely turned grey. She had grown up in the country and had a poor, miserable childhood. Since then her life had not shown much improvement; a small black-and-white television set was the only article of any value in her tiny two-room home.

When our conversation turned to the days of the "cultural revolution", she was not at all proud of the greatest time in her life. The reddening of her face was caused by her embarrassment and repentence. She did not say how she directed that spectacular "revolutionary action", but said that since that "revolution", she had been constantly plagued by nightmares in which Emperor Wanli and the two empresses tried to kill her with a sword. Troubled by nightmares for more than 20 years, she had long ago lost her youth and suffered from serious neurasthenia. She suggested that perhaps this was retribution for her ignorance and arrogance.

When we said goodbye to her, tears filled her eyes. We found it hard to believe that she was once the charismatic revolutionary who played a leading role in the tragedy that saddened the whole archaeological world. Human beings are not least unpredictable.

Every civilisation is the priceless property of mankind. It is a pity that people like S and W failed to realise this at the time.

CONCLUDING REMARKS

Hope for Reparation

On August 21, 1989 the *Beijing Evening News* printed as front page headline news the following item:

Archaeological Study of Ding Ling of the
Ming Dynasty Completed after 30 Years
—Reports on Excavation Being
Published One by One

The excavation of Ding Ling 30 years ago created a sensation worldwide. With the publication of relevant reports on the excavation of the Ming Dynasty tomb complex, which have been delayed for 30 years, the Ming Tombs will once again become a focus of attention among cultural circles in China and the whole world. Thanks to the efforts of the Cultural Relics Publishing House, the first report, a large album of 136 colour photographs of the unearthed objects from the imperial tomb, has been published under the title "The Best of Ding Ling". It includes nearly 40 photos taken at the excavation site. An academic report on the excavation entitled "Ding Ling" with a total of nearly 500,000 characters and more than 380 black ink drawings will soon be released to the press, and will go on sale to the public shortly thereafter. The content of the academic report includes a general description of the Ming Tombs, the construction process and structure of Ding Ling, records of the unearthed objects and appendices of related special-subject reports of archaeological appraisals. Specialists say that the publication of this all-embracing academic report will provide an abundance of basic information for the study of Ming Dynasty history as well as for special archaeological studies in China.

It is a pity that all this came too late for Xia Nai, who had devoted so much of his labour and the last years of his life to the excavation. Xia Nai, who personally guided the excavation of Ding Ling, fully understood the importance of the reports for future research work. If a tomb or ancient site is excavated to show only the objects inside or its original appearance, without investigation into the historical context, and if no definite historical knowledge is obtained through it of the political, cultural and social relations of the period, then the significance of the archaeological excavation is lost. However, Xia Nai, forced to work in a cadre school at that time, was unable to carry out the work that was his most cherished ambition.

In 1971 Xia Nai returned to his office to head the Institute of Archaeology under the Chinese Academy of Sciences. In August 1972 a Vietnamese archaeological delegation visited China. At the dinner for them hosted by Xia Nai, the Vietnamese guests asked:

"Ding Ling was the first imperial tomb excavated

after the founding of New China, and you were the director of the excavation. Our president Ho Chi Minh visited this marvellous excavation. Has a report been published yet? We would be interested to see a copy."

Xia Nai said with regret: "We are still in the throes of the 'cultural revolution'. Both the excavators and their directors are now busy with this work. For the time being, we have no time to write a report on the excavation of Ding Ling. I will let you know when it is written."

The Vietnamese delegate nodded his understanding and expressed satisfaction over Xia Nai's friendly attitude. At that time, it was impossible for them to know about the bitter sufferings of the excavators and their director, or to understand the grief in Xia Nai's heart and the difficulty of the situation he faced.

Xia Nai continued to receive letters from archaeologists, historians and other interested people at home and abroad inquiring about an excavation report. At the beginning he replied to every letter with sincere explanations. With the increasing number of letters and the biting tone of the language used by some of the writers, he found that explanations were no longer of any use. It was more important to finish the report as soon as possible.

On December 6, 1976 a middle school teacher from Shanxi came to Xia Nai's office. He was a keen student of archaeology and had made some studies of Ming history. After news of the excavation of Ding Ling was announced, he had looked forward to an excavation report. During the "cultural revolution", he was branded a "bourgeois rightist who had escaped the net" and was sent to a farm for remoulding through labour. But he never gave up his interest in archaeology and the study of Ming history. He came to Beijing especially to ask Xia Nai some questions on the subject and also to find out about an excavation report.

Xia Nai felt that he could no longer remain silent. After seeing the teacher off, he began to consider how to write a report.

In October 1977 a Chinese archaeological delegation led by Xia Nai visited Iran and attended the annual conference on archaeology organised by the Iranian Archaeological Centre. On the occasion he delivered a report on "Achievements in China's Archaeological Work". As he described the excavation of Ding Ling, the question, which Xia Nai had worried most about, was finally raised: "Mr Xia, has an excavation report been published yet in China?"

"Not yet," he said in truth.

"How is it that no academic report on this great excavation has been published in 20 years? Is this archaeological practice in China?" The questions became caustic.

"Archaeological practice in China is almost the same as in other countries. The report on the excavation of Ding Ling has been delayed due to the 'cultural revolution' of the last ten years. It should be regarded as an exceptional case," Xia Nai replied without hesitation.

"We received only a little information about China's 'cultural revolution'. Could Mr Xia tell us something about the actual nature of this revolution?"

Xia Nai found himself unable to reply directly.

Confronted by the delegates from different countries, Xia Nai summoned his gift of command over exigency:

"The 'cultural revolution' in China is a complicated subject. You would be more than welcome to visit China to learn about it. What I can tell you now is that a report on the Ding Ling excavation will soon be published. At that time, I will seek advice from all our friends."

Immediately after he returned from Iran, Xia Nai hurried over to see Zhao Qichang about the matter. By that time, Zhao had returned to normal work at the Beijing Bureau of Cultural Relics. On meeting for the first time after so many years, both men were overwhelmed with joy and sorrow. When Xia Nai suggested making a concerted effort to produce a report, Zhao Qichang could not hold back his tears. He gave Xia Nai all the letters he had received throughout the years inquiring about the report.

Xia Nai was hard put to control his emotions, but kept calm and said with a smile: "The time has come for us to end this humiliating situation. Let's prepare to do our best to write a first-rate report!"

In April 1979 the Archaeological Society of China was founded and an archaeological planning conference was held in Xi'an. In his capacity as Chairman of the society and director of the Institute of Archaeology, Xia Nai announced at the meeting that the compilation of a report on the excavation of Ding Ling had been listed as one of the major projects in the country's sixth five-year plan for social sciences, and personnel would be organised immediately to take up the work.

After the meeting Zhao Qichang, who had been appointed director of the Capital Museum, and Wang Yan, associate researcher of the Institute of Archaeology, now under the Chinese Academy of Social

Sciences, immediately put their work aside and went to the Ding Ling Museum to begin the huge and complicated writing assignment that was to take them five years to finish.

Belated Report

Zhao Qichang and Wang Yan were joined at Ding Ling by a young archaeologist named Wang Xiuling. When they paid a call on Li Yajuan, keeper of the relics warehouse, she produced what they had come to see — first-hand data of the excavation, which in the "cultural revolution" had been dubbed "evidence of a counter-revolutionary come-back". They were all stunned to find reams of data, thousands of photos, and big thick folios of on-the-spot records in particular, still completely intact after 20 years!

What a great piece of luck in a sea of vicissitudes!

Li Yajuan had been a housewife in Beijing. In 1958 when the unearthed objects were shown to the public in the Forbidden City, she was employed as a guide on a temporary basis. Afterwards she was employed as keeper of the warehouse at Ding Ling. When most people became carried away with revolution, she remained reasonable and calm. She did her best to protect the relics at all costs in spite of all provocations. When the skeletons of the emperor and empresses were seized, forcibly taken out of the warehouse, set on fire by the rebels and burnt to ashes, she shed tears. That was the moment she made up her mind to protect all the other objects in the warehouse even at the cost of her life. The rebels tried to coerce her into handing over the imperial garments and head-dresses; she flatly refused. For this, she was beaten until she bled from the mouth and nose, and had fainted many times. She had four children at home in need of her care, but she remained at the warehouse day and night for the three most difficult years of 1966-1968. The rebels were compelled to give up their plan to destroy or appropriate these valuables. As the political situation improved, she checked the objects and took further measures to protect them. All the negatives for the thousands of photographs first taken were well preserved under her special care.

Li Yajuan had only a junior middle school education. It was out of her sense of duty that she kept and protected all the relics. She remained a warehouse keeper until she died in 1985. On the surface her life was commonplace, but in a certain sense, she was a great woman. In fact, it was the many "small people" like her who, full of loyalty and without fanfare, used their blood to write stirring pages of history during the difficult years of the People's Republic.

In systematising the pile of first-hand data and more than 3,000 unearthed objects, Zhao Qichang, Wang Yan and Wang Xiuling worked day and night. They wrote a general description of the Ming Tombs, explained the construction and shape of Ding Ling, and provided a detailed account of the unearthed objects and their origin. They had also to repair some of the artifacts. The three of them often travelled to Beijing to delve into textbooks on history and to bring in specialists to help check, appraise and analyse the articles as well as to think over which ones should be reproduced.

The unearthed objects from the imperial tomb were divided into different varieties and classes. They represented the cultural cream of the Ming Dynasty, and constituted an extremely complicated research subject. Even the preliminary sorting out involved the cooperation of many separate branches of science and various special fields of knowledge. This was particularly true in the case of the semi-decayed brocades which had become almost non-extant and the techniques of which had long been lost. If they could not analyse and dissect the entire technical process of silk-reeling, thread-twisting, dyeing and weaving to finishing, it would be difficult to know what the original was like, to say nothing of preserving the techniques. Hope of "making the past serve the present" would be even more far-fetched.

The beautiful city of Suzhou was one of the centres of brocade making in the Ming Dynasty. Wu Ping, a 40-year-old female engineer at the local brocade research institute, came to Ding Ling and stayed there for three years. Working day and night, she drew hundreds of brocade designs and garment styles and wrote hundreds of pages of analyses. When the final research work was completed, a special subject report was written by Liu Baimao and Luo Ruilin, specialists of the Beijing Institute of Textile Science.

Gu Wenxia, director of the Suzhou Embroidery Research Institute, formed a special group of highly skilled embroiderers for the reproduction of the imperial ceremonial robe woven by the tapestry method. She led the group on three visits to the Ding Ling Museum to study the unearthed garments. It took them three years to reproduce the rare ceremonial robe. Miss Sun Peilan of the same institute simultaneously produced a technical report on the project.

In the Ming Dynasty Nanjing was also an important

base for the manufacture of silk fabrics. Some of the silk fabrics unearthed from Ding Ling were marked "Woven in Nanjing". Thus it was in this city that Wang Yinran, director of the Nanjing Cloud Brocade Research Institute, with the help of a group of technicians and senior researchers, undertook the project for the reproduction of an imperial dragon robe woven with peacock feathers and gold threads on a gauze base. They built a special Jacquard loom, made special design samples and traced the process back to the dyeing techniques used in the Ming Dynasty. In order to find the unique skill of making goldleaf, they covered the whole of Nanjing in search of a descendant of a Ming Dynasty leaf-maker. He was finally located on the outskirts. A workshop was promptly set up there and soon the rare skill of using goldleaf to cover silk was restored. To weave a permanent dragon pattern with gold threads on transparent gauze together with peacock feathers, Wei Yuqing, head of the relics section of the Ming Tombs Special District Administration, travelled to bird-breeding farms and zoos all over the country to acquire peacock feathers.

The oil in the ever-burning lamps had been in the underground palace for more than 300 years. Oil like that was not seen anywhere else in the country. Data obtained through laboratory tests and analysis would certainly be of use in the modern storage of oils. Fan Tie, a young researcher in the Chemical Research Institute of Cereals and Oils completed laboratory tests and a special subject report.

The teeth of the emperor and empresses also needed appraisal, but the skulls had been destroyed during the "cultural revolution". Zhao Qichang recalled that

Professor Zhou Dacheng of the Stomatological College of Beijing Medical University, a specialist in the history of stomatological medical science, had visited Ding Ling after it was opened. When Zhao Qichang went to see him, he was greeted with glee: "I've got the information ready for you. It's been waiting here a long time!" Professor Zhou had kept the data carefully for 20 years. His report, so quickly and so easily obtained, was like an unexpected gift. Appraisals of the jewellery and wooden artifacts were also readily obtained with the help of the Beijing Filigree Factory and the Timber Industrial Research Institute.

Since the skeletons had been destroyed, no research could be carried out. The appraisal of trace elements in the hair was made by Li Huhou of the Institute of Archaeology. Gao Fuyuan of the Beijing Institute of Criminal Science and Technology tested for their blood types. It was lucky that two fragments of hair from the emperor and Empress Xiaojing had been preserved. Empress Xiaoduan's had been destroyed during the "cultural revolution".

For appraisals of the precious gems and jades, Zhao Qichang and Wang Yan paid a call on the 80-year-old specialist Yang Jie of the Ministry of Geology. Professor Yang was the greatest authority in China in this field. He had studied in Germany for 13 years, majoring in precious gems and jade. He continued his studies in the field after returning home. In 1968 when the jade clothes sewn with gold threads were unearthed at the Han Dynasty tomb in Mancheng, he was called in. It was a pity that they could not get to him earlier, for he passed away before he could finish the analysis and examination of all the objects. The unfinished part was continued by a middle-aged researcher from the Geological Museum named Zhao Songling.

The disappearance of the skeletons was a matter of great regret.

Guo Moruo had suggested early on that laboratory tests should be carried out on the skeletons from many different aspects. He also told Zhao Qichang: "In foreign countries, there is research into ancient pathology. One purpose is to study the cause of death; this is a matter of medical jurisprudence. We want to know the cause of Wanli's death. He suffered from many illnesses in his life and is said to have been a cripple. It is recorded in some historical data that he smoked opium. But what illness caused his body to become deformed and finally led to his death? Whatever test results can be obtained should undergo detailed analysis and study. This will enable us to know what the illnesses were and at what period he had which illness. Syphilis, for example, was first recorded in the late period of the Ming Dynasty. The American Indians did not have this disease until the Europeans arrived. Did Wanli suffer from syphilis?..."

But it was too late. Zhao Qichang, Wang Yan and Wang Xiuling were indignant and repentant. They spent the whole morning trying to find some bones on the square in front of Ding Ling and outside the tomb precinct, but it was to no avail. They failed to find even a tiny fragment. Nothing was left except sad memories which lingered on in the minds of the people.

In March 1985 the academic report on the excavation of Ding Ling was nearing completion. Xia Nai was excited to hear a summary of their progress from Zhao Qichang and Wang Yan. He said: "If you have difficulties, I'll do all I can to help you. Try to have it completed at the earliest possible date."

On the morning of June 15, 1985 Xia Nai was busy as usual in his office, when he coughed heavily all of a sudden. A hot sensation rose from his chest and fluid filled his mouth and nose. When he bent his head, blood splashed on the floor. He felt dizzy and weak. Years of archaeological field work had undermined his health. His stomach, liver and heart had suffered damage. More and more illnesses troubled him in body, mind and spirit, wearing down his vitality. Sensing that the symptoms were unusual and serious, he laid aside the work on his desk to take a walk in the courtyard. He decided to see the doctor when he found free time.

Xia Nai paced up and down in the courtyard, then abruptly went back to his office. He called the Ding Ling Museum, asking Zhao Qichang to send him the first draft of the excavation report immediately.

The report arrived in the afternoon. Xia Nai took the thick copy of the draft in his hands, looked up with a pale face and, smiling weakly, said to Zhao Qichang: "After seeing this, I feel relieved. After I'm gone, it's a good account to hand over to my old schoolmate."

Zhao Qichang at this time did not understand the implication of the great master's remark. By the time he became aware of what was happening, it was already too late.

On June 19, 1985, a staff member went to Xia Nai's office for an instruction, only to find him bending over his desk. He had fallen asleep forever. On his desk was the draft report, with closely-written comments in red ink in the margins.

In the winter of the same year 88-year-old Zhu Xintao, former director of the Ding Ling Museum, also passed away in a hospital in Guangzhou. The Communist Party Committees of Changping County and the Ming Tombs Special District held a memorial meeting at Ding Ling, and according to his last wishes spread his ashes over the Ming Tombs area where he had spent his youth doing underground work for the Communist Party.

Let History Tell the Future

In mid-October 1990, to round out our historical account, we went to the Ming Tombs Special District for our last interviews. It was harvest season, the trees in the fields laden with bright orange persimmons. The autumn leaves on the hill slopes had all turned red in the frost. Standing in the field surrounded by the beautiful landscape, we suddenly felt transported into another world.

The Ming Tombs, a rare scenic landscape, are worthy of their role as the sacred site for the imperial family. This ancient, miraculous tract of land bears the marks of history and reality, of the past and the future. Every hall and every tomb precinct is an album of pictures from history, in which the rise and fall of the nation, the joy and grief of emperors and ministers, and the happiness and misery of the common people are fully displayed. This is a miniature empire, a complete historical record of the Great Ming empire for nearly 300 years.

We travelled from tomb to tomb with heavy heart.

A once all-powerful empire finally declined and fell in this small corner. Except for Chang Ling, Ding Ling and Zhao Ling which have survived all these years of turmoil, the magnificent halls, tall stele pavilions and red walls of the other ten tombs all lie in ruins. The long river of history will never cease, but the surging waves subside from time to time. All things come from Nature, and all can only return to Nature.

We spent the night in the Ding Ling Museum. Although pop music was heard from a television programme, our minds were still searching the long corridor of history.

It is still too early to assess the gains and losses of the excavation of the imperial tomb. However, the many facts it has revealed are thought-provoking enough that one thing is clear: history is the future.

Two thousand, one hundred years ago, the E'pang Palace of Qin Shihuang was set aflame. Twenty centuries afterwards, a big fire raged again in the precinct of Ding Ling — tragedy repeated on this ancient land. Chinese civilisation has risen and fallen, thrived and declined time and again. It has become incomplete and fragmentary, leaving many unmitigated regrets. As writers we feel deeply obliged to tell our people: We need to build up our national cultural edifice so that our ancient 5,000-year civilisation can shine forth in all its past glory and might.

POSTSCRIPT

Zhao Qichang

The New Year's holidays were just over when an editor of the publishing house dropped in with a sheaf of manuscripts under his arm. "It's many years now since Ding Ling was opened," he began, "you are the only one still alive who took part from beginning to end. Here is the manuscript of a book on the excavation of Ding Ling. We were hoping that you would be its first reader. We'd be honoured if you could give us some advice, or even write something for the book. This is our hope, also our duty to the readers." His sincere attitude, and sense of dedication to authors and readers alike moved me. My multifarious duties not withstanding, how could I refuse? More than 30 years have gone by, and frankly speaking, I see them as through a mist. There are many thoughts in my mind, but with the passage of time, some have become vague and some inadvertently cast to the wind. The unforgettable linger on, of course...I really don't know where to begin.

Archaeology is a component part of the science of history. It studies the history of mankind on the basis of the ruins and artifacts left behind through the various activities of ancient peoples. People die and are buried, generation after generation, increasing the number of tombs over the centuries. As society developed, types of burial changed with the times, so did burial procedures, customs and the funerary objects demanded. If all graves and tombs could be dug out and arranged for comparison in chronological and geographical order, the footsteps of our ancestors would become history that is visible and true to life. Whatever our ancestors left us — stoneware, bronzeware, gold- and silverware, tablet inscriptions, ceramics, pots, vases, paintings, sculptures, or even piles of rubbish and disposables — none of these remains are free from the thoughts, ideas, customs and habits of the ancients. They also reflect the respective development stages of science, technology, literature and the arts, built up by the multitude of tribes, clans and ethnic groups through exchange and infiltration. These we refer to as relics. When archaeologists and historians look for historical roots, their work is shown as exhibitions of relics or written essays and books, but lacks popular appreciation. When writers probe for the roots and depict them in the form of literature, it greatly helps to increase understanding of the historical civilisation of our ancestors and its influence will perhaps spread more widely. The roots of our nation and its civilisation are deep and the leaves are luxuriant.

Ding Ling is an imperial tomb. Built with human ingenuity and labour, the material and financial power of the emperor's entire realm, its grandeur is almost beyond words. So far as its construction is concerned, the buildings both above and beneath the ground constitute an integral whole, which encompasses a knowledge of life and death, an understanding of the surrounding influences. The process involved many practical problems like site selection, layout, designing, measuring and construction. The unearthed objects relate to the politics, economy, culture, science and technology of that time. An imperial tomb is not only the recreation of the emperor's life before his death, but is in fact a miniature of his empire. Ding Ling was the first imperial tomb excavated after the founding of the People's Republic. The whole process, as I see it now, has left us both useful experiences and painful lessons.

Archaeological excavations propose to bring out the ruins and objects of the deceased buried underground. In the course of the work, various degrees of damage to the ruins and buried objects are unavoidable. In a sense, any excavation is a form of destruction, in China as well as in other countries. The duty of an archaeologist is to take the strictest and most appropriate measures to reduce the damage to the lowest degree. According to this principle, as shown by the excavation of Ding Ling, the young work team stood the test.

Under the usual practice, completion of the excavation is only half of the work. The remaining, and most important part of the work, is to sort out the unearthed objects and write an overall excavation report. Only then can the work be considered complete. But the excavation of Ding Ling did not follow this procedure. After the excavation was done, the work team was dissolved, with all the members sent back to their original units or to a farm to do physical labour. Although the Ding Ling Museum was set up and opened to the public, nobody took up the unfinished work. When we returned to Ding Ling, more than 20 years later, to sort out the artifacts and write the report, some of the unearthed objects were totally destroyed.

The damage was not caused during the excavation, but after. This was highly unexpected. To our regret and grief, the loss was irreparable. There are many causes —interference by political movements, damage done unwittingly and, chiefly, the lack of knowledge and responsibility of the people involved. If a cultural worker does not have adequate understanding and knowledge, or at least a love for historical culture, losses are inevitable. Thirty years after the excavation Xia Nai concluded, with much regret: "If we were to dig now, the results may be a bit better, but perhaps better still if we put it off another 30 years." Only then was I brought home to the implications of the repeated objections he and Zheng Zhenduo made prior to the excavation and their deep concerns in submitting a letter to the State Council, during the "cultural revolution", requesting a ban on the excavation of imperial tombs.

The opened underground chambers and exhibition of the unearthed relics were far from meeting the needs of various types of research work. Still lacking was the other half of our work — an overall, systematic and comprehensive report on the excavation of the tomb and the unearthed relics. It was precisely for this reason that it became a matter of course for academic circles both at home and abroad to look forward to it, urge it and allow no exception to its delay. It is a pity that 30 years had elapsed before the report was published. In the history of mankind 30 years is not a long time, but for a human being, how many 30 years are there in one's life? The excavation work was finished in 1958, but it was in 1979 when we returned to Ding Ling to sort out the unearthed objects and begin writing the report; and it was just before New Year's Eve of 1991 that I saw the sample book of our excavation report. When I looked at the two thick octavo volumes containing hundreds of thousands of words, hundreds of pictures, rubbings and photos, I was overwhelmed with emotions, thoughts and recollections of the past...

...

Our ancestors have left us an incalculable, priceless legacy buried and hidden deep in the ground. Young people are needed who will work hard to find it and to dig deeper and deeper. I vaguely see their shadows in the cold wilderness, searching, following clues, and digging shovel by shovel. The load on their shoulders is heavy. I wish them success.

Beijing, February 1991.

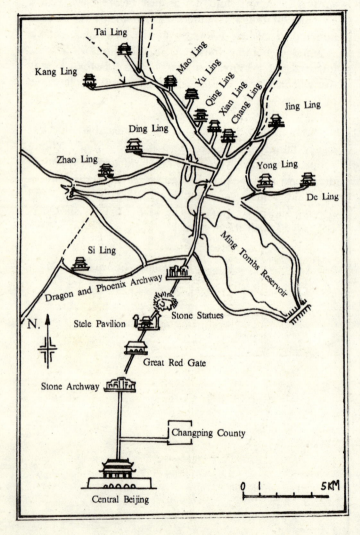

Location of the 13 Ming Tombs

Plan of the Ding Ling Precinct

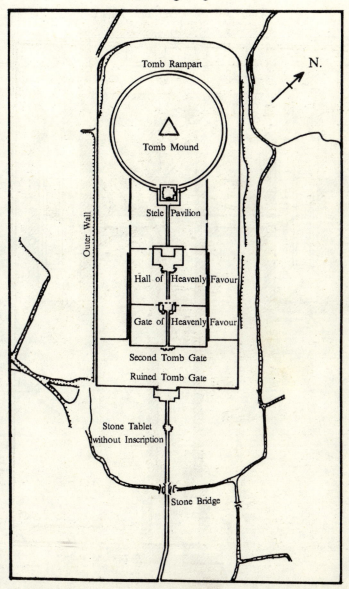

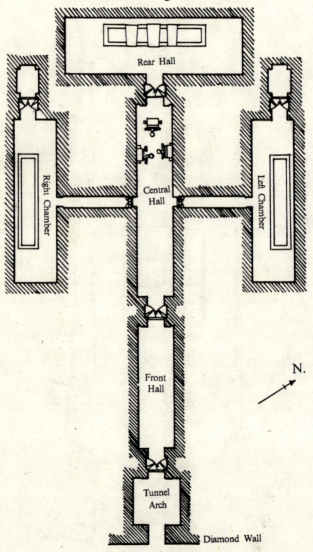

Illustration of the opening of the marble doors

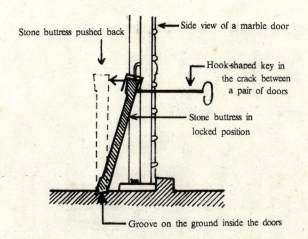

Ink drawing of the 100-boy embroidery jacket (part)

图书在版编目(CIP)数据

风雪定陵:英文/ 岳南著.－北京:中国文学出版社,1996.1

ISBN 7－5071－0298－X

I. 风... II. 岳... III. 报告文学－中国－当代－英文 IV. I25

中国版本图书馆 CIP 数据核字(95) 第 06912 号

风雪定陵

作者 岳南 杨仕
翻译 章挺权
中文责编 王 勇
英文责编 章思英

熊猫丛书
*
中国文学出版社出版
(中国北京百万庄路 24 号)
中国国际图书贸易总公司发行
(中国北京车公庄西路 35 号)
北京邮政信箱第 399 号   邮政编码 100044
1996 年第 1 版(英)
ISBN 7－5071－0298－X (外)
01800
10－E－3069P